RACIAL
IMPERATIVES

RACIAL IMPERATIVES

DISCIPLINE, PERFORMATIVITY,
AND STRUGGLES
AGAINST SUBJECTION

Nadine Ehlers

Indiana University Press
BLOOMINGTON AND INDIANAPOLIS

This book is a publication of

Indiana University Press
601 North Morton Street
Bloomington, Indiana 47404-3797 USA

iupress.indiana.edu

Telephone orders 800-842-6796
Fax orders 812-855-7931

Manufactured in the United States of America

*Library of Congress Cataloging-in-Publication
Data*
Ehlers, Nadine.
    Racial imperatives : discipline, perfor-
mativity, and struggles against subjection /
Nadine Ehlers.
        p. cm.
    Includes bibliographical references and
index.
        ISBN 978-0-253-35656-7 (cloth : alk. paper)
        ISBN 978-0-253-22336-4 (paper : alk. paper)
        ISBN 978-0-253-00536-6 (e-book)
1. United States—Race relations. 2. African
Americans—Race identity. 3. Whites—Race
identity. 4. Racism—United States. 5. Race
discrimination—Law and legislation—United
States. 6. Race—Philosophy. 7. Discipline—
Philosophy. 8. Performative (Philosophy)
9. Jones, Alice Beatrice—Trials, litigation, etc.
10. Passing (Identity)—United States—Case
studies. I. Title.
    E184.A1E37 2011
    305.800973—dc23
    2011030457

1 2 3 4 5   17 16 15 14 13 12

In memory of my mother, Maria Ehlers

CONTENTS

ACKNOWLEDGMENTS

This book would not have been possible without the support, friendship, and guidance of Joseph Pugliese (Macquarie University, Sydney, Australia). I am extremely grateful for his unwavering encouragement and his political commitment to the urgency of academic writing, which has always challenged and inspired me.

For their reading of drafts of an earlier incarnation of this project, and their extensive and invaluable criticism, I would like to thank Elin Diamond (Rutgers University), Dwight McBride (Northwestern University), and Moya Lloyd (then at Queen Mary, University of London and now at Loughborough University). The Center for the Study of Gender and Sexuality, in the Department of Social and Cultural Analysis at New York University provided me with the opportunity to continue working on this project as a Visiting Scholar, and to teach material from the book in a summer course. Don Kulick, the then director of the Center, and Philip Brian Harper who was then director of the Department of Social and Cultural Analysis generously supported my work. I would also like to thank my colleagues in the Women's and Gender Studies Program at Georgetown University—particularly Leslie Byers, Pamela Fox, Dana Luciano, You-Me Park, and Elizabeth Velez—for the community they provide and their advocacy on my behalf.

I would like to thank Robert Sloan, Editorial Director at Indiana University Press, for his enthusiasm for this project. I also thank Sarah Wyatt Swanson, assistant sponsoring editor, for her dedication to detail, and Frank B. Wilderson III and an anonymous reader for the press, who productively engaged the project in ways that helped me to clarify my arguments.

My deepest gratitude goes to the friends who sustain me: Kirsty Nowlan, my rock and my academic interlocutor; Donette Francis, an intellectual ally, and a steadfast and enabling support; and Shiloh Krupar, who has given me a new energy for academic inquiry. Together they have read more drafts of this project than a friendship deserves, and their encouragement and critical engagement with the book (and its surrounding questions) strengthened its outcome. Clare Armitage and Nikolai Haddad have provided crucial sustenance over our years of friendship and they have helped me craft this project in unanticipated ways.

Four previously published essays of mine have lent materials to this book. Parts of them—in various rearrangements—appear in the book with the kind permission of the publishers. "Retroactive Phantasies: Discourse, Discipline, and the Production of Race," *Social Identities: Journal for the Study of Race, Nation, and Culture* 3 (2008): 333–347; " 'Black Is' and 'Black Ain't': Performative Revisions of Racial 'Crisis,'" *Culture, Theory and Critique* 47, no. 2 (2006): 149–163; and "Hidden in Plain Sight: Defying Juridical Racialization in *Rhinelander v. Rhinelander*," *Communication and Critical/Cultural Studies* 1, no. 4 (2004): 313–334, have each been reproduced with the permission of Taylor and Francis Group and are available through the individual journals' websites at http://www.informaworld.com. "Passing Phantasms/Sanctioning Performatives: (Re)Reading White Masculinity in *Rhinelander v. Rhinelander*," *Studies in Law, Politics, and Society* 27 (2003): 63–91 is under the copyright of Elsevier and has been reproduced with their permission.

My family has lived with this project for many years and I thank them—Hans Ehlers, Duncan Ehlers, Domna Daciw, and Imogen Ehlers—for their endless and unconditional love. Most especially, I owe this book to the strength, courage, persistence, and resolute belief of my mother, Maria, who passed away before she could see the completion of this project. The book is dedicated to her.

RACIAL
IMPERATIVES

Introduction

It is not that the beautiful totality of the individual is amputated,
repressed, altered by our social order, it is rather that the
individual is carefully fabricated in it, according to a
whole technique of forces and bodies.

—Michel Foucault, *Discipline and Punish*

Norms are continually haunted by their own inefficacy;
hence, the anxiously repeated effort to install and
augment their jurisdiction.

—Judith Butler, *Bodies That Matter*

Criticism—understood as analysis of the historical conditions
which bear on the creation of links to truth, to rules, and to
the self—does not mark out impassable boundaries or
describe closed systems; it brings to light
transformable singularities.

—Foucault, preface to *The History of Sexuality, Volume 2*

On November 9, 1925, proceedings began in a Westchester County, New York,
courthouse, in the trial of Alice Rhinelander, née Jones. Alice's husband, Leonard "Kip" Rhinelander, had filed for an annulment of their marriage one year
earlier, only a month after the young couple's wedding and at what seemed the
insistence of his family. Their marriage could have been romanticized as a
fairytale union across class lines, for Leonard was the scion of one of New York's
oldest and wealthiest families, descended from the French Huguenots, while
Alice was the working-class daughter of immigrants. In the legal complaint that
initiated the trial of *Rhinelander v. Rhinelander*, however, Leonard charged Alice

with fraud that went to the essence of their marriage, accusing her of having lured him to wed by claiming that she was white and not "colored."[1] Alice had supposedly misrepresented her race, crossed the color line, and passed as white. Yet what came to be the central issue in the case was not whether Alice had indeed passed but, rather, whether she was *able* to pass. Equally important was the question of whether Leonard knew. If Alice had been able to pass, this would unsettle a racial economy that relied on the visual signification of what is supposedly racial truth. And, if Leonard had known that Alice did possess 'colored blood' but married her nonetheless, then he had knowingly transgressed social protocols that censured interracial unions. The answer to these questions was ultimately sought through recourse to the examination of the bodies of the Jones family and, in the most sensational aspect of the case, Alice's own body, which was stripped naked and paraded before the all white, male jury.

The *Rhinelander* case generated so much public interest that it became one of the top ten news stories of 1925, attesting to America's obsession with what W. E. B. DuBois called "the physical differences of color, hair and bone" (2000 [1887], 80). One of the most apparent concerns underscoring the case was that these purported differences might be 'mixed' through miscegenation, particularly via interracial unions between blacks and whites. Despite the fact that New York law did not prohibit interracial marriages, Leonard's attorney, Isaac Mills, positioned the threat of miscegenation as the central aspect of the trial.[2] Indeed, he compared his role in the case to the work of death penalty defense lawyer, stating: "I consider this case of equal importance. I look upon it as a case of life and death. You might as well, gentlemen of the jury, bury that young man six feet deep in the soil of the old churchyard where his early American ancestors sleep, as to consign him to be forever chained to that woman" (*CR* 1277). Within broader white America, this aversion to miscegenation was linked to the fear of racial passing, with both phenomena threatening the taxonomical system of racial classification and the idea of white racial purity. But, in what would seem to be the effort to rule out the possibility of passing, the jury ultimately found in favor of Alice, stipulating that her blackness was indeed visible and that she had not deceived Leonard. In doing so, they suggested that passing could not be successful because it could and would be detected: Alice was unequivocally black. The trial and finding thereby acted as both testament to hierarchies of race and punishment for Alice's attempted interlope. However, the final verdict can also be read as Leonard's punishment for confirming Mills' claim that he was "no ornament to society" (*New York Times*, 3 December 1925, 3).[3] Not only had he defied racial expectations, specifically the imperative to maintain white racial purity through endogamous unions, but it also became clear through the course of the trial that Leonard had failed to fulfill gender, sexual, and class norms. On multiple fronts, then, it was Leonard who was ultimately found to be aberrant and deserving of legal and extra-legal reprimand.

Rhinelander remains a critical account of regulation, punishment, and the centrality of race to understandings of identity. While it may be representative of a particular moment in early twentieth-century America, a series of broader questions regarding race arise from the case, questions that continue to resonate in the contemporary context. For instance, how do relations of power operate in the policing, claiming, and expression of identity? How does categorization function in a disciplinary sense to individuate, identify and distribute, and to condition how subjects are understood, both by others and themselves? What norms—of behavior, corporeality, identity—are associated with categorization? How is the body understood in relation to categorization? And, finally, how are subjects compelled to enact these norms associated with categorization, indeed, how might they be said to be *formed* through this operation? In the course of this book, I proceed to analyze these questions in terms of the normative categories of race, as they are underpinned by demarcations of sexuality, gender, and class. Staging a raciological inquiry into the formations of blackness and whiteness cultivated in North American history and the imaginings of U.S. culture, my concern is to mark out ways that race is cited and recited, the moments or exchanges that identify and form individuals as raced, and the specific techniques of power and regimes of truth through which race is produced. Coupled with these lines of inquiry, I ask: how do individuals participate in their own racialization and how might it be possible to challenge the workings of race in order to realize new socialities?

The three seemingly disparate quotes I open with above trace the trajectory of this project and the propositions around which it is organized. Drawing on the work of Michel Foucault, the first claim explored is that race operates as a disciplinary regime and that racial subjects are formed through racial discipline. The second claim, informed by Judith Butler's theories of subjectivity, is that the mechanism through which this disciplinary formation is inaugurated and sustained is racial performativity, and that all racial subjects can be said to execute a kind of performative racial passing. Finally, while discipline and the performative imperatives of race might seem to delimit ways of being (raced), I examine how subjects can and do struggle against subjection and practice new modes of racial becoming.

DISCIPLINE AND TECHNIQUES OF FORCES AND BODIES

When Foucault states that the individual "is [not] amputated, repressed, altered by our social order . . . [but] is carefully fabricated in it, according to a whole technique of forces and bodies" (1991, 217), he refers to the *disciplines* through and within which subjects are made. For Foucault, the social order—and the forms of power at work within society—do not oppress or constrain a subject who can be said to exist independently from or prior to those mechanisms of constraint. This subject is not amputated, in the sense that an *a priori* capacity has been severed or impaired. Rather, the subject and its capacities are the product of the particular form of power that Foucault calls discipline. Discipline, for Foucault, "'makes' individuals; it is the specific technique of a power that regards individuals as both objects and instruments of its exercise" (1991, 170). In *Discipline and Punish,* Foucault explains that this form of power emerged in eighteenth-century Europe and eventually overlaid an earlier form of power premised on the rule of the sovereign. This earlier form of power, according to Foucault, was a vengeful power. It was punitive in nature and execution; it exerted itself directly on bodies through corporeal punishment and, through spectacle and ritual, confirmed the absolute power of the ruler and their right over life and death. Changing power relations within the social body and the increasing inefficiency of sovereign power, however, resulted in the emergence of disciplinary power. This modern form of power continues to target the body—the individual body—but through different means. Where sovereign power wielded direct force and control over the corporeal, discipline—or what Foucault alternatively calls the anatomo-politics of the body—works through coercion to modify and manipulate the body. This is 'achieved' through various techniques and technologies that *distribute* individual bodies: they are surveyed, organized, separated, and hierarchized in developmental sequence according to a constructed norm. The techniques also operate to *control* the individual body so as to produce a docile and useful—a productive—subject.

If discipline is a set of practices and techniques that 'makes' individuals, my interest here is to establish how *race* might be seen as a form of discipline—a disciplinary practice—that molds and modifies identity through targeting the body. Foucault only specifically considered race as a topic of sustained analysis in the lecture course published as *Society Must Be Defended: Lectures at the Collège de France, 1975–1976* (2003b). In this selection of lectures, however, he was concerned not with this micro-level production of raced individuals but with the question of how racism has been used to control the population *en masse.* Foucault argued that racism has been used in this way—as a functional mechanism of control—from the second half of the eighteenth century when a new form of power, biopolitics, emerged in addition to discipline. This new non-disciplinary technology "applied not to man-as-body but to the living man ... to man-as-species" (2003b, 242) and involved regularizing "the birth rate, the mortality rate, longevity and so on" (2003b, 243). The regularizing nature of biopolitics was enabled through the introduction of mechanisms such as "forecasts, statistical estimates, and overall measures" (2003b, 246). And the use of these mechanisms is never more evident than in the specific ways, from this time, that the species was arranged and regulated into subspecies—or what we know as races. As Foucault states:

> The appearance within the biological continuum of the human race of races, the distinction among races, the hierarchy of races, the fact that certain races are described as good and that others, in contrast, are described as inferior: all this is a way of fragmenting the field of the biological that power [biopolitics] controls. (2003b, 254–255)

While this focus on the structural workings of racism is essential, it leaves unaddressed how race might work at the level of the subject, that is, how the individual is formed as a racial subject. This formation is a product not of biopolitics, the power focusing on the population, but of *discipline*—the form of power that 'makes' subjects. And, while the workings of biopolitics unavoidably condition the lived realities of raced subjects, it remains to be asked how power *creates* the races that biopolitics in turn controls. If Foucault did not specifically consider racial subject constitution, how might his ideas on discipline be productively extended to account for race? This is a question I proceed to explore in chapter 1, where I argue that race is a form of discipline that produces subjects—as raced. The chapter asks: what does reframing race as discipline yield and how might it offer new ways to understand the operations of race, specifically in terms of the construction and maintenance of blackness and whiteness in U.S. history? If subjects are at once formed and form themselves in relation to the norms and dominant relations of power that call them into being *as* subjects, by extending Foucault's terrain of inquiry I demonstrate that, rather than being corporeal 'truths,' blackness and whiteness are (a) normative and regulatory ideals, (b) coercive demands, and (c) forms of power, as they are enmeshed with certain forms of knowledge that invest bodies (what Foucault identifies as power/knowledge). These knowledges that invest the body *create* race as a corporeal reality, the truth of which is supposedly located in (and constructed through the semantics of) color and blood.

Law, as evidenced from the *Rhinelander* trial, functions as a specific site of racial knowledge production and as a key instrument in the technology of power that is racial discipline. This was the case from almost the earliest days of the American colonies, where law was used to identify subjects as raced and to separate subjects through racial designation. I proceed to analyze, in chapter 2, how the deployment of law to these ends can be read through Foucault's notions of anatomo-politics (the political, disciplinary strategies that target 'man-as-body') and biopolitics (those strategies aimed at regulating 'man-as-species'). If discipline is a form of power that is productive, what comes into focus through the course of this study is that law—as a modality of discipline—was used to 'make' racial subjects, raced bodies, and to augment the idea that race is a truth. These ideas, I argue, are legally determined via the concepts of color and blood: though material realities, color and blood are historically produced as the fictive loci of race. During the seventeenth century, race was understood through a reliance on the visual codings of color. Through the course of the eighteenth century, however, this idea was overlaid by codings of blood, when law was used to resolutely secure racial 'truth' in the deep recesses of the body and, through this, organize the population. This securing was achieved through two legal mechanisms: first, anti-miscegenation laws and statutory definitions of race regulated the literal production of race through delineating permitted and forbidden sex and by allocating status; and second, the Court was used as the arena within which to adjudicate racial performance, determine whether it was in line with designated status and, thereby, produce possible ways in which race could be embodied and lived. Importantly, however, though law is enmeshed within, rather than separated out from knowledges that circulate in the broader social realm, it lends dominant knowledges a certain legitimacy. In this way, law enters into a network of relations that together augment what I am calling racial discipline.

RACIAL PERFORMATIVITY, PASSING, AND
THE INEFFICACY OF NORMS

If race is a disciplinary practice, it is also performative. Race is performative because it is an act—or, more precisely a series of repeated acts—that brings into being what it names. In making this claim I situate Judith Butler's work on performativity as central to this analysis. Race, however, is not Butler's focus and has remained largely obscured in her work. Butler has instead been concerned with examining how gender and sex, rather than being ontological realities, are discursive constructs that produce certain kinds of bodies and subjectivities. In *Gender Trouble* she insists that "[g]ender is the repeated stylization of the body, a set of repeated acts within a highly rigid regulatory frame that congeal over time to produce the appearance of . . . a natural sort of being" (1999, 25). In this way, gender is a 'doing'—it is a series of acts that one *does*—rather than the expression of an internal truth or what one 'is.' But, importantly, these acts are not the product of free will—we don't just get to choose how we act—because they are executed within a 'rigid regulatory frame' or what can be thought of as discipline.

For Butler, subjects are compelled to enact the compulsory norms of gender —those ascribed to masculinity and femininity—in order to become and exist as viable social subjects, and efforts to enact these norms work, in turn, to condition the body. However, these norms are a product of disciplinary power and, as such, constructed and ultimately unattainable. They are, as Butler states, "continually haunted by their own inefficacy." Precisely because of this, the norms are endlessly asserted within discourse, marking "the anxiously repeated effort to install and augment their jurisdiction" (1993, 237).

While Butler has claimed that race is performatively produced in ways similar to gender, a consideration of racial performativity is not integrated into her work. This study aims to provide such an account and to explore the implications of thinking about race as performative: a performative compulsion always inter-articulated with gender, sex, and class. Let me be clear, however, that I am not concerned with whether gendered performativity is analogous to racial performativity; this is not my study, and I would insist that the performative compulsions of gender and sexuality that bring the subject into being are always already enmeshed within racial performative demands, and vice versa. I demonstrate this enmeshment through the course of this book, most specifically (in chapters 4 and 5) in relation to productions of black femininity and white masculinity within the overarching economy of heteronormativity. My primary interest in using the concept of performativity is to see how it extends understandings of racial subject formation. Ultimately, I bring into focus how racial discipline and the performative imperative of racial enunciation are inextricable; they work together to *produce* subjects as raced. In addition to these claims, however, I specify that this production functions as a form of (performative) *racial passing*. In saying this, I rework the traditional understanding of racial passing, where the term is usually used to refer to a subject who passes for a racial identity from which they are discursively prohibited. But, in stipulating that race is performative, I point to the fact that there is no internal 'truth' to race. Rather, through being read as 'belonging' to a particular racial category— that is, visually appearing and conducting one's acts, manners, and behaviors in accordance to disciplinary racial demands—*all* subjects are passing-*for* a racial identity that they are said to *be*.

Butler's account of performativity is provocative in the context of this inquiry for a number of reasons. Among these are that Butler's particular model of performativity takes Foucauldian paradigms of discourse, power, and subject formation as its primary point of departure. On the basis of this genealogical commonality, I put Butler and Foucault into conversation to see what this might yield in relation to my investigation of racial subject constitution. This particular constellation—race, Foucault, Butler—is not, to my knowledge, one that has received sustained scholarly attention. Also, Butler's repeated gesturing toward race, but only fragmentary attention to how the theory of performativity might revise contemporary questions regarding racial construction demands analysis. In deploying Butler's formulation of performative theory, however, it bears mentioning that I don't engage with the psychoanalytic component of her analysis. This choice is informed by my interest in the overlay between her work and Foucault's: Foucault's critique of psychoanalysis and the fact that the inclusion of such an investigation would generate another book in itself underlie my decision to not consider this dimension of Butler's scholarship here.[4]

The inextricability of racialized discipline and performative imperatives of race is the focus of chapter 3, where I situate the compelled performative enactment of norms as the *mechanism* through which racial discipline is sustained. Racial discipline, as I establish in this chapter, relies on surveillance—on what Foucault calls the panoptic power of continual observation. This regime requires that the body visually announce 'racial truth' and that the subject self-discipline in line with designated status. However, I am interested in what the ability to evade efforts of disciplinary surveillance—through passing for a prohibited racial identity—exposes about the general performative process of racial subject formation. The discursively defined black subject who passes-for-white 'fails' in terms of both of the requirements marked above: they disrupt the notion that race is visible and secured in the body, and highlight the tenuous foundations upon which the system of racial discipline rests. Through redeploying Butler's theory of gendered performativity to account for race, I explore how the passer's production of identity is parallel to *all* racial subject formation. The chapter examines the significance of applying the theory of performativity to the workings of race; analyzes how these ideas relate to the earlier elaboration of Foucault's theory of discipline; and shows that citations of racial norms do not reflect racial internality but, rather, produce what they name.

In order to flesh out these ideas and ground them in a tangible empirical example, I turn, in chapters 4 and 5, to *Rhinelander v. Rhinelander*. My aim in looking to *Rhinelander* is not, however, to provide a cultural history.[5] Rather, the case is strategically operationalized or put to work, to elucidate the multivalent and contingent processes through which social subjects come into being as raced. Thus, I use the *Rhinelander* court records alongside popular media coverage in order to test the theoretical claims I have made regarding the disciplinary and performative production of racial identities and to excavate the role of law in the production and maintenance of these identities.

Beginning in chapter 4 with a focus on Alice, I consider how law is used to detect acts of racial passing, and how law 'domesticates' the liminal passing subject by 'making' them signify blackness. What we see through this case is that the legal realm becomes a space in which to recuperate defiance and to insist on the commensurability between supposed 'internal racial truth' and external expressions of race. The Courts' resecuring of Alice as black ultimately highlights the productive capacity of law and the workings of performative discipline. My claim, however, is that it is not only Alice who passes. Rather, because all racial subjects are formed through the compelled and never-ending recitation of norms associated with particular categories of race, racial identity in general operates as a pass that is *a becoming,* one that never assumes the fixed status of 'being.' To address these ideas, I turn, in chapter 5, to an analysis of Leonard Rhinelander and what is deemed by the Court to be his failed performance of white masculinity. I show that despite having a white body and white legal title, Leonard is unable to pass as a white male because he does not successfully recite the normative imperatives of white masculinity. Regardless of the form of passing—those in line with or in defiance of racial status—we see that subjects never *occupy* the site of identity. The significance of such a claim underscores one of the key points of this inquiry: acts rather than corporeality are the means through which racial identity is produced and this identity is only ever a (passing) phantasm devoid of ontological security. Ultimately, an analysis of both Alice and Leonard enables us to see (a) the workings of legal summons and the compelled citation of 'racial truth' before the Court, (b) the labor that the production of racial identity requires and how this might 'fail,' and (c) the legal and extra-legal discipline that constrains the subject's ability to pass-*for* a given racial identity, whether that be one that is in line with legal status or not.

THE QUESTION OF AGENCY AND
TRANSFORMABLE SINGULARITIES

In analyzing the triangulated operations of racial discipline, performativity, and passing, my scope is limited to considering the formation of race along the black/white binary axis. In doing so, I am conscious of the danger of reinscribing an artificial opposition that has been set up between these identity sites. Yet it is precisely the continuing force that this binarism yields and its ongoing currency in the contemporary U.S. racial landscape that motivates this concentration. This book engages scholarship that questions the prevailing power of the black/white binary by illuminating the complexities of its functionings, and by identifying its points of weakness that might be exploited to disturb its political centrality and power.[6] In exploring the binary, I use the term 'whiteness' to simultaneously encompass both *the process of being white* and *a discursive systemic social power* supported by practices and beliefs. I use the term in a broad sense, in a similar way to my generalized use of the terms 'black' and 'blackness.'[7]

While I deploy these terms for analytic convenience, the study pivots on the desire to make clear the false homogeneity of subjects that are denoted by these terms and the arbitrariness of race *per se*. In the same moment that I employ these terms as critical tools of analysis, then, I hope to expose the mechanisms of their production and mark possibilities for their rearticulation.

The final portion of this study is concerned with examining what forms of agency and resistance are possible within the context of this binary construction of black and white identities. Guiding this analysis is the question of how individuals struggle against subjection and how racial norms might be recited in new directions, given that the coercive demands of discipline and performative constraints make it seem like race is an insurmountable *limit* or closed system. That race operates as a limit appears particularly so for black subjects. For despite the fact that *all* subjects are produced and positioned within and by the discursive formations of race, the impact of that positioning and what it means for experience is markedly different. Black subjects are situated within an anti-black context where the black body/self continues to be torn asunder within the relations of civil society. This means that, as Yancy (2008, 134 n. 11) insists, "the capacity to imagine otherwise is seriously truncated by ideological and material forces that are systematically linked to the history of white racism."

A number of scholars have examined these realities and advanced critical accounts of what they identify as the resulting *condition* of black existence. David Marriot, for instance, argues that "the occult presence of racial slavery" continues to haunt our political and social imagination: "nowhere, but never-theless everywhere, a dead time which never arrives and does not stop arriving" (2007, xxi). Saidiya Hartman, in her provocative *Lose Your Mother: A Journey Along the Atlantic Slave Route* (2007) refers to this haunting as slavery's afterlife. She insists that we do not live with the residue or legacy of slavery but, rather, that slavery lives on. It 'survives' (Sexton 2010, 15), through what Loïc Wacquant (2002, 41) has identified as slavery's functional surrogates: Jim Crow, the ghetto, and the prison. For Hartman, as echoed by other scholars, slavery has yet to be undone:

> Black lives are still imperiled and devalued by a racial calculus and a political
> arithmetic that were entrenched centuries ago. This is the afterlife of
> slavery—skewed life chances, limited access to health and education, pre-
> mature death, incarceration, and impoverishment. I, too, am the afterlife of
> slavery. (2007, 6)

Frank B. Wilderson III, in his *Red, White, and Black: Cinema and the Structures of U.S. Antagonisms* (2009), powerfully frames slavery's afterlife as resulting in a form of social death for black subjects and, more than this, he argues that black subjectivity is constituted as ontological death. For Wilderson, "the Black [is] a subject who is always already positioned as Slave" (2009, 7) in the United States, while everyone else exists as "Masters" (2009, 10).[8]

Studies of slavery's afterlife and the concept of social death have inarguably made essential contributions to understandings of race.[9] The strengths of such analyses lie in the salient ways they have theorized broad social systems of racism and how they have demanded the foregrounding of suffering, pain, violence, and death. Much of this scholarship can be put or is productively in conversation with Foucault's account of biopolitics that, as I noted earlier, regulates at the level of the population. Where sovereignty 'took life and let live,' in the contemporary sphere biopolitics works to 'make live.' However, certain bodies are not in the zone of protected life, are indeed expendable and subjected to strategic deployments of sovereign power that 'make die.' It is here that Foucault positions the function of racism. It is, he argues, "primarily a way of introducing a break into the domain of life that is under power's control: the break between what must live and what must die" (2003b, 254). Thus, certain bodies/subjects are killed—or subjected to sovereign power and social death—so that others might prosper.[10]

In *Scenes of Subjection: Terror, Slavery, and Self-Making in Nineteenth-Century America* (1997), Hartman examines the 'must die' imperative of social death—understood broadly as a lack of social being—but she also illuminates how, within such a context, slave "performance and other modes of practice . . . exploit[ed], and *exceed[ed]* the constraints of domination" (1997, 54, my emphasis). Hartman analyzes *quotidian* enactments of slave agency to highlight practices of "(counter)investment" (1997, 73) that produced "a reconstructed self that negates the dominant terms of identity and existence" (1997, 72).[11] She thus argues that a form of agency is possible and that, while "the conditions of domination and subjugation determine what kinds of actions are possible or effective" (1997, 54), agency is not *reducible* to these conditions (1997, 55).[12] The questions that I ask in this analysis travel in this direction, and aim to build on this aspect of Hartman's work. In doing so I make two key claims: first, that despite undeniable historical continuities and structural dynamics, race is also marked by discontinuity; and second, race is constantly reworked and transformed *within* relations of power *by subjects*.[13]

For Vincent Brown, a historian of slavery, "violence, dislocation, and death actually generate politics, and consequential action by the enslaved" (2009, 1239). He warns that focusing on an overarching condition or state potentially obscures seeing these politics. More than this, however, it risks positioning relations of power as totalizing and transhistorical, and it risks essentializing experience or the lived realities of individuals.[14] I scale down to the level of the

subject to analyze both (a) how subjects are formed, and (b) how subjects—
black and white alike—have struggled *against conditions* in ways that refuse
totalizing, immutable understandings of race. This book does not seek to mark
a condition or situation then, but instead takes up Brown's challenge (made
within the context of studies of slavery) to pay attention to efforts to *remake*
condition. Looking to those efforts to remake condition and identity grapples
with the microphysics of power and the practices of daily life, enacted by individuals and in collective politics, to consider what people *do* with situations:
those dynamic, innovative contestations of (a never totalizing) power. Echoing
the call raised by Brown (2009, 1239), my work focuses then on "examining . . .
social and political lives rather than assuming . . . lack of social being" in order
to think about how subjects can and have "made a social world out of death
itself" (Brown 2009, 1233) or how, more generally, race can be reconfigured
within the broader workings of what I am calling racial discipline and performative imperatives.

But in addressing the quotidian and those efforts to remake condition and
identity, this study insists on a shift in perspective in terms of how power is
thought about. As I have remarked, I am not focused on biopolitics or what can
be seen as solely sovereign forms of power that are deployed to condition who
will live and who will die. Instead, I am concerned with disciplinary power,
which is articulated simultaneously but at a different level to biopolitics (and
despite the exercise of sovereign forms of power) (Foucault 2003a, 250). For
Foucault, this form of power is not absolute, nor does it exist in opposition to
resistance. Rather, power is seen as always fragmentary and incoherent, and
power and resistance are seen as mutually constitutive. Disciplinary power is
productive, in that it generates particular capacities and forms of subjectivity
(and, necessarily, agency). And finally, though subjects are formed in power,
they are not reducible to it, not determined by power.

With these ideas in mind, I proceed, in chapter 6, to examine how both
Foucault and Butler frame agency within their theories of subject constitution,
and the possibilities these framings invite. To map the complexities of agency I
return to an analysis of *Rhinelander,* specifically focusing on Alice's agential
practices. What *Rhinelander* highlights is that resistance and power are not
antithetical and that agency is not the product of free will or choice. Rather, we
see that it is *within* the very imperative to recite discursive norms that the ability
for agential rearticulation resides. Precisely because disciplinary power has unintended effects and because performative demands rely on faithful performances, it is in the embodied performance of identity that power can be re-
deployed and race recited in new directions. Through thinking about power in
the ways I mark out, racial agency comes into view as that which, though

truncated, is not foreclosed. And by tracing race's historical, mutable, contingent, contradictory, and thus changing formations, it becomes possible to see the articulation of spaces and embodiments that *enable* agency, exceed constraints of domination, and pursue transformation.

In chapter 7, I more concretely examine how the individual might practice race in ways that problematize notions of truth, resignify racial norms and, in so doing, craft new modes of being. I begin with analyzing Henry Louis Gates Jr.'s theorization of the African American practice of signifying, which, I argue, represents a cogent example of efforts to critically recite the force of racial discipline through restylization. What underscores this practice is an insistence on critique—of received signs, meaning, language, discourse, knowledge, and identity. This concept of critique is central to Foucault's later work on what he calls 'technologies of the self,' where he was specifically concerned with how sexual subjectivity might be refashioned. While much of the current scholarship that takes up this aspect of Foucault's later work continues in this vein, my interest is to ask how racial identity might be both formed and transformed in the often vexed practices of self-critique that struggle against subjection and how racial rearticulation might be seen as a technology of self.[15] Foucault explains that this form of self-critique, or criticism, is an ethical practice that involves analyzing the power/knowledge relations through which subjects are formed—examining "the historical conditions which bear on the creation of links to truth, to rules, and to the self." Such an analysis, and understanding of the self as a product of historically produced truths, does not, Foucault insists, "mark out impassable boundaries or describe closed systems." Instead, this critique "brings to light transformable singularities" or points where identity might be problematized and subjectivity crafted anew (Foucault 2010, 335).

In arguing that racial identity is disciplinary and performative, I am building on the work of scholars such as Siobhan Sommerville (2000), Dwight McBride (1998), Henry Louis Gates, Jr. (1987; 1988; 1992), George Yancy (2004a; 2008), Philip Brian Harper (1996), Rinaldo Walcott (2000; 2003), and E. Patrick Johnson (2003) whose scholarship, while never forsaking analyses of the complexities of what being black means and how race operates, have critiqued notions of racial authenticity. These writers have challenged received wisdoms about race and racial hegemony, and have questioned African American investments in supposed 'authentic' racial performances. Critique in this vein can be seen as evidence of several decades of theoretical and political agitation, which has compelled a rethinking of black subjectivity. Feminists brought gender specificity to the analysis of black identities; diaspora theorists demanded the contextualization of distinct forms of racial oppression and formations of identity; and black queer theorists have shown how heteronormativity has shaped racial discourse in the United States. In addition to engaging scholars working in these areas of inquiry, this project also participates in dialogue—generated from within the fields of African American and African Diaspora Studies—that has demanded that whiteness be interrogated. Unsettling the 'taken-for-granted-ness' of whiteness, the work of scholars such as Robyn Wiegman (1995), George Lipsitz (1998), Richard Dyer (1997), Julian B. Carter (2007), David Roedigger (1998), and Ladelle McWhorter (2009) has insisted that specific attention be directed toward mapping the particularities of white subject constitution as a discursive production. My discussion of racial discipline and performativity seeks to contribute another dimension to these important conversations.

Analyzing race in the ways explored in this study elucidates that what we understand as race is not a self-evident truth and that it does not reflect an 'essence' or essential self that is conveyed through skin. Instead, race is seen to be a discursively generated set of meanings that attach to the skin—meanings that, through various technologies and techniques, come to regulate, discipline, and form subjects as raced. Addressing the ways that race is disciplinary and performative does not, as I argue, simply point out closed systems that can't be altered. What we see instead is that the supposed 'obviousness' of subjectivity can be questioned and that this might, as Foucault has suggested, "contribute to changing certain things in peoples' way of perceiving and doing things" (1981, 12). Working within discursive constraints, subjects always *do* negotiate concepts of race, racial identity, and racial definition, and it is precisely here, in these spaces of negotiation, that the possibilities for innovative reworkings of performative imperatives of race might be—and are—seized. To say that race can be reworked is not to say that we should seek to (or could) do away with it. Rather, it is to suggest that as racial subjects we might consciously think about the processes of our development as raced, our investments in racial systems and identity, how these investments might be lived more ethically, and ultimately, how we might practice race in new ways—and thus forge new realities.

1

Racial Disciplinarity

In the age of Reconstruction America, where slavery had been abolished and a new era of racial politics supposedly embarked upon, the presiding Judge in *Scott v. Georgia* (1869) emphatically declared that "the laws of civilization demand that the races be kept apart in this country."[1] He recited, here, the insistent historical desire within dominant American racial ideology to maintain unequivocal distinctions between disparate races. And he called upon the very 'laws of civilization' as the origin of and justification for these apparently immutable divisions drawn along the lines of race. Echoing this call, the opinion delivered in *Kinney v. Commonwealth* (Va. 1878) stated:

> The purity of public morals, the moral and physical development of both
> races, and the highest advancement of our cherished southern civilization,
> under which two distinct races are to work out and accomplish the destiny
> to which the Almighty has assigned them on this continent—all require that
> they should be kept distinct and separate, and that connection and alliances
> so unnatural that God and nature seem to forbid them, should be prohibited
> by positive law, and be subject to no evasion.[2]

Divisions deemed to be ordained by God were to be unhampered by human intervention, and the very well-being and future of the cultural dominion meant adhering to this supposed natural and omnipotent law. For, "[a] sound philanthropy, looking at the public peace and the happiness of both [the white and black] races would regard any effort to intermerge the individuality of the races as a calamity full of the saddest and gloomiest portent to the generations that are to come after us."[3] This *individuality* (marking that which is supposedly separate) speaks to the fundamental principle upon which the notion of race rests: more than simply describing physiological differences, race has been used to denote *absolute* distinctions between 'types' of humans who have been figured as intellectually, psychically, emotionally, and culturally incommensurate. Physiological markers were seen to be simply the external manifestation of these internal racial differences, differences that *rendered* racial groups as discreet in that they were seen to possess distinguishable and independent traits and characteristics. Though differences existed *between* racial types, individuals *within* these types were seen as generally homogenous in their shared attributes. It was these attributes that were used, retroactively, to continually reenforce racial lines, positioning race as that which signifies a resolute and unalterable boundary that cannot be traversed.

Despite producing powerful and distinct lived experiences, race is a social fiction. As Haney López (1996, 14) notes, race "can be understood as the historically contingent social systems of meaning that attach to elements of morphology and ancestry." This historical contingency can be seen in the various and often contradictory distinctions that have been made between 'types' of humans in different temporal and spatial contexts. Between the earliest notions of modern racial ideology, where human types were hierarchically organized (between the Creator and all other living beings) within the 'Great Chain of Being,'[4] to contemporary formulations of race, what *constitutes* different racial groups and what race *means* has undergone radical revision. Even though racial meaning has been disparate in content as well as context, the very force of race as a signifier has derived from this disparity, leading David Goldberg (1992, 558) to claim that the power of race "has consisted in its adaptive capacity to define population groups, and by extension social agents, as self and other at various historical moments." The possession of certain traits or characteristics have, accordingly, been (temporarily) stabilized as denoting one's belonging or nonbelonging to a particular racial group. Yet "[t]o be capable of this, race itself must be almost but not quite empty in its own connotative capacity, able to signify not so much in itself as by adopting and giving naturalized form to prevailing conceptions of social group formation at different times" (Goldberg 1992, 558). While race classifies individuals in a system of inclusion and exclusion, it must be understood as more than simply categorization. Race is a practice: it is a system of meanings *deployed* in the racing of individuals and, as a concept, race must be *maintained* in order to survive. The categories accepted as natural and inevitable must be consistently reiterated in discourse in order for these categories to be sustained. They must constantly be called upon, called forth if you will, for without possessing ontological grounding, the 'truths' of racial categorization and demarcations exist only in their 'retelling.'

It is through this retelling that race is understood and through which we come to see the demarcations of race as natural. And it is only through this reiterative practice that the "social systems of meaning," to which Haney López (1996, 14) refers, can be connected to individuals based on physiology. It is these social systems of meaning that render race comprehensible. The question of what 'marks' or is the 'cause' of racial difference (whether it be seen, for instance, as that which is imposed by biology or divine decree) has been the object of multiple and conflicting scientific, social, religious, and legal inquiries. Yet it is important to stress that all such efforts to understand race, or make racial distinctions, have been generated through sets of abstract injunctions that dictate (a) the way in which race has been (and can be) thought about and, in turn, (b) the manner(s) through which 'difference' is recognized. Individuals only connect themselves with those who supposedly share their racial identity and distinguish themselves from others who are supposedly distinct, based on these rules of racial recognition. For these injunctions structure how we see race: we can *only* see race through these injunctions. In being unable to even comprehend race outside of these injunctions, racial distinctions become figured as prior to culture, as residing in the domain and by the decree of nature.

It is discursive power that 'makes' race perceptible, because it teaches or instructs people to read by it. And the racial meanings that are generated within this form of power condition the organization of an individual's relations, their world, their comprehension of others and of themselves. As Foucault has argued, this form of power works through hegemonic disciplinary mechanisms such that it "applies itself to immediate everyday life[,] categorizes the individual, marks him by his own individuality, attaches him to his own identity, imposes a law of truth in him that he must recognize and others have to recognize in him. *It is a form of power that makes individuals subjects*" (2000c, 331). In this chapter, I consider how the practice and notion of race can be figured as a type of discipline that functions to achieve the subjection of the individual—to make the individual a racial subject. The questions that interest me here include: what initiates and propels the marking of the individual; what attaches the individual to that which is apparently their 'identity'; in what manner and through what means is a 'law of truth' forcefully bestowed on an individual so that they come to recognize themselves *as raced,* a recognition that parallels the way they are perceived by others; and how are the injunctions that structure racial meaning and identity generated?

To begin thinking through these questions, I look to Foucault and, more briefly, Butler because, while neither of these theorists has given extended attention to race, each provides accounts of subject constitution that are compelling when deployed in the service of such an inquiry. Butler has been principally concerned with interrogating how sex and gender function as normative ideals in the production of subjectivity. Taking her work as a point of departure, I enquire how race and the raced subject might be "marked and formed by discursive practices" in a manner similar to that of the 'sexed' subject (Butler 1993, 1).[5] And Foucault only specifically considered race as a topic of sustained analysis in the lecture course published as *Society Must Be Defended: Lectures at the Collège de France, 1975–1976* (2003b), but focused on the regulatory functions of modern racism, a technology of power that, as Foucault explains, is employed by the state in order to 'manage' and 'protect' *the population*. Here, however, I look to his work in order to reflect on how *the individual* is inaugurated as a racial subject *through the workings of discursive discipline*.[6] I argue that the specter of race is itself a disciplinary regime that discursively generates, forms, and constructs the racial subject.

THE COERCIVE DEMANDS OF RACE

In *Bodies That Matter: On the Discursive Limits of Sex*, Judith Butler begins her introduction with the following claim:

> The category of "sex" is, from the start, normative; it is what Foucault has called a "regulatory ideal." In this sense, then, "sex" not only functions as a norm, but is part of a regulatory practice that produces the bodies it governs, that is, whose regulatory force is made clear as a kind of productive power, the power to produce . . . the bodies it controls. Thus, "sex" is a regulatory ideal whose materialization is compelled, and this materialization takes place (or fails to take place) through certain highly regulated practices. (1993, 1)

Butler's claim is that the sexed categories of male and female, and the correlative gender assignments of masculinity and femininity, are normative and idealized discursive models that function to produce, or bring into being, the very sexed subjects that these categories supposedly only demarcate. Through regulating or disciplining the body, discursive power *manifests* sexed bodies. While Butler's investigation specifically critiques the constitution of the subject in terms of sex and gender, I want to shift this analysis to consider how her ideas might be pertinent in mapping the formation of racial subjectivities. It is important to note at this point, however, that neither of these facets of subjecthood can stand alone or be considered in isolation.[7] For the purposes of analysis, though, I want to consider race temporarily as if it can be divorced from other discursive categories of identity.

If Butler's claim is refigured in terms of race, then it is possible to begin with the notion that race is normative. The racial categories of black and white can be seen, consequently, as normalizing regulatory ideals that generate and form the very bodies that race governs. In such an understanding, race functions as a component in the broader workings of discipline as a *practice* that *produces the very bodies and subjects that it controls*. The notion of race (the demarcation along lines of 'difference') is disciplinary precisely due to the various methods of control that are exerted over the body; methods are instituted in the name of race that, in turn, racialize the body and condition racialized subjectivity. One of the primary and foundational regulatory devices in the disciplinary regime of race is, fundamentally, the process of classification or codification, that is, the division of different 'types' of racial bodies. Codifying, by way of division between 'types,' acts as a gate-keeping mechanism whereby bodies are separated—rendered as distinct in their difference.

Race, like sex, is regulated by "the discourses of truth that have taken charge of it" (Foucault 1998, 97)—discourses that work, moreover, to set the limits of how race is conceived. Racial discourse can be understood in Foucauldian terms as the group of statements that govern and condition racial 'truths,' practices, value systems, beliefs, and assumptions.[8] These discourses mark the possible limits or enforce a conceptual grammar on what kinds of knowledge can be generated in terms of race and what can, in turn, be 'known' about race. In order to achieve this form of containment, these racial discourses must have "a repeatable materiality" (Foucault 2002, 122); they must retell, indeed reinscribe similar statements about race.

When it comes to thinking about racial discourse, though, it is important to remember Foucault's "cautionary prescriptions" (1998, 98) or the rules that mark the production of any form of discourse, for these rules structure the matrices in which racial subjects emerge. When applied to notions of race, they can be thought about in the following ways. First, the *power* that governs the formation of racial subjects and the *knowledge* that is generated in relation to racial subjects cannot be extricated. Race only came to be considered as that which was worthy of interrogation (whereby various medical, legal, and social 'truths' have been formulated in order to 'understand' the racial subject) because relations of power had already marked it as a possible target or object. Yet relations of power were only able to mark race as a target because knowledge had been "capable of investing it" (Foucault 1998, 98). Knowledge and power, and the manner in which they regulate race, are indissoluble. Second, the distribution of power that governs racial subjects is always modified or shifting so that various forces control the racial subject; these forces are never fixed (Foucault 1998, 99). Third, when considering the production of discourse in relation to race, it is important to analyze how microscopic (or localized) power and macroscopic power, or what Foucault (1998, 99) refers to as "over-all strategy," mutually condition each other in order to engender the regulatory formation of racial subjects. Foucault stresses here, though, that these two forms of power do not operate on different levels. Localized power, rather, acts as "the anchor point" (Foucault 1998, 99) for broader systems of power. Finally, discourse joins (multiple sites and forces of) power and (multiple and contesting forms of) knowledge; power and knowledge meet here. As a consequence, discourse must be understood as fractured, multiple, and contradictory. In Foucault's (1998, 100) analysis, "discourse [is] . . . a series of discontinuous segments whose tactical function is neither stable or uniform." Following from this, then, we cannot claim that there is an accepted discourse of race and, in opposition, unaccepted discourses. Instead, multiple discursive 'truths' exist in circulation and come into operation at different moments and in different sites. In order to claim, then, that the subject is formed in discourse is to acknowledge that this formation is marked by the inextricable workings of power and knowledge; that power, in this operation, is always mutating or shifting; that power works at both local and broader levels in a system of double conditioning; and that contradictory discourses exist simultaneously.

Yet certain discourses have maintained critical force within the Western racial economy and have generated the dominant conceptualizations of 'blackness' and 'whiteness' that are their legacy. This has been achieved because these 'discursive truths' have been grounded (or located) as material practices within specific institutional sites of power. And it is within these sites of power that racial discourse is rendered a "repeatable materiality." Here, racial 'knowledge,' or what are considered to be racial 'truths' are inscribed over and over again; they are reproduced and maintained through repeated reference. It is these discourses that configure bodies and engender a racializing of the subject, a 'reality' fabricated in what Foucault (1991, 194) refers to as a "specific technology of power . . . called discipline."

What, then, is this 'technology of power' that Foucault calls discipline? And how can it be seen to form, to craft, to fabricate individuals into subjects that can be recognized and that recognize themselves as raced? Foucault insists that above all else, this is a form of power that *produces:* "it produces reality; it produces domains of objects and rituals of truth. The individual and the knowledge that may be gained of him belong to this production" (1991, 194). Where technology denotes the capacity 'to make,' discipline constitutes the racial subject; racial subjects are the historical products of technologies of representation and apparatuses of power, in short, *techniques* of power. Power forms the racial subject through the disciplinary process of *subjection,* a dual process that denotes both the subordination of the subject through external control *and* the process of becoming a subject through being attached to an identity that one recognizes as 'self' (Foucault 2000c, 331). Butler (1997b, 11) elaborates on Foucault's argument, stating: "A power *exerted on* a subject, subjection is neverthe-less a power *assumed by* the subject, an assumption that constitutes the instru-ment of the subject's becoming." There is no racial subject that can be said to exist prior to power and that is then retroactively acted upon by power. Rather, the *racial* subject comes into being precisely through their discursively con-stituted identity *as raced*. In this way, then, there is no subject that can be viewed as black prior to the discursive mark that designates them as such. Once discur-sively marked, discipline 'works' to "mold conduct, to instill forms of self-awareness" (Gordon 2000, xix) and to inculcate a racialized identity in line with the discursive designation. External power (exercised within various institu-tional sites) simultaneously 'acts on' this individual as a racial subject. Above all, subjection is, as Butler (1997b, 84) claims, "the principle of regulation according to which a subject is formulated or produced." This regulation takes place through disciplinary measures in which certain signs (behaviors, manners of being, bodily markings, comportments) are excluded or ruled out as denoting 'racial belonging' (to a particular 'type') while others are produced. In Foucault's formulation, the subject is the (never fully achieved, because always in process) result of both juridical power (power that acts on the subject) and productive power (the power that constructs).

This power that forms the racial subject works through a process of normal-ization in which racial bodies are compared, differentiated, hierarchized, ho-mogenized (into set 'types'), and in which the abnormal is defined (Foucault 1991, 182).[9] In this way, only certain racial bodies (and hence, racial subjectivi-ties) are configured or accepted as viable. This can be seen in the measuring of distinct 'types' of racial bodies, distinctions that have only been made through a process of comparison and that have hierarchized the various 'types' of racial bodies that have been identified. The identification of 'fixed' racial possibilities have generated the normalized racial positions of black and white.[10] For Fou-cault (1991, 193), those identified as existing 'outside' of these normalized posi-tions are more highly marked and regulated than those within. These 'non-normalized' or 'abnormal' others become subject to rigorous interrogation that, in terms of race, seeks to fix the limits of racial intelligibility and augment the discursive power of the normalized racial positions. Consider, for instance, the discursive imperative to quantify and label racial subjects that complicate the normalized subject position of 'black.' In order to maintain the dominance of racial norms, various relations of power have persistently endeavored to align racial subjects that exist *between* the oppositional categories of white and black with blackness. Consequently, law and science, among other discursive forces, have generated an intricate catalogue of racial demarcations such as mulatto, quadroon, octoroon, and so forth that chart and fix differentiations from the norm, yet resecure the norm by way of connecting each of these racial categories to normalized blackness.

The norms of black and white function, ultimately, as coercive demands, as the imposition of one of these terms upon the subject is a disciplinary decree that operates to form that subject in alignment to the bestowed racial term. As noted previously, Foucault (2000c, 331) outlines that disciplinary power categorizes the individual and, in the process of this marking, attaches them to the categorization in a manner that ensures that they recognize themselves in the categorization. In regards to race, the discursive process of naming the individual as 'black,' for instance, is coupled with a co-extensive process; carried with the name are the workings of external power that compel the individual to assume this position that is marked out in discourse, a movement that sees the subject simultaneously "being occupied [by] and occupying the law" (Butler 1993, 122). This subject is called into being through various processes of constraint that determine and set the limits of the enunciative possibilities of the subject.[11] If only certain positions are marked out in discourse as possible and viable racial sites, then in order to be recognized as a subject (who must inevitably be raced), one must occupy the site within which one is placed. Consequently, the marking of the subject, as raced, can be seen to engender a double movement that (a) imposes and (b) activates identity, as this marking enters the subject into social existence and, in doing so, requires that the subject occupy this term so as to maintain discursive intelligibility.

Let me return to Butler's account of the gendering of the subject in order explore this movement. According to Butler, the discursive naming that is initiated by the doctor's call at a child's birth of "It's a girl!" transforms the child from an 'it' into a sexed subject. As a marking or placement within one of only two possible subject locations, this naming sees the girl 'girled,' "brought into the domain of language and kinship through the interpellation of gender" (Butler 1993, 7). This is, however, not a decree that sees the girled subject formed in totality in this instance. For Butler, rather, this "founding interpellation is reiterated by various authorities and throughout various intervals of time to reenforce or contest this naturalized effect. The naming is at once the setting of a boundary, and also the inculcation of a norm" (Butler 1993, 8). Coupled with the individual's participation in this 'girling' of the self—through the assumption of various normalized practices and bodily comportments and so forth that are seen to be the signifiers of the 'natural' expression of this subject position—the gendered subject is formed.

As a system of categorization or naming, the racializing of the subject functions in a similar manner. This can be seen in Frantz Fanon's (1967, 111) account that recalls the violent effect of a discursive proclamation that is cast his way. He hears "Look, a Negro!" and knows that this call is directed toward him. His recognition of the call is witnessed with his statement to himself, "It was true."[12] It was true—or he recognized this as a truth—because this discursive call is one of the key means through which his sense of sociality has been fashioned. He is unable to form a sense of identity that is not influenced by broader social norms that designate him as black. Like the naming ritual enacted through 'girl,' the discursive call of 'Negro' in Fanon's example is not a momentary designation but one that continues over and over again, called forth in a myriad of social institutions and practices so as to repeatedly race the subject.[13] Imprisoned by discourse, Fanon states, "I am given no chance. I am overdetermined from without. I am the slave not of the 'idea' that others have of me but of my own appearance" (1967, 116). Obviously the factors at work here are complex, and in subsequent chapters I explore them in more detail. For the present analysis, though, I want to mark that the individual is compelled to assume a normalized racial position, they validate this exercise of power through observing discipline (proclaiming 'It was/is true') and, thus, the individual *participates* in the discursive constitution of himself or herself as raced.[14]

THE POLITICAL TECHNOLOGY OF THE BODY

As Fanon's account illuminates, it is the body that bears the limits of subjectivity. This body determines discursive designation. Simultaneously, however, this body is itself a *product* of the meanings that are discursively attached to it. This raises a certain circularity in which one is invested with racial knowledge premised on a supposed corporeal 'truth' or a prior mark of race—an exteriorized mark that is figured as that which articulates an internal essence. Yet it is this supposed inner essence that determines one's allocation within a discursive site and it is this allocation that will then discursively mark the subject through the formation of subjectivity. Put another way, race is fabricated as a prediscursive corporeal 'truth,' and this 'prior' signifier relegates the subject to a certain racialized subject position. The discursive designation of racial status retroactively *racializes* the body (or constructs it as raced) and compels the subject to assume (or take-up) this position in order to supposedly reflect this inner essence.[15] Foucault (1991, 25) argues that this is achieved due to the body being "directly involved in a political field: power relations have an immediate hold upon it; they invest it; mark it; train it; torture it; force it to carry out tasks, to perform ceremonies, to emit signs." This 'political investment of the body' is initiated and sustained through what Foucault refers to as a *political technology of the body*, that is, a series of techniques in which the corporeal is subject(ed) to various disciplinary mechanisms that regulate and produce embodied subjectivities. Subjection is obtained through various forces that generate not only knowledge of the body, but utilize this knowledge in an attempt to contain, to master the body (Foucault 1991, 26). Historical efforts within the sciences to chart intricate repertoires of racial divisions, to mark, dissect, and typologize corporeal differences between black and white bodies and to 'uncover' various 'racial truths'—based on these corporeal distinctions—can be seen as one particular series of techniques that have operated to regulate and invest the body. Similarly, legal endeavors have labored to codify, classify, and designate racial status in order to maintain racially demarcated subjects, and themselves represent another series of techniques that have disciplined bodies. Both series of techniques are examples of the investment and regulation of bodies—operations of discipline that are exercised by making bodies *objects of knowledge.*

The body is rendered an object of knowledge (and a vehicle of power/knowledge) in that it is appropriated and interrogated in order to gain access to that which is supposedly *beyond* the body—that is, the putative internal racial 'truth' of the individual. This is not, as I have stated, a preexisting 'truth': this individual is *endowed* with a soul—a 'psyche, subjectivity, [or] a consciousness'—that functions as the 'prison of the body' (Foucault 1991, 29). The soul is, as Foucault (1991, 29) argues,

> produced permanently around, on, within the body . . . [and] born . . . out of methods of punishment, supervision and constraint. This real, non-corporeal soul is not a substance; it is the element in which are articulated the effects of a certain type of power and the reference of a certain type of knowledge, the machinery by which the power relations give rise to a possible corpus of knowledge, and knowledge extends and reinforces the effects of this power.

The racial body in and of itself, then, was not of primary concern in either the scientific or legal efforts to differentiate bodies. For what these ventures sought, instead, was the acquisition of knowledge pertaining to the *nature* of black and white subjects—a nature that was perceived as only accessible (and necessarily articulated) through the body—a materiality that was figured as pre-social. This body was seen to be the locus of 'essential' racial character and these efforts went to great pains to locate the physiological markers that apparently enunciated these racial truths in a manner that was beneficial to the racial economy of white dominance.

As such, the specific techniques that comprise the political technology of the body fabricate the racial subject as an object of knowledge by coming to 'know' the subject. This knowledge subsequently operates in a dual capacity in order to simultaneously (a) mark the parameters of the subjects' existence and nature, and (b) *constitute* the subject within this knowledge. This knowledge comes, ultimately, to *define* the individual. If we return to the process of normalization, it is possible to claim that 'racial experts' in the sciences and legislators (among various other legal actors) have normalized certain external corporealized traits and characteristics as indicative of distinct racial groups. For example, those who possess the phenotypic markers of white skin, straight hair, aquiline nose and thin lips have been typologized as 'Caucasian.' In opposition, those possessing "black skin-pigment, 'wooly' hair . . . [and] thick lips" have been identified as being of the 'Negroid race' (Davenport 1913, 34). Through the meticulous observation of the likes of technicians, legislators, and scientists, norms have been generated in regards to target groups. These norms work to homogenize the group that is targeted, but also to individualize those within the group by positioning all differences within that group as relative to a norm. However, these normalized traits of race ultimately work to enforce and maintain distinctions *between* racial groupings. As never simply external markers, corporeal distinctions have been invested with discursive meanings that come, through the workings of power/knowledge, to represent the supposed internal racial truth of individuals, and make the body the grounds for subjectivity. The political technology of the body is, then, as Foucault (1991, 28) states, "a set of material elements and techniques that serve as weapons, relays, communication routes and supports for the power and knowledge relations that invest human bodies and subjugate them by turning them into objects of knowledge." This investment and subjugation is achieved through the workings of discourse, the arena in which power and knowledge meet.

The respective 'technologies of power' of science and law can be seen as particular 'weapons' that serve the workings of power/knowledge relations in the subjugation and production of embodied racial subjects. Scientific and legal 'truths' generated in regard to race are repeatedly deployed to construct and regulate raced subjects. The communication routes that Foucault refers to can be seen to be the various networks of textual, discursive, and representational power that fabricate and maintain certain power/knowledge 'truths' of racial existence. And finally, multiple relays operate between these disparate technologies of power—networks of connection that enable these technologies of power to reinforce one another. For instance, if certain racial 'truths' are generated within particular scientific discourses and these same discursive 'truths' are reiterated in law and implemented as legal decrees in the regulation of racial subjects, then science and law have mutually augmented their respective roles in the subjugation of individuals as raced.

These techniques of power are not coherent in their ability to subjugate, however, nor are they able to be unilaterally imposed on subjects. Rather, these techniques are refractory and marked by multiple contradictions and disjunctions. The contesting capabilities, for example, of the legal arena to subjugate certain subjects into black racial subject status can be seen in the often-contradictory definitions of what *constituted* this status. This is clear in the disparity between definitions of race as they existed in two antebellum states. South Carolina repeatedly refused to impose an absolute definition of blackness. Instead, in 1835, Judge William Harper (cited in Williamson 1995, 18) insisted that an individual could "by reputation, by his reception into society, and his having commonly exercised the privileges of the white man" escape a definitive legal ruling as to whether they were black or white. During this same period, however, the State of Virginia legislated that an individual with one black grandparent was legally defined as black.[16] This suggests, then, that a subject could move between states and, in doing so, alter not only their racial status but also their ability to access the privileges that are legally attached to that status. This instability (or inability) to establish systematic and encompassing definitions of what constitutes black racial status attests to the incoherence of power. For power, as it pertains to race, is never exercised as totalizing control. The various and contradictory discourses that inform conceptualizations of race, and the subsequent methods of control that are instituted to maintain subjects within certain racial designations, create fissures that can and do result in innovative contestations of power.

The racial subject is disciplined and produced through multiple forces; external operations of power, such as those exercised in institutional settings, the disciplinary practices enforced in intersubjective exchanges, and the discipline of the self in relation to regulatory maxims, operate *together* to ensure that the subject recites the historically and spatially specific norms of their discursive constitution. One can only 'achieve' a racial subjectivity—that is, exist and survive as a recognizable and tenable subject—through the ratification of these imperatives. Foucault (1991, 26) is adamant, though, that we take note of the particularities of the workings of the political technology of the body. He states:

> this technology is diffuse, rarely formulated in continuous, systematic discourse; it is often made up of bits and pieces; it implements a disparate set of tools or methods. In spite of the coherence of its results, it is generally no more than a multiform instrumentation. Moreover, it cannot be localized in a particular type of institution or state apparatus. For they have recourse to it; they use, select or impose certain of its methods. But, in its mechanics and effects, it is situated at a quite different level. What the apparatuses and institutions operate is, in a sense, a micro-physics of power, whose field of validity is situated in a sense between these great functionings and the bodies themselves with their materiality and their forces.

Though diffuse, the workings of the political technology of the body, as it functions in relation to race, have been reliant on knowledge that insists that race is evident in corporeal distinctions.[17] While this view has historically received general consensus, debates have waged over *where* in the body this 'racial truth' has resided, that is, which specific bodily traits determine race. Theorists, scientists, theologians, legal agents, and natural historians could also come to no agreement as to how to measure racial distinctions or which criteria to use. And further confusion arose because some argued that humans were one species that could be divided into subgroups or categories while others maintained that blacks were a distinct species that descended from separate origins. This was the view considered by America's third president and principle author of the Declaration of Independence, Thomas Jefferson, who, in his *Notes on Virginia* (1786), "advance[d] . . . as a suspicion only, that the blacks, whether originally a distinct race, or made distinct by time and circumstance, are inferior to the whites in the endowment both of body and of mind" (quoted in Gossett 1964, 44). The very notion of 'whiteness' to which Jefferson refers was only a vague concept in the late eighteenth and early nineteenth centuries. As Higginbotham and Kopytoff (1989; 1983) note, "Pure white race as a legal [and social] concept was a vigorous and powerful social construct. It gained force in the late nineteenth and early twentieth centuries, and was called on to justify an ever harsher set of repressive legal [and extra-legal] measures against blacks."

The racial lines that have been drawn between supposedly 'distinct' subjects have been security measures established at the peripheries of European ancestry to ward against possible 'racial pollution.' In this manner, race has operated as a literal and figurative vehicle of containment to imprison individuals within a discursive designation based on a supposed 'essence.' And this racial essence has been *made* evident in two corporeal sites, color and blood, which have become the fictive loci of race. Racial meaning has been articulated and produced through the semantics of color and blood, which have worked in a metaphoric capacity (Jones 1993): social phenomena—that is, the construction of division along lines of differences inaugurated in the name of race—have been described "*in* and *as* metaphor" (Saks 2000, 63). If color and blood have functioned metaphorically it has been in their capacity to consume virtually all meaning pertaining to race and, simultaneously, to fashion all racial meaning. Race as color has referred to the phenotypic or external differences upon which notions of race have been premised, such as skin pigmentation, hair curvature, cranial shape, and various other corporeal traits. Race as blood has referred to the genotype of individuals and has utilized the idea of lineage or descent in order to describe and identify race. These dualistic understandings of the locus of race have been reflected within two standards of racial classification; race has been designated in terms of appearance and in terms of ancestry. Together, the notions of blood and color have diligently functioned so as to locate race *in* and *on* the body as a corporeal 'truth' that can be ascertained and, thereby, discursively fixed.

While I've marked these two conceptualizations of the locus of race as distinct, they are not separate: blood and color cannot be extricated in determining or thinking about race, because one cannot be secured without recourse to the other. Establishing the race of an individual by lineage, for instance, cannot be sought without referring to a racial group to which that individual supposedly 'belongs,' a group that is marked by externally distinct physical characteristics that are read as raced. Likewise, to racially classify individuals based on appearance inevitably establishes appearance as that which signifies blood. Blood and color, as metaphoric markers of race consequently collapse into one another and together comprise the corpus of racial knowledges that generate racial 'truths.' The racial subject becomes an object of these fields of knowledge, is invested with this knowledge, and is constituted through the rituals of truth production that contribute to this body of racial knowledge (that can also be defined as racial discourse). This constitution entails that the racial subject be regulated or disciplined according to the injunctions that are erected within and between these fields of knowledge. Below I briefly outline the contours of how blood and color have been understood, because it is these ideas that underscore the remainder of the analysis.

THE DISCOURSE OF COLOR

Skin color has generally been the medium through which racial classification is recognized and determined. As Zuberi (2001, 107) has noted, "such a grouping is based on our arbitrary distinctions"; nevertheless, it is the visible markers of skin that have come to stand for the most powerful differentiations between peoples. Within the elaborate spectrum of racial difference that has been fabricated based on the differentiation of skin pigmentation, it is those skins identified as black and white that have been formulated as antinomies.[18] Derrida argues that "Western thought . . . has always been structured in terms of dichotomies or polarities: good vs. evil, being vs. nothingness, presence vs. absence, truth vs. error, identity vs. difference, mind vs. matter, man vs. woman, soul vs. body, life vs. death, nature vs. culture, speech vs. writing" (cited in Johnson 1981, viii). Within this oppositional logic, these terms gain meaning only in relation to one another and "[t]he second term in each pair is considered the negative, corrupt, undesirable version of the first, a fall away from it . . . In other words, the two terms are not simply opposed in their meanings, but are arranged in a hierarchical order which gives the first term *priority*" (Johnson

1981, viii). Within this system, black is positioned as antithetical to white, with whiteness being invested with positive meaning and blackness with negative meaning. This dichotomous logic works such that the primary term in the pairing, in this case white, only gains its positive meaning against the negative meaning that is invested in the secondary term of black. Yet this is a product of the fact that the power of definition lies with those that claim occupation of the primary term, such that the meanings that are attributed to the secondary term are those that the inhabitants of the primary term refuse to claim as their own or use to identify themselves. Consequently, in order for whites to position and interpret themselves as superior, all that is deemed to be inferior must be attributed to those that are defined as diametrically opposite to whites. In this manner, those that have been discursively defined as black have been fabricated as the embodiment of evil.

As Ahmed and Stacey (2001, 4) insist, this mark of skin—as black or white—is not only "assumed to be a sign of the subject's interiority (for example what it means to be black or white . . .), but the skin is also assumed to reflect the truth of the other and to give us access to the other's being." Hence, a reciprocal relationship exists between the meanings that have been attributed to black skin and the internal 'truths' of black subjects that are supposedly articulated through the tangible materiality of the skin. The conceptualizations of blackness (and, by implication, whiteness) have been fashioned through intricate historical processes. Yet the term black, according to Winthrop Jordan (1968, 7), had been utilized to signify negative meaning even before English contact with Africa. He argues that during the Elizabethan era, the English had valorized 'white and red' beauty—'lily whiteness'—and associated the term black with evil and danger. When the English first encountered Africans they viewed them as repulsive because, in contrast to the (European) epitome of beauty, "the Negro was [seen as] ugly, by reason of his color and also his 'horrid Curles' and 'disfigured' lips and nose" (Jordan 1968, 8). Subsequently, color has become a discursive instrument not only in the differentiation of racial subjects but also in a generative sense to fabricate racial 'essence' and 'truth' as that which is heralded *by* and *through* the skin.

THE DISCOURSE OF BLOOD

The second, but by no means secondary way race has been conceptualized is through the semantics of blood. Blood and race have been conflated such that blood has come to denote race: blood is understood as one of the primary sites in which race is located and to be synonymous with race itself. According to Winthrop Jordan, the notion of blood has been formulated within Western thought "as much more than a convenient metaphor"; it was conceptualized as the "principle of life" (Jordan 1968, 165–166) and the carrier or determinant of race. Blood was figured as the very 'essence' of racial subjectivity, as genealogy was believed to govern racial 'truth.' In reconfiguring social practices as biological essences, the discourse of blood established the individual as *possessing* racial blood (Saks 2000, 62). This essence of race was seen as that which could be pure and, thereby, exist as discrete from other types of racial blood. Consequently, an individual was said to possess either black or white blood; white blood, however, could only be claimed if it was undiluted. For white blood was conceptualized as that which carried the identity, integrity, and currency of whiteness. In the words of the influential twentieth-century American eugenicist Lothrop Stoddard, the white subject was seen to have "clean, virile, genius-bearing blood, streaming down the ages through the unerring action of heredity, which, in anything like a favorable environment will multiply itself, solve our problems, and sweep us on to higher and nobler destinies" (quoted in Gossett 1964, 395). In opposition, the discourse of blood, as influenced by the discourse of color, rendered 'black blood' as that which denoted negative meaning; it functioned in terms of signification as pollutant, contaminant, contagion, and stain.[19]

Racial theories of the late nineteenth and early twentieth centuries saw heredity as key to the character of the individual. The racial sciences of this era proclaimed that, above all else, racial blood needed to be diligently regulated so as to thwart the contamination of whiteness. Yet this notion reaches back further to the earliest stirrings of modern racial thought, where the mixing of racial blood through miscegenation was identified as the absolute threat to dominant whiteness. If white blood gained and maintained its potency only in undiluted form, mixing with black blood represented danger for the economy of whiteness. Not only did this mixing of racial bloods suggest that the boundaries of whiteness might be blurred, it also threatened that in doing so the integrity of whiteness might be corrupted, as this introduction of foreign strains would supposedly produce individuals of inferior psychological, physical, and temperamental ability.[20] Blood, consequently, held omnipotent power in that it was, as Foucault states, "*a reality with a symbolic function*" (1998, 147). According to Foucault:

> Blood constituted one of the fundamental values. It owed its high value at the same time to its instrumental role (the ability to shed blood), to the way it functioned in the order of signs (to have a certain blood, to be of the same blood, to be prepared to risk one's blood), and also to its precariousness (easily spilled, subject to drying up, too readily mixed, capable of being quickly corrupted). (1998, 147)

In conclusion, these concepts of color and blood are inextricable from what has been my central concern in this chapter, namely, the idea that race is constructed through arbitrary divisions, ones that must be continually recited in order to be maintained. Race does not exist ontologically, rather, it is a system of meanings and practices that I have argued is disciplinary: race as discipline produces and regulates subjectivity in that mechanisms of control and techniques of power form the subject as raced. It is the body, I have insisted, that bears the limits of this subjectivity and is itself produce by the meanings attached to it. Thus, this chapter has underscored that the body is rendered an object of knowledge, that the subject is formed and regulated within this knowledge (of the body), and that this knowledge, in turn, secures race in the body. Principally, race as a corporeal truth has been believed to inhere in color (or skin) and in blood, and it is these ideas that have both structured racial discipline and exhausted racial logic.

2

Racial Knowledges

SECURING THE BODY IN LAW

> An aversion to their corporeal distinctions from us . . .
> militates against a general incorporation of them with us.
> —St. George Tucker, letter to Jeremy Belknap, June 1795

Racial distinctions based on supposed truths of color and blood were made from the earliest days of the North American colonies and confirmed in slavery, where blackness became synonymous with servitude and whiteness with freedom. In this chapter I trace the codification of these racial distinctions within law, because it is in this arena that the broader discursive workings of racial discipline have been secured. The law has been deployed in the service of whiteness to construct and maintain it as a pure and superior racial category. Militating against the 'incorporation' of racial others, law (echoing St. George Tucker) has historically been used to create and institute a complete division between black and white racial subjects, and to reinforce that these divisions—or absolute distinctions—are grounded in the body, in the fictive loci of race: color and blood. In order to map how this was achieved, in what follows I examine the relationship between law and racial knowledges, truth, subjectivities, and what I have called racial discipline. I argue in this chapter that law must be seen as a core modality or technology of discipline that works—in the sense of labor—to 'make' racial subjects, raced bodies, and to formulate the idea that race is a truth. This making of race has been augmented and maintained through what can be called 'racial purity laws,' which encompass statutory definitions of race and anti-miscegenation regulations. Before going on to this analysis of how race has been articulated and secured in law, however, I want to first mark some of the core ideas that have informed and conditioned the production of blackness and whiteness, for it is in the context of these ideas or knowledges that law operates.

EPISTEMOLOGIES OF BLACKNESS AND
THE FIGURE OF THE SLAVE

Slavery was not immediately linked to blackness, as the early colonies did not institute a perfect system binding the concept of slavery solely to the black body. When the first blacks were forcibly brought to Jamestown in 1619, they served no differently than white bondservants and, consequently, the inheritance of slave status as evident in Virginia "was, as written, technically independent of race" (Higginbotham and Kopytoff 1989, 1970). During these early days of settlement, blacks entered a society in which the majority of people were indentured laborers who lacked what is understood as 'complete freedom.' No meaning existed within English jurisprudence regarding the word *slave* and so these early black subjects were regarded as servants. Gossett (1964, 29) explains that the fact that there was no point of termination to this servitude did not differ in structural relation to the common understandings of indentured labor. The plentiful labor force in England accustomed employers to a system where servitude generally did not expire because social circumstances compelled servants to continually renew their term. It was not until 1664 that the colony of Maryland finally made a distinction between blacks and other servants. In this year, an absolute division was drawn with a bill enacted that decreed: "All Negroes or other slaues already within the Prouince and all Negroes and other slaues to bee hereafter imported into the Prouince shall serue Durante Vita [for life]" (cited in Fowler 1987, 41). The language of slavery was set and a clear linkage between the notion of the slave and 'the Negro' was articulated.[1] In 1662, Virginia law made a connection between black subjectivity and slave status in adopting the civil rule of *partus sequitur ventrum*. The act read: "some doubts have arisen whether children got by any Englishman upon a Negro woman should be slave or free. Be it therefore enacted and declared . . . that all children borne in this country shalbe held bond or free only according to the condition of the mother."[2] In a society where whiteness and freedom were becoming synonymous and blackness and slave coterminous, this act ensured that the children born of black women would be slaves. It was not until 1670, however, that Virginian law made a specification that all servants *imported by sea* who were not Christians were to be servants for life.[3] While not explicitly referencing blacks, there is no doubt that they were the targets of this act. As the only non-Christians brought by sea, blacks subsequently became distinct from other servants. Their enslavement was made to depend on color and religion and it was made explicit that their servitude did not expire.

By the 1680s, the institution of slavery had spread to create a society that was premised on race. And, as whiteness became an attribute of the free, white identity came to function as a "shield from slavery" (Harris 1993, 1720). The figure of the slave, however, came to obscure the ideals upon which the new nation would be built a century later and to call into question the principles of the Enlightenment as articulated in the Declaration of Independence. It became essential, then, to reconcile the contradiction that slavery represented in North America. How to account for humans in bondage when calling for human freedom? The contradiction was reconciled, as Marvin Jones has noted, within and through the prism of Enlightenment thought, "in terms of Cartesian dualities, by splitting off one dimension of a slave's being—her mind—and reconstructing her only as a body—a pair of hands; or, relying on the same mind-body dualism, reconstructing her as subhuman or beast lacking the intellectual facilities of whites" (1993, 458). This positioning of blacks as separate and hierarchically inferior to whites was perhaps most evident in the United States constitutional decree that established blacks as only three-fifths of a man.[4]

In this way, slave status came to constitute the black individual *as a slave;* black subjects were not simply enslaved, rather, the status of slave pervaded their very being. The slave became reduced solely to a body that was seen as capable of being rendered completely docile, and the ability to achieve this molding into disciplinary 'obedience' was utilized as confirmation that the slave was simply a body without a mind.[5] Slave status became linked to an internal 'essence of the slave' that retroactively replaced the effects of the institution of slavery with what were perceived as the cause(s) of black enslavement (Jones 1993, 459). By divorcing the enslaved from the realm of the mind and figuring them simply as corporeal instruments in an elaborate labor force, the system of slavery erased the slave as a subject. The enforced divisions between master and slave became naturalized such that the slave was seen to embody all traits that were opposite to the privileges, dues, and characteristics of the free. If the white master was imagined and operated in the world as a free human subject who possessed agency, autonomy, culture, and all the concomitant inalienable rights that were associated with subjectivity, then the slave was discursively constructed in an inverse relation. To be a slave became coterminous with the complete lack of subjectivity: the slave *was* property and, therefore, had no rights; they lacked agency, culture, and the accompanying access to knowledge. In short, the slave was a 'sub-human object' to be directed and controlled by the white subject.

Justification for this form of treatment towards blacks was sought and found among the early myths and conceptualizations of Africa and its peoples. Within the European imaginary, Africa was configured as *terra incognita:* a land that was unknown, vast, and impenetrable due to its perceived extreme naturalness. For the Europeans, the 'unknown' came to represent the 'uncivilized' and those that populated this 'unknown' land were cast as the epitome of that which lacked civility and culture, that is, they were relegated to the realm of the animalistic. Travelers' accounts, according to Wiegman (1995, 56), "emphasized both the primativity of blackness and its incomplete humanity." That which was identified as marking the most noticeable disparity between whites (or more correctly, Europeans) and blacks were the corporeal distinctions that were made in regards to sexual characteristics. Many scholars, including Lisa Duggan (2000), Siobhan Somerville (2000), Robyn Wiegman (1995), and Sander Gilman (1985), note that blackness was produced as *sexual difference,* and these differences were often framed within the language of bestiality.[6]

By the eighteenth century both the black female and male had become "icon[s] for deviant sexuality" (Gilman 1985, 81). This perceived deviancy was seen to begin at the surface of the skin, in that physical differences were simultaneously viewed as the indicator and evidence of differences in physiology and physiognomy. The figure of the southwestern African Hottentot came to stand as the exemplar of this deviancy that was imagined through the prism of sexual difference. Her enlarged breasts and buttocks and the form of her genitalia were perceived as external corporeal excesses that marked an internal libidinal excess. She was contrasted to the normalized 'healthy' European as *pathology,* for her difference was conceptualized as a disease, or congenital disorder (Gilman 1985, 88) that was supposedly evidence of degeneracy and bestiality. Justification for black masculine depravity was found in the purported extravagance of his penis size.[7] The idea of the black male as totalized within the image of the penis is one that has maintained discursive power. As Fanon (1967, 170) has noted, "The white man is convinced that the Negro is a beast; if it is not the length of his penis, then it is the sexual potency that impresses him."[8] Yet while the black male member may impress, it simultaneously, and perhaps more forcefully, threatens. For it is seen as the very instrument of the possible contamination of white blood through interracial sex. This black male penis may have represented an anomaly to the European male, but it has also represented that which could captivate or compromise the virtue of the European female through the perceived wanton lasciviousness of its owner. Subsequently, it is this "threat . . . to civilization itself" (Mercer 1993, 353) against which the maximum of vigilance was required.[9]

By conceptualizing blacks as inherently distinct due to differences in appearance, Europeans formulated a 'blackness,' and by implication a 'whiteness,' that conflated color with fictionalized racial *identities*. The initial distinctions that were made based on skin pigmentation, facial lineaments, and body conformations were seen (and fabricated) to denote inherent subcutaneous differences of blacks—characteristics of blackness—that *determined* identity. Sexual behavior, mental aptitude, the ability to access culture, indeed, all the traits of 'normal human subjects' were seen to be lacking in those of African origin. Consequently, the aberrant African other was depicted as less-than-human, a position that in one and the same moment determined and validated their designation as slaves in the North American colonies.

Law, as I explore in more detail below, played a key role in this production of blackness and whiteness as defined identities. But it must be remembered that laws pertaining to race emerged within the context of these broader circulating racial knowledges. To trace the specific ways that race was augmented and secured within the legal area, what needs to come into view is the constellation of legal imprimatur, epistemologies of racial truth, and the workings of what I have called racial discipline.

LAW AND DISCIPLINE

Law has often been seen as oppositional or antithetical to disciplinary power. The technology of power that is discipline operates through normalization, not prohibition, through control instead of punishment. Where law is sovereign and unyielding, discipline is capillary, diffuse, invisible, non-uniform. Law might impose rule, but discipline, through a series of 'quiet coercions' shapes how individuals see themselves and the world around them. While I go into these operations further in the next chapter, here I want to refute this supposed opposition between law and discipline and instead map ways that law has supplemented and extended racial discipline. In *Foucault's Law* (2009), Golder and Fitzpatrick have argued that, for Foucault, law and discipline are not opposed, nor is law subordinate to or the pliable tool of discipline. Rather, law and discipline operate and exist in relation to one another (2009, 53). Further, they've shown that disciplinary power *needs* law: unable to ultimately 'prove' the truth claims generated by various knowledge systems and used to discipline subjects, disciplinary power needs to be able to have these ideas 'made' truth by being enshrined in law (thus naturalizing discipline); and unable to absolutely enforce discipline, disciplinary power requires the legal arena in order to reprimand, punish, and correct the recalcitrant subject.[10]

If law works to supplement and extend discipline, here I consider how 'racial purity laws' do more than work at the biopolitical level to regularize and regulate the population: they condition the disciplinary creation of race and racial identities.[11] 'Racial purity laws' denote "those externally imposed definitions of a group that the state creates for its own ends" (Scales-Trent 2001, 261). They encompass both statutory definitions of race that are created through legislative decree and the specific mechanism of racial purity maintenance that has been implemented in the form of anti-miscegenation laws. These laws are *disciplinary*. The 'intention' of the various and often contradictory racial purity laws may have seemingly been to classify, codify, or define racial status (in ways that reflect 'fact' or 'truth'), but they have functioned in more complex ways to become a core component in the political technology that is discipline. For in a Foucauldian understanding where technology means 'to make,' law has contributed to the (disciplinary) *making* of racial subjects: it has conditioned the production of racial subjectivities in line with the dominant extra-legal dictates of racial discipline. In the imposition of a classificatory racial schema, juridical power consolidates discursive demarcations of races. However, in enforcing these imprimaturs, law "also comprises the intention to teach, to mold conduct, to instill forms of self-awareness and identities" based on the normalized differentiation of races (Gordon 2000, xix). As Hyde (1997, 222) has argued, "race is performatively [re]enacted in legal discourse, a discourse that constructs and naturalizes what it claims [only] to find."[12] Law has defined not only what bodies *are* and *mean* in relation to other bodies but also *how* those bodies and attendant subjectivities *come to operate in the world;* law racializes the corporeal and seeks to confine and regulate the subject within the 'truth claims' of racial epistemology that are discursively attached to that racialized corporeality. Analyzing the particular 'body of law' that applies to the racial body highlights that law and discipline cannot be extricated and that law has been intimately involved in the disciplinary construction of race.

Before addressing the particularities of race and law, I want to mark several points. First, precisely because law is involved in the disciplinary construction of racial subjectivities, it cannot be seen as that which is imposed on preexisting subjects. Instead, subjects are formed through their enmeshment with law (and other social institutions). Second, law does not exist in any abstract sense, because it is not independent of extra-legal social discourses. Law is not self-sustaining or self-contained. It is, rather, "constitutively attached," as Golder and Fitzpatrick (2009, 60) tell us, "to a whole range of different entities, bodies of knowledge, or modalities of power." Thus, "the condition of law is that of a perpetual hyphenation, reliant in some measure upon" other forms of knowledge (Golder and Fitzpatrick 2009, 60). In regard to race, law has historically been most reliant on those often contradictory knowledges formulated within the 'sciences of man.' Science, particularly from the eighteenth century, lent knowledge to law and, in turn, law granted science legitimacy.

These laws have augmented racial epistemologies that have sought to secure race *in* the body. Through employing the discourses of color and blood, they have established race as a corporeal 'truth' that can be detected and measured as an objective 'fact.' Racial 'facts' are established in the demarcation and statutory classification of distinct racial subjects. Likewise, these supposedly 'natural' and 'essentially' delineated racial entities have been the focus of rigorous juridical surveillance and regulation in the form of anti-miscegenation laws that have operated to prevent any form of 'sexual mingling' that might compromise the 'purity' of whiteness. To these ends anti-miscegenation laws came "to function as the ultimate sanction of the American system of white supremacy" (Pascoe 1996, 49).[13] The 'finding' or 'uncovering' of this 'fact' of race (a 'fact' upon which the prohibitions against interracial sex have rested) was achieved and implemented within law through recourse to two intertwined and mutually conditioning classificatory schemas. The first of these was the classification of race by *appearance* and the second was of race as a classification based on *descent.* As Scales Trent (2001, 278) has noted, "the two tests often collapsed into one: high theory about genealogy and descent was conflated with the reality of visual clues." Yet, if appearance/color did not 'obviously' indicate 'blood,' it would be sought out through other means in order to racially classify.[14]

Race, then, has been *conceived (of) as an embodied 'truth'* that must be protected through various methods of racial purity maintenance within law. Two primary mechanisms have been implemented within law in order to chart the boundaries of 'distinct' races and, in so doing, discipline racial subjects. The first of these mechanisms, which I focus on below, was the regulation of the *production of race;* anti-miscegenation laws attempted to patrol the literal production of racial subjects and statutory definitions of race attempted to patrol the *discursive* production of race through interpellating possible subject positions for the products of miscegenous unions. Miscegenous unions were in turn prohibited on the basis of these statutory definitions of race. In subsequent chapters I analyze the second of these legal mechanisms, those efforts that regulated the *take-up of race:* that is, how law assessed the manner in which certain racial subjects had come to operate in the world or perform their race. Put another way, then, law can be seen to generate 'knowledge' pertaining to the *meaning* of supposedly disparate bodies and, in attaching this meaning to the corporeal, has contributed to (a) the kinds of racial subjectivities that emerge and (b) the regulation of 'appropriate' articulations of racial subjectivity, based on the designation of racial status. Ultimately, this juridical policing of 'racial borders' functioned as a method of containment. It is a containment that has been executed through constraining the possible interpretations and articulations of racial subject-hood—constraints that have functioned to call into being or produce (at the level of discipline) the very racial subjects that law has claimed only to classify and keep separate (at the level of biopolitical efforts to regulate the population). Establishing a history of racial production within law is not, however, as Foucault tells us, about reconstructing a 'genesis of race' or about finding an absolute 'truth':

> It would involve [instead] the genealogy of regimes of veridiction [truth tell-ing], that is to say, the constitution of a particular right (*droit*) of truth on the basis of a legal situation, the law (*droit*) and truth relation finding its privileged expression in discourse, the discourse in which law is formulated; the regime of veridiction, in fact, is not a law (*loi*) of truth, [but] the set of rules enabling one to establish which statements in a given discourse can be described as true or false. (Foucault 2008, 35)

It is to these regimes of veridiction that I now turn.

MAKING RACE IN LAW

The term 'miscegenation' was not coined until 1863, when the journalist David Goodman Croly published a pamphlet entitled *Miscegenation: The Theory of the Blending of the Races, Applied to the American White Man and Negro.*[15] What *American Jurisprudence* (1941) defined as the "intermarrying, cohabiting, or interbreeding of persons of different races" (quoted in Saks 2000, 62) had, however, been a persistent concern from the earliest days of the North American colonies. This act of interracial mixing (previously often referred to as "amal-gamation") was viewed by white society as the ultimate threat to the purity, sanctity, and integrity of the race. Laws that prohibited miscegenous unions were rapidly enforced in the new colonies and concentrated on criminalizing white and black unions. While judicial measures to maintain separation be-tween supposedly disparate racial groups "came to include . . . American In-dians, Chinese, Japanese, Hawaiians, Filipinos, and other groups . . . *all* such laws," Sollor's notes, "restricted marriage choices of blacks and whites, making the black-white divide the deepest and historically most pervasive of all Ameri-can color lines" (2000, 3). Within an elaborate racial spectrum, blacks were considered to be antithetical to whites and, hence, not to be 'incorporated' in any capacity. The "racial hierarchy could be maintained primarily through the development of a *rigid* color line: if whites and blacks could not have chil-dren together, then racial categories could be preserved" (Hodes 1993, 72, my emphasis).

The racial delineations established within anti-miscegenation laws were premised on supposed incommensurable racial 'truths.' These internal truths of essential blackness and whiteness needed to be kept separate; to allow the union of these disparate racial entities would compromise the supposed innate workings of nature that had established black and white as absolute opposites. Anti-miscegenation laws sought to regulate subjects within the 'truths' of racial ontologies or 'facts of race' which were clearly evident in the visible. While distinctions were made at the surface of the skin—the epidermis functioning as the signifier of racial difference—the visible was perceived as that which indicated a subcutaneous natural difference between the races. The irreconcilable visible differences invoked concomitant differences of *blood*. Thus, when the early colonists "called sexual union between Negroes and whites a mixture of bloods they were expressing a strong sense of radical distinction between two kinds of people" (Jordan 1968, 166). As a consequence, miscegenation was viewed as a crime *against* and *of* blood. Within the discourse of white supremacy, it represented the ultimate disregard for that which inhered within white blood.

Under the system of slavery white blood had come to be seen *as a form of property.* Slavery rendered race and property synonymous. Blacks were figured as property, chattel that could be bought and sold through the complete deprivation of liberty. However, white racial identity and property also became conflated, as whiteness became the 'property of the free' and white skin (which invoked white blood) became the signifier of free status. This was a prized possession that set one apart from those who could be possessed. Consequently, as Cheryl Harris (1993, 1720–1721) has insisted:

> the racial line between white and black was extremely critical; it became a
> line of protection and demarcation from the potential threat of commodifi-
> cation, and it determined the allocation of the benefits and burdens of this
> form of property. White identity and whiteness were sources of privilege and
> protection; their absence meant being the object of property.

In this sense, what had previously been an aspect of identity became reconfigured as legal status, such that a privileged identity transformed into a "vested interest" (Harris 1993, 1725). The key to this vested interest resided in the blood of whiteness. Black blood did not entitle one to any form of privilege. White blood alone was valuable. Harris has shown that the notion of whiteness as property created a property right in an abstract or intangible *thing* (1993, 1725). Whiteness, then, is not a physical property but a metaphysical one that resides within the symbolics of blood.

As whiteness became a property interest, the protection of its boundaries was vigilantly sought so that the benefits of whiteness could be maintained *for those defined as white.* The beginning of 'white' as an exclusive category that required the utmost attention from 'crimes of blood' is evident from the first colonial legislation that pertains to miscegenation. Passed in 1630, just eleven years after the first Africans were forcibly brought to Jamestown, this initial legislative enactment in Virginia merely concerned the suggestion of interracial sex. It decreed that a white manservant, Hugh Davis, was to be subjected to public confession and "soundly whipped . . . for abusing himself to the dishonor of God and shame of Christians by defiling his body in lying with a negro."[16] The necessary question becomes, why was Davis punished? The case and the reasons for censure have been variously interpreted.[17] Some have speculated that this punishment simply targeted fornication and worked to make and maintain a distinction between Christians and heathens, so that perhaps the punishment was not racialized in the strictest sense.[18] Yet it can be assumed that Hugh Davis's whiteness was indicated by default, through the explicit racialization of the 'negro' with whom he lay. Moreover, Christianity and European whiteness worked as synonymous concepts at this time and, thus, an implicit racialization was at work. Christians were to set the example for appropriate conduct, and it was only the 'souls' of the 'godly' that needed to be corrected and saved. Regardless of a definitive interpretation, at this moment in time a distinction between black and white was established, and the language of defilement used foreshadows the notions of pollution and pathology upon which anti-miscegenation rhetoric came to be predicated.

The first definitive pronouncement against interracial sex was not made in Virginia until 1662. In this year a statute was passed that was the first in a long series, continuing over two centuries until after the Civil War, that punished whites for consensual interracial sex and marriage while ignoring non-white partners (Higginbotham and Kopytoff 1989, 1994). This decree held that "if any Christian shall commit ffornication with a negro man or woman, hee or shee soe offending shall pay double the ffines imposed"[19] by former acts that punished adultery and fornication without regards to race.[20] So began a regime of discipline that positioned whites as those needing to maintain the sanctity of their privileged condition. It was this same act, however, that also imposed that status would be inherited through the matrilineal line: adopting the civil rule *partus sequitur ventrum*, the act only concerned and was directed toward "the children got by" 'Englishmen' and 'Negro women.' It stipulated that "all children born in this country shall be held bond or free only according to the condition of the mother."[21] Jordan (1974, 70) stresses that "[i]n most colonies virtually all the offspring of interracial unions were illegitimate . . . and [these unions have] typically involved white men and black women." As the overwhelming majority of black women were slaves, their progeny were burdened immediately with slave status. To say, then, that whites were punished for mis-

cegenous acts requires clarification. White men who took advantage of their
slaves presumably escaped such discipline. Black women and their progeny
may not have been *explicitly* punished, but the demarcation of status (and its
synonym—race) was, itself, the pinnacle of a racialized discipline that definitively contained the products of 'admixtures of blood' within a subordinate
classification.

The first legislative decree that directly prohibited miscegenous marriages
was not enacted until 1664, when the colony of Maryland specifically addressed
white women who engaged in interracial marriage. This ruling held that "whatsoever free borne woman shall inter marry with any slaue . . . shall Serue the
master of such slaue dureing the life of her husband And that all the Issues of
such freeborne woemen soe marryed shall be Slaues as their fathers were."[22]
Beyond the white woman being required to serve her husband's master for the
term of his life, the act stipulated that any children were to serve the master of
their parents for a term of thirty years. The Virginia legislature, similarly, turned
their attention toward interracial marriage in 1691. In this act, the white partner
involved in a miscegenous union was to be "banished and removed from the
dominion forever."[23] The "abominable admixture and spurious issue" of the
union (the mulatto child of a white woman and a Negro man) was to be bound-
out in servitude to the parish until they were thirty years old.

The fate of the 'mixed' children of black/white unions was established definitively in Virginia in 1705, when the colony deemed that "the child, grandchild, or
great-grandchild of a Negro" was a mulatto.[24] Hence, one-eighth black blood
was sufficient to outweigh any white blood and demarcate one as black in a
racial economy that stipulated that Negro and mulatto comprise *one* single legal
category. Virginia was not alone in this maneuver to clearly define 'mulatto.'
During this period, North Carolina made a stricter designation by which an
individual with one-sixteenth black blood was deemed to be a mulatto.[25] As
Jordan (1962, 185) states, "there is no reason to suppose that these two colonies
were atypical." What was happening in these early days of the colonies was
presumably an acknowledgement that the effort to control interracial sexual
activity was a logistical impossibility. What was required, instead, was that the
products of these unions be definitively placed within the social order so as to
protect the peripheries of whiteness.[26] Legislative decree, therefore, had to endeavor to control *how* these products were classified. The boundaries of whiteness were being drawn such that proportional admixture of black blood relegated an individual as *beyond* the realm of whiteness—they were pushed instead
toward blackness.

One can assume that interracial marriage became a target, above and beyond
interracial sex, because it was within this arena that both reproduction was

legitimized and property inherited. By making laws such as these in regards to miscegenous unions, the governing legal bodies essentially ensured four factors. First, they increased the property of the master. Second, these laws functioned to discourage white women from participating in relationships with black men due to the extreme punishments that were involved. Third, the laws dissuaded black men to become sexually involved with white women. Ultimately, however, what these laws accomplished was the ability to generate, regulate, and fix statutory definitions (and the attendant discursive positionality) of racial subjects. The external *imposition* of racial status was actually the *production* of race because it was an interpellation of possible subject positions. It was inextricable from that which followed from being designated as black or white; in this movement, legal apparatuses circumscribed the individual's being-in-the-world. In determining to which race a subject belonged, law inserted the individual into a network of relations of power, specifying their access to the "benefits [or lack thereof that] accrue to that status . . . [and] what *legal* entitlements [or disadvantages] arise from that status" (Harris 1993, 1725). Within these early colonial decrees the territories of racial identities were already being demarcated; individuals were being *produced* as raced through the judicial enforcement of rules of inheritable status, a status that was based on ancestry and which was, inevitably, seen as fixed.

While the drawing of racial lines was being executed within the legal arena in terms of descent, during the eighteenth century and into the first years of the nineteenth century the visible was still considered to be the most potent indicator of blood.[27] In *Hudgins v. Wright* (1806), for instance, this was clearly articulated when Judge Roane observed the following:

> The distinguishing characteristics of the different species of the human race are so visibly marked, that those species may be readily discriminated from each other by mere inspection only. This, at least, is emphatically true in relation to the negroes, to the Indians of North America, and the European white people.[28]

In Judge Roane's findings, the eye is privileged as the fundamental tool of racial perception. Race is read through the eye that can perceive racial 'truth' because it has been instructed to divide individuals according to certain readable and meaning-laden traits and characteristics that code *for* and *as* race.[29] Another of the presiding judges on this case, St. George Tucker, insisted that certain corporeal 'facts' facilitate the determination of racial status. For Tucker, the 'African's' "flat nose and woolly head of hair" were characteristics that enabled black racial coding to be made.[30] He claimed that long after the complexion of 'the Negro' had faded, these two other physical features remained as verifiable somatic indicators of blackness. The last of these features to fade, Tucker believed, was the distinctive hair of 'the Negro,' a trait that would inevitably give away racial 'truth.'

Through these examples, law can be seen in its operative capacity as 'truth-maker.' It is the actions of the Court that establishes race as a natural truth that is visually evident and an objective fact. What is veiled in this operation is law's own role in the construction and maintenance of this belief system: law fabricates race as an innate ontology residing on the surface of (and by implication, at a subcutaneous level *in*) the body. Juridical power is instantiated at the moment in which race is designated and this allocation functions as a device of disciplinary initiation and maintenance of subjectivities.

THE REGULATORY MECHANICS OF BLOOD

Legal faith in the visible declined throughout the nineteenth century. As racial intermixture continued and the supposed physical manifestations of racial 'truth' became more confusing to read, vision faltered as a reliable tool through which racial designation could be made. The visual order was no longer a sufficient medium upon which to base judicial discipline, whether it was classification or the administering of prohibitions against miscegenation. This shift was also reflected in scientific conceptualizations of race.[31] While in prior centuries skin color was the organizing principle of race, by the nineteenth century the racial sciences invested an increasing emphasis on the idea that race was an *interior* corporeal 'truth.' Taxonomies of skin were replaced by investigations that sought to locate racial essence beyond the skin and, instead, in the deep recesses of somatic functioning. And as the search proceeded, racial difference became located in every conceivable *invisible* part of the body, but most especially in the blood. These notions were reflected in miscegenation jurisprudence and legislative demarcations of race that began to rely more readily on the supposed "biological *res* of blood" (Saks 2000, 67). If the physical features of blackness could be altered through interracial mixing, blood was perceived as that which would always continue to carry this 'truth.'

Thus, the trend reflected in *Hudgins v. Wright* that stipulated that visible distinctions could determine race, became increasingly coupled with references to blood. This was especially so in the South in the period immediately before the Civil War and became only more pronounced following the war.[32] As the regulatory device of slavery was abolished, new mechanisms were sought for racial demarcation. The method that was turned to was a more rigorous and vigilant regulation of blood. Racial subjects needed to be kept separate in order to maintain the lines between blackness and whiteness. Black subjects needed to be clearly demarcated because, while slavery may have been eroded, the system of social dominance that relegated blacks to subordinate status had not. New methods of oppression were enforced to simply absorb and rearticulate the old distinctions between black and white that had been formulated under the slavocracy.[33] And in this postwar period, miscegenation was that which was most zealously regulated so as to keep racial bloods apart. In reality, miscegenation decreased significantly during and following the Reconstruction era. The demise of slavery resulted in an increase in the physical segregation between the races and, as such, opportunities for interracial mixing became rarer. The plantations of the South became smaller farms; slave gangs dissolved into family-based groups; and schools, churches, and homes became rapidly divided along racial lines. "Consequently, the relatively plentiful opportunity for bodily contact between the master class and slaves afforded by the particular institution [of slavery] diminished drastically in freedom" (Williamson 1995, 90). White antagonism toward miscegenation, however, increased.[34] As Hodes (1993, 60) notes, "the separation of blacks and whites was essential to Southern whites who were determined to retain supremacy after the Civil War; consequently, the 'mixture' of people of European ancestry and people of African ancestry became a much more serious taboo." The demise of slavery and subsequent new legal rights of blacks threatened to undermine prewar racial delineations that had been enforced through rules pertaining to matrimony (Grossberg 1982, 203). The concerns that these factors raised can be seen in the new legal rulings passed during this period. The possibility of nuptial equality was refused and miscegenation, instead, came under greater judicial scrutiny. State intervention operated within nuptial law to strictly criminalize interracial marriage, enabling the white racial, sexual, and class hegemony of the prewar years to be maintained through the institution of matrimony.[35]

The passing of these laws seriously compromised the meaning of the Fourteenth Amendment to the U.S. Constitution that was designed to ensure due process and equal protection before the law.[36] Laws prohibiting miscegenation were yet systematically enforced and, in general, reinterpreted the Fourteenth Amendment in order to guarantee continuing sexual division between the races. In *Bowlin v. Commonwealth* (Kentucky Supreme Court, 1878), for instance, the right to ban interracial marriage was defended on the basis that to suspend this rule would "legalize inter-marriage between the races, [thereby] deteriorating . . . Caucasian blood [and facilitating the destruction] of the social and legislative decorum of the States."[37] Other courts also maintained that to forbid interracial marriage did not violate the Fourteenth Amendment or the Civil Rights Bill. These prohibitions were generally justified via arguments such as those offered by the Texas Court of Appeals in 1887:

> Marriage is not a contract protected by the constitution of the United States
> or within the meaning of the Civil Rights Bill. Marriage is more than a
> contract . . . it is a civil status, left solely by the Federal Constitution and the
> law to the discretion of the states under their general power to regulate their
> domestic affairs.[38]

By claiming the relative autonomy of state nuptial law, the postwar restrictions against miscegenation were able to continue as they had under slavery.[39] They continued, however, in increased capacity—more anti-miscegenation laws were passed in the post-bellum period and well into the twentieth century than had been during slavery—and the punishments became considerably more pronounced.[40] This stricter stance toward miscegenation is evident in both the lead-up to the Civil War and the decades that followed, as the fear of abolition mounted and was finally realized. A statute enacted in Mississippi in 1865 decreed that the marriage of a white person and an individual that descended from a 'Negro' to the third generation was a felony punishable by life imprisonment for both parties.[41] Florida enacted legislation in 1881 that established that the marriage of a white person and an individual with one-eighth black blood was a felony crime, and mandated that the punishment should entail imprisonment for a period of between six months and ten years (cited in Fowler 1987, 355).[42] Maryland passed a similarly rigorous punishment; in 1884, the legislature branded miscegenation (between individuals classified in the same manner as the Mississippi law of 1865) an 'infamous crime' to be met with an eighteen-month to ten year prison term.[43]

In order to enforce these prohibitions against miscegenation, the law had to become more reliant on attempts to adjudicate *fractions* of blood. Anti-miscegenation law could not exist, could not be passed or administered in the absence of statutory definitions of racial subjects: racial intermixture could only be prohibited on the basis of definitive legislative classifications of blackness.[44] It is these laws that operate to produce racial subjects in the second capacity in which I utilize this term. Anti-miscegenation laws may have regulated the literal production of race—stipulating who could legally have sex and reproduce with whom—but statutory definitions of the products of these unions (and the courts' interpretation of these definitions) regulated the production of race in a different way. For in defining the products of miscegenous unions on the basis of fractional amounts of blood, these statutes achieved more than simply the imposition of status. They functioned to interpellate possible subject positions and endeavored to condition racial subjectivities. By providing only certain viable and permissible racial categories, law has contributed toward the discursive inauguration and maintenance of delimited racial identities. The imposition of status *attaches* an individual to a racial subject position and conditions both society's and the individual's recognition of themselves as occupying that category as an ontological and pre-cultural reality.

But if blood was the ultimate corporeal 'truth' upon which this racial ontology was premised, what portion of black blood constituted an individual as black? The various states implemented a confusing and contradictory array of statutory definitions (and legal interpretations) that attempted to delineate various 'shadings' of those of African ancestry. For all intents and purposes, however, this intricacy simply produced a tapestry of blackness: the subjects that these classifications divided were all conceptually encompassed within the category black. The quest to establish racial blackness by portions of blood is clear in the 1890 federal census that sought to distinguish between blacks, mulattoes, quadroons, and octoroons. The census enumerators were instructed to classify individuals on the basis of the following definitions: "The word 'black' should be used to describe those persons who have three-fourths or more black blood; 'mulatto,' those persons who have three-eighths to five-eighths black blood; 'quadroon,' those persons who have one-forth black blood; and 'octoroon,' those persons who have one-eighth or any trace of black blood."[45] In one and the same moment, this census divided those with black blood and homogenized them as *socially black*. What is perhaps of more significance here, however, is that this allocation of degrees of blackness was to be made by the enumerators on the basis of visual inspection alone. This raises a certain paradox in which the visible was called upon to ascertain the invisible: legal codings of race that counted fractions of blood still relied on the visible as a medium through which to measure racial truth. But the visible alone could not function as an epistemological guarantee; how would a court, an enumerator, or an impartial observer register three-eighths of black blood? As Saks (2000, 74) states, "[t]o substantiate blood, to substantiate what is neither a mimetic description nor a tangible entity, but instead a semiotic figure, is impossible." Consequently, in cases of racial determination, courts were led to attempt to find the 'proof' and 'truth' of race through other means so that "even Blacks who did not look Black were kept in their place" (Diamond and Cottrol quoted in Harris 1993, 1740). They called upon what Gross (1998) has referred to as factors of 'ascriptive identity': an individual's reputation, associations, and reception in society were utilized in order to designate race. If these failed, or were not 'proof' enough, courts would scrutinize the individual's comportment and behavioral traits with the view that this would render race transparent.[46]

The judicial and legislative debate as to what specific portions of 'black blood' determined black racial status was, for all intents and purposes, put to rest in the precedent-setting case of *Plessy v. Ferguson* (1896).[47] Homer Plessy, who had seven-eighths white ancestry and one-eighth black ancestry, contested as unconstitutional the Jim Crow statute that endorsed racially segregated seating on the Louisiana railway. Plessy argued that in being forcibly ejected from his seat he had been deprived of racial property in whiteness. According to his counsel, "[t]he mixture of colored blood was not discernable in him." As such, "he was entitled to every recognition, right, privilege, and immunity secured to citizens of the United States of the white race by its constitution and laws."[48]

While the holding in this case did not determine a set definition of blackness, it may as well have done. The opinion of the Court found that although Plessy may have been able to visibly pass as white, the portion of black blood dispossessed him from a property right in white legal title.[49] *Plessy* inaugurated the legal acceptance of what had implicitly been in social operation from the earliest days of slavery, for the U.S. Supreme Court took 'judicial notice' of the 'fact' that an individual with any fraction of black blood, regardless of quantity, is black.[50] What was achieved in this ruling, consequently, was a federal judicial endorsement of the 'one-drop rule.' This notion has been referred to in sociological and anthropological circles as 'hypodescent,' and deems that an individual with any trace of known black ancestry is "assigned the status of the subordinate group" (Davis 1998, 5), that is, they are racially black.[51]

That Plessy looked white was not enough. That Plessy had a majority portion of 'white blood' was also not enough. What the law was constructing here was a forceful articulation of whiteness as a 'pure' and exclusive category that, as Dyer has argued, only the "utterly white could inhabit" (1997, 25). Through this ruling, law established that blood eclipsed the visual and, in so doing, enforced blood as a more potent (albeit, more difficult to ascertain) locus of race.

The logics of blood—as the essence within which race was seen to inhere—only gained increasing momentum throughout the twentieth century. The rise of eugenic thought compounded the importance of blood and the notion of black blood as a pollutant or stain that would not fade regardless of the degree of intermixture. Legal arguments and judgments incorporated eugenicist principles that maintained that racial bloods needed at all cost to be kept separate. To do otherwise would be to the detriment and devaluation of whiteness; it would result, as eugenicist Edward Reuter (1931, 3) claimed, in the "increase of hybrids[, the] disappearance of racial lines, and the ultimate mongrelization of the entire population." While eugenic ideas were expressed in law from the late 1880s, the most extreme eugenic argument was established by the landmark legislation enacted by the Virginia General Assembly in 1924. Entitled "An Act to Preserve Racial Integrity," this bill was masterminded by two leading eugenicists, John Powell and Walter A. Plecker.[52] Powell was the founder of the Anglo Saxon Clubs of America (A.S.C.O.A), and his comrade, Plecker, was a physician and administrator in the Virginia Bureau of Vital Statistics. Together with the support of other 'reputable' eugenicists, such as Madison Grant, Lothrop Stoddard, and Franklin Giddings, they advanced a proposal for a bill "for the preservation of the white race" (A.S.O.C.A. newsletter cited in Lombardo 1988, 429). Believing that interracial mixing was deteriorating white racial integrity they put forward four regulations:

> [A] registration system that required birth certificates to show the racial
> background of every citizen; regulations that forbade the issuance of mar-
> riage licenses to any person who did not possess a racially keyed birth certifi-
> cate; a definition of "white persons" that included only those with "no trace
> whatsoever of any blood other than Caucasian"; and the strict prohibition of
> a "white person" from marrying anyone other than another "white person."
> (Lombardo 1988, 429)

The bill was amended so that racial registration was optional for those born before 1912, and was passed by the Senate, signed by the governor, and enacted. Various points of the proposed bill had been opposed, but the "chief feature . . . passed through all of its tribulation unscathed, that is the definition of a white person as 'one who has no trace whatsoever of any blood other than Caucasian'" (Plecker quoted in Lombardo 1988, 435). This bill would appear, then, as the pinnacle of blood-based attempts at racial regulation and definition.

The idea that race must be pursued *beyond the skin* had already received judicial endorsement in *Plessy* and its progeny, such as *Ozawa v. United States* (1922)[53] (where the Supreme Court found, simply, that skin color could not be used as a reliable marker or determinant for race).[54] So, although courts continued to employ the visible and to classify according to appearance, during the nineteenth and early twentieth centuries they came increasingly to call upon descent—bloodlines and fractions or drops of blood—as a crucial tool in racial definition and as the natural essence that *constituted* racial 'truth.' What had always been present in the rhetoric of racial purity laws was now firmly entrenched; the property of racial blood that had been of utmost importance for the earliest colonists—and figured as that which required protection through the implementation of laws against amalgamation—was only articulated more forcefully as time progressed. Taxonomies of skin coupled with taxonomies that adjudicated the supposedly quantifiable minutiae of blood in order to fabricate race as a prediscursive biological ontology. These endeavors, in turn, *manifested* the raced body; the technology of law—the legal practices of racing individuals—created race as that which the corporeal enunciates. Charting these practices exposes not only the 'how' of racial construction but also the paranoia and surveillance that accompanied the quest to maintain the apparent integrity and purity of whiteness. The vigilance with which this care for whiteness was at-tended to can be seen in the legal demarcations of who could *be* a white subject, that is, who could lay claim to this subjectivity. These laws functioned to in-stitute rigid boundaries around different racial subjects and to prevent sexual mixing between people of distinct origins so that, as Haney López states, "mor-phological differences that code as race might be more neatly maintained" (1996, 117). Law, thus, enters into a network of relations that operate to con-stitute and police racial subjectivity, positioning law as a key participant in the reproduction of a disciplinary regime of racial 'truth.'

3

Passing through Racial Performatives

Race and the laws regulating it have been premised on a paradox, or what can be understood as an internal contradiction. For there has been a belief that race is at once *in plain sight* and is yet *potentially hidden*. Race is seen to be a 'truth' that the body of the subject announces; the body is viewed as a *legible text* upon which the schema of race is inscribed and through which it is transparently conveyed. The subject becomes synonymous with the body, which functions as the disciplinary mechanism through which the social and legal position of the subject is defined and regulated, and it is this body that marks the parameters of subjectivity. At one and the same time, however, the racial body has been positioned within this rhetoric as that which could *belie* 'truth,' escape detection and confound the workings of the hegemonic racial economy that desperately relies upon identifiable demarcation between racial subjects. This epistemological loop is a recurrent motif in American racial ideology. For while social discourse and legal measures have advanced that race is inevitably pronounced by the body, the fear has always been present that race may defy visibility.

The disciplinary regulations of race within law are technologies employed in the service of attempting to 'uncover' racial 'truth,' an 'uncovering' that was itself a fiction which contributed to the *creation* of racial subjects. As I discussed in the last chapter, racial purity laws attempted to control the *production* of race in two senses. First, they endeavored to control what 'kinds' of racial subjects were produced (in a literal capacity) through the regulation of sexual contact and reproduction. This technique of discipline was premised on the idea that races were 'true' and 'discrete,' and were, therefore, groupings that could be marked and kept separate. In the event of the inevitable failure of these laws, legal methods were instituted in order to control the definition and classification of the offspring of interracial unions so as to maintain the fictional boundaries between these supposedly disparate races. Second, and as I will explore in further detail in chapters 4 and 5, law monitored and assessed the manner in which racial subjectivity could be enunciated (that is, the 'take-up' or performance of race) by determining the supposed truth of the performance and, subsequently, the race of the subject before the bench. These dual technologies delineated possible and permissible racial subject positions, instituting law as one of the discursive mechanisms in the arbitration and disciplinary enforcement of race.

All methods that were utilized in order to achieve this 'uncovering' collapsed, reinforcing or contradicting each other, but all such efforts were premised on the belief that there *was* a racial 'essence' that could be revealed. This pursuit of and insistence on the inevitability of racial 'disclosure' highlights what I've called the epistemological loop that underscores racial rhetoric in the United States. The emphatic contention that race could and would be detected (because, ultimately, it was perceived as that which was *in plain sight*) was grounded in the fear that race would become/could be *hidden*, and as that which would then have compromised white 'purity' and have infringed upon white privilege. It was precisely this fear—the inability to ascertain and code racial difference—that propelled the legal measures that were instituted for these ends. This dual notion of race as being in plain sight and yet potentially hidden is significant in that through cumulative historical force it has dictated contemporary conceptualizations of race and racial subjectivity. While it is not my intention to explore these issues here, these ideas are important in the contemporary context where the legacy of racial surveillance, generated by racial purity ideology, continues to inform the discursive reproduction of raced bodies within the arenas of both societal and judicial law(s). America's present still desperately requires the body to speak 'the truth' (consider racial profiling or new biometric technologies,[1] for example) and is destabilized by the possibility that the body will 'fail' to articulate this 'truth.' What happens when we are unable to definitively tell the race of a body? In order to begin exploring this question, this chapter proceeds to demonstrate that racial discipline requires the clear visual signification of supposed racial truth and that the subject self-disciplines in relation to this truth. I then consider the possibilities that the ambiguous or liminal subject—the person who passes-for-white—presents in terms of complicating ideas of race as a corporeal truth; the passer exposes the tenuous foundations upon which the system of race rests, and they show the labor that is involved in the production of racialized identity. Ultimately, I argue that this figure highlights that racial discipline is sustained through the performative compulsions of race, and that all subjects are produced and produce themselves through a kind of labor (discipline) that can be seen as (performative) racial passing.

THE DISCIPLINARY PURSUIT OF RACIAL DOCILITY

> What the eye sees is not a neutral moment of reception but an arbitrary and disciplinary operation, one in which experience is actually produced in the subject.
>
> —Robyn Wiegman, *American Anatomies*

In *Discipline and Punish*, Foucault establishes that the employment of and authoritative investment in vision is paramount to relations of power, to the distribution of subjects, and to the various apparatuses of discipline. Foucault concentrates on penal practices in order to explore the technologies of power and mechanisms of discipline that rely on vision as the means through which to order social subjects and punish dissent. To the sixteenth and seventeenth centuries he attributes the regime of the spectacle as the primary means of penal legislation and punishment: punishment centers on the display of "the tortured, dismembered, amputated body" (Foucault 1991, 8). This sovereign system of punishment was replaced in the eighteenth century with what Foucault refers to as discipline or "the gentle way in punishment" (1991, 104)—a system of power that relied on what he called the panoptic schema and its methods of surveillance. As Wiegman (1995, 37), following Foucauldian terms has noted, "the organization of vision and the relationship between visibility and invisibility are central" in this latter method of disciplinary punishment.[2]

In what follows, I consider the mechanics of the visually based schema that has produced specific modes of racial subjection. Before doing so, however, I want to revisit the operation of discipline that I have outlined up until this point. I have analyzed what Foucault would identify as some of the "mechanisms of power which have invested human bodies, acts, and forms of behavior" (1980a, 61). These technologies, comprising what Foucault calls the microphysics of power,[3] have generated multiple racializing discourses (produced within religious, scientific, or juridical formulations of racial thought, for instance) and the racial subject is the object of these discourses.[4] The subject is both constituted and constitutes themselves through and in relation to these discourses. In the 1984 interview, "The Ethics of the Concern of Care for the Self as a Practice of Freedom" (1988, 11), Foucault explains that this process is a dual operation: discourse *declares* the subject—in this case as 'black' or 'white'—and the subject constitutes themselves in a parallel manner "in relationship and in the presence of the one who declares him [so]." The constitution of racial subjectivity thus involves the mutual enforcement of these two operations and can be seen as an intersubjective manifestation. The technique that enables this achievement—whereby the self is imbued with the disciplines that dictate acceptable beliefs and corresponding permissible manners of behavior—is a "generalizable mechanism of panopticism" (Foucault 1991, 216) in which the subject is perpetually "coerce[d] by means of observation" (1991, 170).[5]

Foucault's theory of panopticism is based on the architectural form of the Panopticon devised by Jeremy Bentham (1785). This structure is representative of subject formation within the disciplinary method of power that emerged in the eighteenth century:

> at the periphery, an annular building; at the centre, a tower . . . the periphetic building is divided into cells . . . they have two windows; one on the inside, corresponding to the windows of the tower; the other, on the outside, allows the light to cross the cell . . . They are like so many cages, so many small theatres, in which each actor is alone, perfectly individualized and constantly visible. (Foucault 1991, 200)

The one who surveys or supervises within the Panopticon is obscured from the subject that is surveyed, so as to induce in the subject "a state of consciousness and permanent visibility that assumes the automatic functioning of power" (Foucault 1991, 201). The effects, then, can be unceasing and without exercise, because the subject cannot tell when or if the gaze is upon them. As in the structure of the prison, in broader society visibility is everywhere and "is a trap" (Foucault 1991, 200). The subject, as a consequence, takes responsibility for conducting themselves in line with the constraints of regulatory behavioral decrees. They *inscribe in themselves* the power relation within which this same subject plays a simultaneous dual role; they are at once the subjugator and the subjected, for in regulating the self the subject "becomes the principle of his own subjection" (Foucault 1991, 203). What Foucault describes as the "infinitely minute web of panoptic techniques" (1991, 224) enables this schema to be polyvalent in its applications: it is an arrangement of power that is discrete, diffuse, pervasive, and above all, invisible.

The political anatomy of panopticism, so Foucault (1991, 208) explains, has the relations of discipline as both its object and end result. Within this schema discipline becomes generalized and subjection becomes intensified due to the subject's participation and investment within the process of its own formation. While this chapter goes on to explore the intricacy and extent of the individual's role in the constitution of the racial self, I want to briefly outline the operation here.

If we consider that the racial subject is called forth in discourse as white or black, and that this individual then partakes in the normalizing process of constituting themselves in relation to the sanctions, decrees, and prohibitions of that racial status, then this individual fabricates themselves in a manner that reflects the discursive norms of that discursive racial identity. They do so in relation to the power that is exercised within the disciplinary panoptic schema: under, against, through, and because of the potentially ever-present watchful eye of discursive power. Racializing discipline operates by shaping behavior, and in incorporating and conforming to racial norms the individual who observes this discipline is shaped as a racial subject.

The discipline—or what Foucault also called the anatomo-politics—of race has sought totalizing control; within this regime the body that can be analyzed and the body that can be manipulated have been combined so that the body may be "subjected, used, transformed, and improved" (Foucault 1991, 136). In a Foucauldian understanding, this racial body would be referred to as a docile or passive racial body—a body, and commensurate subjectivity, that had been molded and subjected in accordance to the disciplinary mechanisms of the racial schema. The discipline that is at work in the constitution of racial subjectivity is comprised of two interrelated processes:

> [It] increases the forces of the body (in terms of utility) and diminishes these same forces (in political terms of obedience) . . . [I]t dissociates power from the body; on the one hand, it turns it into an 'aptitude,' a 'capacity,' which it seeks to increase; on the other hand, it reverses the course of the energy, the power that might result from it, and turns it into a relation of strict subjection. (Foucault 1991, 138)

Racial subjectivity, of which the body bears the limits, is regulated and constrained such that racial subjects form and conduct themselves in relation to the naturalized 'truth' of racial discursive discipline. George Yancy, in line with this Foucauldian reading of race, argues that "from the moment that the first black body was placed in shackles, it was being disciplined to embrace the 'truth' about its 'inferiority' " (2004a, 109).[6] 'Truths' of race, as I marked in the preceding chapters, have been figured as inherent, pre-cultural, and 'fixed' realities of corporeal 'innerness.' And the individual—under the ever-present subjection of panoptic surveillance—is compelled to abide by the disciplinary injunctions of the racial 'site' within which they are discursively positioned and through which they are constituted. So despite, for instance, transitioning in and out of what Yancy calls "white racist semiotic spaces" and creating complex "counter-semiotic systems (that sustain and reconfigure) internalized white constructions of the world" (2004b, 11), black subjects cannot escape the regulatory dimensions of these norms that call them into existence. For Yancy (2004a, 111), "the black body/self is kept obedient and disciplined by the process of instilling certain beliefs and habits that produce a new subjectivity, a subjectivity which is imbued with a sense of self-surveillance, a mode of seeing blackness through white eyes."[7]

THE "CROSSING OVER": PASSING FICTIONS OF RACE

Two assertions can be made from the analysis that I have outlined. First, the disciplinary regime of race is based on surveillance. This is a surveillance that depends on visual signs or codings of race (that are seen to announce racial 'truth') in order to 'achieve' the regulation of individuals within particular demarcations of racial status. Second, this surveillance exists within a panoptic schema in that it relies on the notion of the permanent yet invisible watchful eye of power, an invisibilized gaze that operates to coerce the individual into exercising self-discipline in the formation and enunciation of racial identity. In self-disciplining, the subject regulates their behavior so as to maintain an assigned discursive position.

A particular body, however, fails to articulate racial 'truth.' This might enable an individual to refuse to self-discipline in accordance with discursive decrees and instead manifest a racial identity at odds with the supposed 'truth' of the body. This subject that I refer to is the passing figure, the subject who executes a 'crossing-over' of any line or border that separates social groups (Sollors 1997, 247). The terminology 'passing' is most often utilized to denote the action of an individual who, based on genotype is defined as black, but crosses the racial line into whiteness through winning acceptance as white. Thus, 'passing' is identified in Carl van Vechten's addendum—a "Glossary of Negro Words and Phrases"—to his novel, *Nigger Heaven* (1926), as simply "passing for white" (cited in Sollors 1997, 247), and it is in this way that I use the term. The act of passing-for-white problematizes the two assertions that I have proposed. As Ahmed (1999, 88) has noted, "the conviction [that we can know and see the difference between black and white] is the organizing principle for a system of racial classification which assumes that racial identity marks the subject in the form of the absence or presence of colour." In a racial economy that presumes, then, that blackness is visible, the discursively designated black subject who phenotypically appears to be white challenges the veracity of the visual realm. Significantly, in executing the act of passing, this subject evades the technologies of power and mechanisms of discipline that maintain the regime of race, a system premised on the visible signification of 'racial truth.' Visibility falters, in what Danzy Senna (1998, 107) calls a game of "phenotypic peek-a-boo." In addition, the act of passing-for-white challenges the second assertion I've made, because this subject defies the invisible force of panoptic power. The subject may be constantly aware of the invisible 'threat' of regulatory visual surveillance, but this gaze fails to coerce the individual into a state of submission to discursive demarcation. An example of this can be seen in Nella Larsen's 1929 novel, *Passing,* where Irene Redfield reflects on her 'pass' while under the inquisitive eyes of a stranger:

> Feeling color heighten under the continued inspection, she slid her eyes down. What, she wondered, could be the reason for such persistent attention? . . . Something wrong with her dress? . . . Again she looked up, and for a moment her brown eyes politely returned the stare of the other's black ones, which never for an instance fell or wavered . . . Still looking . . . And gradually there rose in Irene a small inner disturbance, odious and hatefully familiar . . . Did that woman, could that woman, somehow know that here before her very eyes . . . sat a Negro? (Larsen 1986, 149–150)

Although Irene may be aware of the ever-present threat of the detection, she persists: "No, the woman sitting there staring at her couldn't possibly know" (Larsen 1986, 150). Her 'invisible blackness' enables a clandestine break from the classificatory dictates of the racial schema.

In passing-for-white, Irene Redfield defied 'racial truth,' the confines of the normalized racial body, and naturalized racial knowledges. Later, I consider the relation of passing to racial performativity and how 'to pass' might function as anti-discipline. Before doing so, however, I want to be clear on what I mean by passing and the multiple ways in which it has been pursued. It is an act, for instance, that may be executed *voluntarily,* such as when a subject 'reflexively' and decisively executes a pass-for-white. Some of the possible motivations for this form of passing would have included the desire to escape social disadvantage, whether it be slavery, segregation, or any other form of racially based discrimination. A voluntary pass could also have been inspired through a will to pursue a prohibited interracial relationship, to gain economic advantage that was denied to black subjects as a result of discriminatory practices, or to temporarily access certain rights that would be denied to a visibly black subject. Sollors (1997, 250–251) suggests that other motives could have included "curiosity, [a] desire for kicks . . . [a] love of deception [or] preparation for political acts of subversion or revenge." These latter forms of passing can be described as discontinuous passes, because the desire to access the privilege of whiteness might only take place on an occasional basis. One of the primary incentives for this kind of passing was the possibility of gaining economic security. Cheryl Harris (1993) relays the story of her grandmother's pass-for-white, a movement that involved a daily transition from a black to a white identity for the purpose of accessing and maintaining a higher-paying job. Harris (1993, 1711) describes her memory of her grandmother's sacrifice in the following way:

> Each evening, my grandmother, tired and worn, retraced her steps home, laid aside her mask, and reentered herself. Day in and day out she made herself invisible, then visible again, for a price too inconsequential to do more than barely sustain her family and at a cost too precious to conceive.

The traversing of racial space may have also been executed for social reasons. For instance, a subject might have passed in order to gain entry to a venue, such as a theatre, restaurant, or hotel. The protagonist of Larsen's novel, Irene, undergoes the scrutiny that is quoted above when she shelters from the summer heat in a white-only hotel. As an alternative to these efforts to gain specific privileges at specific times, the passing-for-white that a subject executes may be continuous, whereby they pass-over into 'invisibility' and live as white.

Passing may also be an act that is 'achieved' *inadvertently* or *unwittingly*, such as when a subject is (mis)taken for being white. This might be without the individual's knowledge, or if this individual realizes that a white identity has been assumed, they might continue the pass without protest, thereby generating a *de facto* whiteness from silence.[8] Alternatively, passing may be practiced *unknowingly*, such as when a child is raised as white without any knowledge of their black ancestry,[9] or this pass may be executed *involuntarily*, when a child is forcefully compelled to formulate a white identity.[10]

Whatever form this passing took, and regardless of the motivation, this defiance of what Hortense Spillers (1987) has called the "American grammar" of race, was undoubtedly a panacea (of sorts) to subordination.[11] It was availed in different capacities and raised different issues for men and for women, rendering it an act that was implicitly gendered. Barbara Christian (1980, 45), for instance, has remarked that in fiction it is generally women who have been depicted as passers.[12] This may have been due to the economic security and mobility that could have been achieved through such a maneuver. Albeit, other writers, such as Judith Berzon (1978, 142), have suggested that a greater number of males passed due to their ability to utilize their occupational skills. The dynamics of passing—who passed, how many, why, and when—are beyond mapping because, as Carole-Anne Tyler has stated, "the mark of passing successfully is the lack of a mark of passing" (1994, 221). The very nature of the act—as secret—rules out the answers to such questions. It seems plausible, however, to argue in line with Joel Williamson (1995, 102), that the rate of passing would have altered with the corresponding rate of subordination. During Reconstruction, when the potential for the transformation of racial dynamics seemed possible, the rates, conceivably, were low. However, the instances of passing have been assumed to have reached their height as discrimination and oppression rose throughout the Restoration period and into the early decades of the twentieth century (Sollors 1997, 247).

Regardless of the temporal, spatial, or gendered specificities of the act of passing, the costs were considerable. To pass meant to leave behind, to subject oneself to the loss of a prior identity. While to perceive the phenomenon of passing in this vein is to mourn for a *phantasmatic* originary racial identity, to pass-over or pass-through into whiteness was undisputedly to abandon a 'real' and substantive social identity. The notion of loss is present in the very terminology of passing. 'Passing' and 'crossing-over' are both metaphorically employed to describe the transition from life to death, or to signify a journey to a realm beyond the earthly plain. Thus, to pass or cross-over racial lines calls forth imagery of an experience that is a form of death, a social death that is a passing-on, a passing-away.[13] As the authors of *Deep South* (quoted in Sollors 1997, 252) describe it: " 'passing' has the characteristics of sociological death and rebirth . . . [The passer] is as completely removed from his former social relations as if he were actually dead . . . He must be reborn as a new social identity."

An additional cost of passing-for-white is the perpetual fear of detection or a fear that the 'invisible blackness' will suddenly become visibilized. In passing, an individual enables a movement *from* a space or status that is simultaneously hyper-visible yet invisibilized *and into* a structurally different space of invisibility. Blackness is typically understood as a racial subjectivity that is visually and conceptually overdetermined. As Fanon (1967, 111) has established, black skin calls-forth "a thousand details, anecdotes, [and] stories" that function to trap black subjects within an essentialist notion of blackness. Or as Patricia J. Williams (1993, 222) describes it, "white people see all the worlds beyond me but not me." As a black person she may be visible in an objectified sense, yet Williams is *not seen* as a subject.[14] She states: "I could force my presence, the real me contained in those eyes, upon them, but I would be smashed in the process." In this description, Williams marks the distance between being visible, as black, and at the same time being socially invisible. This stands in distinction to the state of invisibility that is coterminous with whiteness; to pass into whiteness is to transition into an invisibility of sorts, but this invisibility is a not a consequence of not being seen. Rather, the white subject—or person who is read as white—is invisible in the sense that they are presumed to be racially unmarked.[15] In passing from a status as black to a status as white, the passer invisibilizes the self and is, therefore, passed-over as 'normal' (rather than marked out as different). Yet this form of invisibility is fragile because it is always under the threat of detection. The pass could be 'uncovered' through an association with others that might somehow 'give away' and fracture the passing identity, for instance.

Nella Larsen describes such a scenario in *Passing*. The story revolves around Clare Kendry's pass for white, a pass that her white husband, Bellew, had no knowledge of. In order to protect Clare, her friend, Irene, had been shielding her own black identity from Bellew, through passing-as-white in his company. One day, however, the illusion is compromised when Bellow sees Irene accompanied by a visibly black friend, Felise:

> A sudden bluster flung them around the corner with unexpected quickness and they collided with a man.
>
> "Pardon," Irene begged laughingly, and looked up into the face of Clare Kendry's husband.
>
> "Mrs. Redfield!"
>
> His hat came off. He held out his hand genially.
>
> But the smile faded at once. Surprise, incredulity, and—was it understanding?—passed over his features.
>
> He had, Irene knew, become conscious of Felise, golden, with curly black Negro hair, whose arm was still linked in her own. She was sure, now, of understanding on his face, as he looked at her again and then back at Felise. And displeasure. (Larsen 1986, 226)

Irene's association with blackness, through her literal association with a black subject (her friend Felise, whose arm is linked through her own), calls Clare's whiteness into question by default. One of the primary ways in which whiteness has been constituted is through the absolute disavowal of blackness. In early twentieth-century America, then, the simple association with blackness potentially taints whiteness.

Clare's ability to access white privilege is also under threat from a persistent fear known as *Natus Aethiopus;* the threat that black blood will be detected through the birth of a child who may appear more visibly black than the parent who has been passing. In a discussion that Clare has with Irene and Gertrude, Clare claims that she does not think that she will risk having anymore children. She says, "[i]t's awful the way it skips a generation and then pops out . . . nobody wants a dark child" (Larsen 1986, 168). Yet Clare is quick to point out that "[i]t's only deserters like [her] who have to be afraid of freaks of nature" (Larsen 1986, 169). To pass, consequently, is to engage in a practice of silence, a silence that is marked continually by the possibility that the line that has been crossed will be revealed.

Cheryl Harris (1993, 1711) has described passing as a "spinning on margins, [a] travel[ing] between dualities of Manichean space [that are] rigidly bifurcated into light/dark, good/bad, white/Black." While the passer *traverses* the racial divide, at one and the same time they *pass-over* the borders or peripheries that demarcate discursively separate realms. These legal and social borders of white-ness have been in continual flux, arbitrarily altering in accordance with the needs, desires, and interests of dominant whiteness. This has meant that who is thought of as white has also shifted. Despite this, borders always function, as Anzaldúa notes, to "define the places that are safe and unsafe, to distinguish between *us* and *them*" (1987, 3). In doing this definitional work, these borders have simultaneously protected and confined: they have policed the peripheries of the 'privileged' white racial group and constrained racial others within a subordinate status. To access this protected space, consequently, is not simply to pass, but to *trespass*. As whiteness became figured as status property under slavery, the act of passing enabled an individual to (illegally) access the accom-panying rights that this property entitled one to.[16] Thus, the passer transgressed a legal and cultural boundary.

Viewing passing as a transgression or flagrant disregard of 'truth' only gained force after the demise of slavery, as the desire for racial demarcation took on greater importance. And, as the property right in whiteness was firmly estab-lished as a right carried through blood, passing became unequivocally associated with the notion of deception. It was seen as a duplicity that belied a legal, cultural, and somatic truth or to mark an abandonment of one's 'authentic' identity. As a consequence, passing has been represented by images of camou-flage, masquerade, concealment, denial, and imposture (Bradshaw 1992, 79), and castigated as a forged or counterfeit identity.[17]

Yet passing can only be understood in this way if the notion of hypodescent is accepted. As Sollors (1997, 249) notes, " 'Passing' can . . . justly be described as a social invention, as a 'fiction of law and custom' (Mark Twain) that makes one part of a person's ancestry real, essential, and defining, and other parts acciden-tal, mask-like, and insignificant." That black and white exist as binary 'truths' is an idea only made possible through the notion of hypodescent, a concept that both *solicits* the necessity to pass and *produces* the pass. If individuals with black ancestry could have been identified as other than black, passing would not have been necessary, moreover, it would not have existed as a phenomenon.

Passing, we see, raises pressing challenges to the disciplinary regime of race. The simple possibility of passing 'works' (and I mean this in the sense of labor) to expose the tenuous foundations upon which this system rests. Most notice-ably, the individual who is discursively demarcated as black (due to their geno-type), yet escapes or evades reigning regulatory strictures of black subject status, highlights the extent to which disciplinary control is premised on the visible. The passer illuminates that race is, essentially, a scopic regime because it relies on the ability to visually identify difference as the means by and through which to delineate subjects. If the subject cannot be visually coded as black, then the possibility of regulating this subject within black subject status becomes com-promised. Thus, passing disturbs the accepted axiomatic relation between visi-bility and epistemic 'content' as it were. It evacuates the capacity to perceive racial 'truth' and challenges the knowledge(s) and meaning(s) that are sup-posedly carried with the visual and which the subject supposedly embodies. The subject who passes fails to signal racial 'truth'; indeed, they expose the fragility of the notion of true racial identities by demonstrating that these categories are mutable and non-essential.

STYLIZATIONS OF RACIAL "INNERNESS"

The passer's ability to defy visual identification has led Robert Westley to argue that "the phenotypically qualified accept a racial identity in order to function within a system of racially justified privileges and exclusions" (2000, 309). The claim here is that because the individual phenotypically appears to be white and is socially perceived as white they are then "qualified to adopt a white identity," a qualification that the "visual idiom . . . confirms" (2000, 309).

Two key limitations arise in this formulation of passing. First, white skin is not always enough and the visual alone does not ensure that a white identity will be read. If this were the true, how could the myriad cases where individuals were called before the court to 'prove' their race be accounted for? Rather than simply looking white, for the subject to successfully pass-into-whiteness they must also *act* white. This 'fraudulent' construction of a white identity is contingent on the ability to perform whiteness through the technique of *assuming the image of whiteness*. This image of whiteness or the semblance of a white identity is produced through rehearsing certain 'acts' (that is, resignifying existing sig-nifiers of whiteness) that enable the passer to be read as white. The passer must approximate whiteness through reciting the embodied signs of whiteness, sig-naling that the pass is not an 'ability' solely determined by the visual confirma-tion of white skin.[18] The second limitation in framing the phenomenon of passing as the adoption or acceptance of a white identity is that it fails to account for the complexity at work within the very possibility of passing. In previous chapters I've outlined the rigor involved in the disciplinary production of race. This production is fabricated and implemented by multiple discursive pro-cesses. As such, the subject cannot cast-off that by which they are constituted and simply 'adopt' a new racial identity. Moreover, the use of these terms sug-gests that the passing identity can be 'acquired' (in the sense that one comes to *occupy* the identity) and implies that the passing identity can be inaugurated and determined by the subject. Yet the very possibility of passing is only ever tenuous or provisional as it relies on those around the individual recognizing and validating the performance of white subjectivity. It is the reader, rather than the passer, who at one and the same time *enables* the performance of race executed in the pass and *constitutes* the performance. As Amy Robinson has noted, a pass can only be said to be successful once the passer appears to the reader "to *be* the category into which she has passed" (1994, 718, my emphasis). The pass is contingent on the reader, for if they do not recognize the performance of whiteness then the performance does not exist. Thus, passing is a (precarious) collaborative venture that requires that the passer's 'aim' be commensurate with the spectator's reading of race. In light of these provisions, the pass-for-white can only be ensured through the *sustained* acceptance of the performance of whiteness, a validation that would only be granted on the basis of the continued ability to reiterate the conventions of whiteness and, thereby, to maintain a white identity.

In addition to these factors, passing needs to be thought about in terms of a movement from a black identity to a white one; it is a transition. In making this transition, a subjectivity that has *already been* formed or constituted is subsequently disavowed. Rather than being an effortless discarding of one identity and the adoption of an-other, this is an elaborate operation. And it is this operation, I suggest, that invites further consideration because it highlights the techniques involved in *all* productions of racial subjectivity. I look to passing, accordingly, to ask: what does the passer 'do' when they manufacture an-other racial identity?

This technique—passing—demonstrates that the 'expression' of race and, thereby, race itself is not an intrinsic essence that is naturally and inevitably articulated. Passing reveals that race is a performed embodied practice, performed in a sense as a restylization of identity for self-authorized ends. What might it mean, then, to claim that race is performed? As Elaine Ginsberg (1996, 8) notes, passing incites the need to ask: "if 'white' can be 'black,' what is white?" Framing this question in alternate terms I ask: if a 'black' individual can be 'white' through acting white, what can this contribute to understandings of how racial subjectivities are produced?

In answer to this question, I want to suggest that passing echoes the general production of racial subjectivity in that it parallels the formation of a self that is derived from a false claim to bodily truth.[19] As I've discussed, the individual who passes-for-white forms or stylizes a white identity through the approximation of the 'idealized' norms of that discursive position. This production of a white identity is marked by regulation and constraint, as there are only limited behaviors, comportments or stylizations that are acceptable in order for the pass to 'succeed.' The act, thereby, correlates to the account of the performative constitution of subjectivity proposed by Judith Butler.

In *Gender Trouble,* Butler is concerned with interrogating how gendered categories and the materiality of sexed bodies are produced through the disciplinary operation of discursive regimes of power rather than existing as ontological givens. Butler (1999, 173) writes:

> acts, gestures, and desire produce the effect of an internal core or substance, but produce this *on the surface* of the body, through the play of signifying absences that suggest, but never reveal, the organizing principle of identity as a cause. Such acts, gestures, enactments, generally construed, are *performative* in the sense that the essence or identity that they otherwise purport to express are *fabrications* manufactured and sustained through corporeal signs and other discursive means.

Gender, Butler tells us, is 'acquired' through the performative reiteration of norms and normalizing procedures. Consequently, gender is formulated as "always a doing, though not a doing by a subject who might be said to preexist the deed . . . [rather] gender . . . is performatively constituted by the very 'expressions' which are said to be its results" (1999, 33).

My particular interest in light of these ideas is to ask how they might work in terms of the formation of racial subjectivities. The aim, here, is not to mark out ways that racial performativity might be different—and operate in distinct ways—to gendered performativity, while this has been the focus of other studies.[20] This, I believe, is to ask the wrong question. Instead of attempting to sort out the differences and name what racial performativity *is* in isolation, I want to focus on how racial performativity *works* and how it is always a relational operation: racial performativity always works within and through the modalities of gender and sexuality, and vice versa, and these categories are constituted through one another. In this understanding, one is never simply called into being as 'woman.' Rather, norms of gender are always already racialized such that one is formed and forms themselves as a 'white woman' or a 'black man' and so forth. While I suspend considerations of gender and sexuality here momentarily to think about race, I go on to show how race is always gendered within an overarching economy of heteronormativity. I demonstrate this impossibility of disentangling race, gender, and sexuality through examining the production of black femininity in chapter 4 and white masculinity in chapter 5.

To think about race as performative shifts attention away from looking at the effects of race to instead focus on the means of its production and maintenance. It also allows for analysis to move beyond the accepted idea that race has no biological basis or scientific veracity. This is important because the claim that there is no biological truth to race often works to consolidate or legitimize the *social* demarcations of groups based on color (in the very same moment that the claim insists on the scientific illegitimacy of this practice). By proposing a performative model of race, it is possible to see that these social groups do not exist in an a priori sense but are, rather, constructed and diligently maintained: race is a *practice* that requires tenuous attentive labor in order to 'survive.' If the disciplinary economy of race is fragile and requires the ever-attentive operations of discursive power in order to maintain its currency, it is then unstable and open to the possibility of rearticulation. The ability to consider race in these terms means, in a general sense, that the operations of racial practice and oppressive racial prescriptions can potentially be reworked. To think about race in this way exposes the complex mechanisms through which marginal racial identities are constituted. Simultaneously, the necessary correlative *against* which 'othered' identities are formed is brought into focus; a performative understanding of race is particularly useful for thinking about whiteness because it enables an analysis of 'white' as a racial category such that it can be marked and visibilized. Thus, the belief that white peoples' lives or subjectivities are not influenced by race can be exposed as a contentious one. Interrogating the performative aspect of racialization shows, instead, the highly regulated and constrained processes that racialize *all* individuals.

Taking Judith Butler's work on performativity to think about race, however, raises the following important questions: what are the implications of thinking about race as performative; and what kinds of 'doings' or embodied acts are involved? Furthermore, what formulation of subjection is being proposed in a performative account of race and how does this relate to the Foucauldian understanding of subject formation that I have outlined? And what is perhaps of primary importance is the question of how *agency* might be imagined through a performative understanding of race. These, however, are concerns that I address in subsequent chapters. First I want to retrace my steps and expand on Butler's notion of performativity in order to then move on to thinking about race as performative.

PERFORMATIVE CITATIONS: WHEN NAMING IS A DOING

> If a performative provisionally succeeds . . . then it is . . . only because that action echoes prior actions, and *accumulates the force of authority through the repetition or citation of a prior, authoritative set of practices.*
>
> —Judith Butler, *Bodies That Matter*

When Butler writes that performatives only succeed when they *recite* conventional and authoritative practices, she draws on a tradition of thought initially proposed by J. L. Austin in 1955 in his *How To Do Things With Words*. Austin was concerned with examining how certain kinds of language *perform actions,* that is, how certain forms of language accomplish the act that is designated in the words that are uttered rather than simply describing them. These he called performative utterances. They differed, Austin insisted, from constative utterances which " 'describe' some state of affairs, or . . . 'state some fact,' which [they] must do either truly or falsely" (Austin 1980, 1). This criterion did not apply to performatives for Austin, because performatives can only be assessed in terms of the success or failure of the act(ion) to which they refer. Thus, the performative utterance of "I promise"—in which the *act* of promising is *performed*—cannot be judged as true or false but simply assessed in terms of efficacy or inefficacy, or deemed as 'felicitous' or 'infelicitous' to use Austin's words. Austin reworked the distinction between these two forms of language, however, to argue that rather than being discrete and distinct statements, constatives are, instead, implicit performatives. The statement "the dog is hairy" may appear initially to be a constative statement of true or false fact but becomes, for Austin, an elliptical version of a performative statement in which the explicit performative verb has simply been deleted. Read without the omission, this statement becomes "I hereby affirm that the dog is hairy." This is an utterance that *accomplishes the action* of affirming that to which it refers. From this, Austin proposed that all language is performative, because to speak is to act. But a speech act can only be felicitous or successful (what Austin called 'happy') if it follows certain rules or conventions: it must follow "an accepted conventional procedure having a certain conventional effect"; it must be invoked by persons and within circumstances that are 'appropriate'; and it must be "executed by all participants correctly and . . . completely" (Austin 1980, 14–15). Two additional stipulations are set: "Where . . . the procedure is designed for use by persons having certain thoughts or feelings . . . then a person participating in and so invoking the procedure *must in fact have those thoughts or feelings, and must intend* so to conduct themselves"; and these participants "must actually conduct themselves subsequently" (Austin 1980, 15, my emphasis). *Intention*—the conscious presence of meaning—is, for Austin, an essential element in the success of performative communication. The performative would be unsuccessful should any of these stipulations not be met.[21] The primary distinction that Austin went on to make, however, was between performative speech acts and what he defined as *etiolations*, or non-serious utterances of language such as words uttered by an actor on a stage. These he excluded from consideration because he perceived them to be *parasitic* on the normal use of language. For Austin, these are "hollow and void" pseudo-statements in that they merely imitate performatives (Austin 1980, 22).[22]

In "Signature, Event, Context," Derrida (2000) critiques and ultimately displaces the binarism between serious and non-serious language that Austin establishes.[23] Derrida takes Austin's contention that non-serious forms of language exist as derivatives of serious forms of language and reverses the relationship of dependency. Derrida argues instead that the division Austin marks between success and failure is insufficient as they are enabled through one another; the failure that is inherent to non-serious utterances is a "necessary possibility" (2000, 15) in order for there to be utterances that can be said to be serious and felicitous. Going beyond this, however, Derrida takes Austin's notion that non-serious forms of language exist as mere imitations or citations of serious forms of language and establishes that *all utterances* (whether they be performative or not) are subject to the need to be recognizable as citations. Every utterance, in order to be intelligible, therefore, is derivative; they are "the determined modi-fication of a general citationality—or rather, a general iterability" (Derrida 2000, 17). Utterances must follow a convention and, as such, cannot be said to originate with the subject or be initiated by an 'autonomous intention.' This works to challenge the liberal humanist view that the speaker can control language, be-cause it highlights that the speaker's intention is always constrained by and contingent on convention and context.[24]

The account of 'general citationality' proposed by Derrida is critical because, while it maintains a distinction between performative and 'pretend' speech acts, it destabilizes their oppositional placement (as introduced by Austin). A 'relative purity,' Derrida insists, may exist between performatives and other types of iteration, yet this "does not emerge *in opposition to* citationality or iterability, but in opposition to other kinds of iteration within a general iterability which constitutes a violation of the allegedly rigorous purity of every event of discourse or every *speech act*" (Derrida 2000, 18). Thus, the structure of this system of language proposed by Austin is destabilized, as the citation—that which for Austin was an anomaly to be excluded from consideration—becomes, for Der-rida, the *very condition* of the speech act.

I have briefly charted the parameters of these two theoretical models in order to identify some of the key influences within Butler's theory of performativity. Her work is also indebted to Foucault, specifically his paradigm of subject formation.[25] She stresses the normalizing power of discourse, the importance of the disciplinary apparatuses that form subjects, and the power of language and discourse to generate and condition power/knowledge relations that fabricate the subject in terms of 'truth.'[26] Following from the interstices of these Foucaul-dian arguments, Butler reinforces that the subject is the *effect* rather than the origin of discursive practices. She echoes Foucault when she argues that the subject is formed in gendered terms through both the grammar or language of gender and the power/knowledge mechanisms of discipline that are discursively produced surrounding/concerning sex and gender.

Butler begins her analysis of performativity with the claim that rather than being ontological, gender is fabricated within the social realm, which is "the realm in which subjects interpellate and hail other subjects, in which the performative enactment of gender occurs" (Lloyd 1999, 196–197). This idea is central for Butler and leads her to insist that interpellation—or the process of social recognition—is a performative act. These are "forms of authoritative speech: most performatives . . . are statements that, in the uttering, also perform a certain action and exercise a binding power" (Butler 1993, 225). Put another way, performative acts produce what they name (Butler 1993, 23). In positioning her argument this way, Butler calls upon the legacy of both Austin and Derrida. But although Butler may be indebted to Austin, she rejects his idea that there is an autonomous author who is the origin and instigator of these performative speech acts. Instead, Butler follows the Derridean argument that states that any intention and any performative utterance is always constrained by or limited to the general iterability of the sign. In this way, the performative reenactment of gender is only ever a reiterative 'expression' of gendered norms that the subject performs in order to be recognized, intelligible, and ultimately formed as a gendered subject. This subject is not the author or origin of these gendered acts, for the normalized acts are discursively generated 'manners of being' that the subject approximates in a repetitive or reiterative process. Generalized iterability is critical for Butler, in that performativity only " 'works' to the extent that *it draws on and covers over* the constitutive conventions by which it is mobilized" (1993, 227). Thus, any performative utterance is only/ever a derivative citation, because a citation must conform to an iterable model in order for it to be intelligible.

The formation of the subject through performative citation is not, however, achieved in a single act of interpellation. Rather, the gendered subject is formed through the continual process of interpellating 'calls.'[27] The subject is called into being through what could be identified as an initiatory performative—recall the example of the doctor's exclamation, "It's a girl!" Through this call, which is always a recitation of a preexisting norm, the individual is situated within discourse. This is an assignment that is an interpellating demand or imperative. In *assuming* this position *the subject becomes the appropriated effect of performative demands,* demands that stipulate the behavioral norms of that site of identity (the site of 'girlness'). These performative norms of gender that "precede . . . and condition . . . the formation of the subject" (Butler 1993, 226) function, and are maintained, through performances that are the *embodied practice of* gendered *identity.* Thus, the individual recites these norms that carry citational force—a force or power that is formed through historicity—and they are compelled to do so "in order to qualify and remain a viable subject" (Butler 1993, 232).

By deploying Derrida's notion of citationality, Butler extends Foucault's account of subject formation. In the preceding chapter I outlined that for Foucault, the individual is simultaneously *subject to* and *enabled by* the normalizing conventions or constraints of power. In answer to how the individual could be constituted as a subject by both of these mechanisms at once, Butler presents citationality. Citational force within a general iterability thus constrains and enables, forecloses and produces. The notion of citationality rules out seeing the subject as wholly and definitively determined from and by exterior forces, because norms must be incorporated and recited *by subjects* in order to survive. It is these discursive norms, then, that operate in the same overall process to subordinate the subject and to enable (produce) the subject through enunciative possibilities. As Lloyd (1999, 200) has argued, gender functions at once as (a) a regulatory mechanism of constraint (in which norms are established that demarcate subjects as normal/abnormal, and (b) the 'locus of productive activity' (the means through which subjects are produced).

For Butler, though, idealized norms can only ever be *provisionally* recited because the reiterative constitution of gender always involves a repetition with a difference—a repetition through which the idealized norm is necessarily altered or transformed.[28] Thus, as gender is only the acts and behaviors that constitute it, it cannot be perceived as a fixed or stable 'reality.' Instead, the "failure to become 'real' and to embody 'the natural' is . . . a constitutive failure of all gender enactments for the very reason that these ontological locales are fundamentally uninhabitable" (Butler 1999, 186). If the gendered locale of 'girlness' can never be fully occupied it is because the subject never 'arrives,' as it were, at a point where their 'girlness' is secured. Instead, the subject must persistently rearticulate the norms of 'girlness' in order to continue to be identified as a girl. It is this very impossibility of inhabiting or occupying the idealized identity site that opens up a space for transformative practices, ones that alter or rework the conventional injunctions that constrain any given subject position.[29]

By presenting gendered identities as always in a process of 'becoming,' Butler destabilizes the binarism between determinism and voluntarism. Instead, gendered identity is an *effect* that is "neither fatally determined nor fully artificial and arbitrary" (1999, 187): if the subject is always under construction and constructing themselves within the limitations of available gendered citations or enunciations then they are neither unilaterally constructed nor the autonomous practitioners of free will.[30]

RACE AS PERFORMATIVE PRACTICE

Various theorists have suggested that race be analyzed as a performative practice.[31] Butler herself makes reference to this need, most notably in *Bodies That*

Matter, where she remarks that "recent race theory has underscored the use of 'race' in the service of 'racism,' and proposed a politically informed inquiry into the process of *racialization,* the formation of race" (1993, 229). Despite this recognition, race is not Butler's focus. What, then, would it mean to say that race is a performative practice that produces the very bodies and subjects that are said to *be* a particular race? As I explored in chapter 1, the construction of race, or the process of racialization is, essentially, a disciplinary operation. But this is a discipline that can only be reenforced through the perpetual reiteration and reinscription of performative decrees of race. Thus, while race may have the appearance of reflecting an 'inner essence,' this is a phantasy. It is only the continual reenactment of racial norms that retroactively produces the appearance of race as a fixed essential truth. Racial subjectivity is constituted through the mandatory reiteration of regularized racial 'norms.' The *expression* of this subjectivity *is* the compelled recitation of normalized learnt acts and behaviors that are seen to mark one's 'belonging' to a particular racial group—'belonging,' that in the case of race, is linked to and conditioned by discursive interpretations of physical markers. Recall, though, that these markers themselves are discursively produced such that they come to denote interior depth. Thus, race is discursively rendered as that which is supposed to mark the racial subject prior to their social fabrication. But both the racial body (that is perceived to be pre-discursive) and racial subjectivity are governed by and called into being through performative reiterations of discursive norms.[32] As with the norms of gender, these exist prior to, and are themselves the means through which the racial subject is formed (Butler 1993, 226).[33] We are born *into* these norms and our subjectivity is fashioned in, by, and through them. In order to qualify and be validated as a viable racial subject, one must perpetually strive to inhabit the perceived discursive norms (or performative dictates) of the racial subject position one is assigned. For the very possibility or "discursive condition of social recognition" (Butler 1993, 225) is premised on the adherence to the power of normative decrees of discursive allocation. As more than simply an assignment, the 'sign of race,' then, is *a command* or an imperative; the individual cannot be recognized, and therefore cannot come-into-being or exist as a certain racialized subject without occupying the regularized norms of that subject position. They are compelled to recite these norms (of blackness or whiteness) in order to survive as a discursively recognized and tenable racial subject. Yet it is precisely *the very reiterative repetition* of said normalized acts that give the semblance that the identity being expressed *is natural and unified* rather than a performative fabrication: an identity that 'succeeds' only because it recites the various signifying conventions by and through which that subject position is mobilized. These conventionalized norms become 'ideals' that the subject seeks to embody through the performance or practice of identity.[34] But they are ideals that are illusory because they are discursive fictions devoid of ontological security. Race is, as a consequence, a perpetual labor of reenactment with the aim of (ineluctably) inhabiting an 'ideal,' and the subject becomes raced not through the enunciation of a constative utterance, a factual statement, but through a continual process by which one is inserted into and interpellated through discourse that functions to *create* that which it names. Thus, occupying a socially, legally, and discursively sanctioned racial subject position is "not . . . an expression of what one is, but . . . something that one does" (Lloyd 1999, 196).

As with gender, the performative reenactment of racial subjectivity is a precarious and ever-tenuous affair. An individual must continually reiterate racial norms and they must be repeatedly called-forth as a particular (and normalized) racial subject by discursive power. As Mirón and Inda (2000, 100) state, "[t]he racing of the subject is a never-ending process, one that must be reiterated by various authorities in order to sustain the naturalized effect of race." It becomes important, then, to ask the following questions: which forms of authority exercise this force? In which ways do authorities participate in the interpellative process of racialization? Moreover, what are the norms of blackness and whiteness that condition racial subjectivity and how does the individual participate in the process of self-disciplined racialization? How too might performative disobedience be pursued in regards to race? If identity is a site of ambivalence, then the subject is neither fully determined nor a free agent (free in the sense that they are liberated from discursive compulsions). However, subjectivity is "the space . . . which opens up the possibility of a reworking of the very terms by which subjectivation proceeds—and fails to proceed" (Butler 1993, 124). Mirón and Inda discuss one example of reworking in regard to race. They highlight the way in which the term 'black' has been resignified by subjects of 'African origin' in new and positive assemblages of meanings. These reworked meanings move beyond dominant discursive or performative utterances of 'black' that have historically been employed to shame, subordinate, and marginalize the group encapsulated by the term. My particular interest in the chapters that follow, however, is to address specific processes through which *individuals* are formed as subjects, how individuals navigate these processes, and how the performative imperatives through which these individuals are formed might be rearticulated.

In pursuing such an analysis several important factors require noting. First, the macro-level or superstructure of performatively prescribed discipline must be considered alongside the experience of discipline at the micro-level. Looking at this micro-level yields a nuanced account of disciplinary power as the constituting force in subject formation. Second, and as discussed in chapter 1, because the disciplinary fabrication of subjects takes place within particular institutional sites, it is these same sites that must be analyzed in terms of thinking about the constraints of identity and the possibilities for agency. I have focused specifically on the disciplinary apparatus of law and the role that various and often conflicting legal actors have played in the constitution of racial 'truths.' If, as Mirón and Inda suggest, we were to consider the ways in which "various authorities" reiterate performative injunctions of race, law would be one of the primary authoritative arenas in which racial performativity can be investigated. In light of the theory of performativity that I have outlined here, it is possible to interpret the legal designation or classification of race as a performative utterance, whereby the legal decree of blackness *performs the action* of racing the subject and exercises a binding power (Butler 1993, 225).[35] Following from this instantiation of identity, any action that complicated or reinterpreted the performative injunctions sanctioned by law could be analyzed in terms of the agential possibilities that they suggest. Finally, Butler only gestures toward ways that race might be thought of as performative and how racial agency might be realized. A historically specific reading of what is involved in constructing the racial subject—the *materiality of subjugation,* both by external power and through a practice of self-discipline—seems essential, then, in order to consider the localized resistances to disciplinary power that are enabled or, indeed, generated. This last problematic is one to which I specifically return in chapter 7. In the next chapter, however, I revisit the question that I have already raised and subsequently suspended: what happens when the race of a body challenges demarcation, that is, when the racial subjectivity that is enunciated seemingly complicates the performative dictates pertaining to race that are augmented in law? How might this subject be seen to pass-through racial performatives?

4

Domesticating Liminality

SOMATIC DEFIANCE IN *RHINELANDER V. RHINELANDER*

> Miscegenation . . . has been abhorred by men for ages . . . if young
> Rhinelander had gone no farther than to place the battered crown of
> illicit love upon the brow of Alice Jones . . . recent spectacle would now
> be an unwritten and unacted drama . . . [I]nstead . . . he and the girl
> he married are viewed today by the millions as degraded violators
> of an age-old human law. The reasons that marriage is more
> abhorred than illicit connection are two in chief: First, marriage
> is an open defiance, a rebellion against the code which forbids
> miscegenation: and, second, marriage is more likely
> to produce children and mix the races forever.
>
> —*New York Amsterdam News,*
> 25 November 1925, Editorial page

In 1924, the former laundress and nursemaid, Alice Jones, married Leonard
Rhinelander, the scion of one of New York's oldest and wealthiest families. In
doing so, the *New York Times* (11 March 1925, 1) claimed, Alice "passe[d] over
hundreds of persons on the fringes of society and [made] her debut therein."[1]
But "[w]ithin a few hours of the wedding announcement," the newspaper reported, "town gossip recalled that Alice Jones's sister was married to a colored
butler, and then it was found that a census taker had written down Mr. Rhinelander's bride as a mulatto. Shortly afterward the youthful bridegroom separated from his wife and the annulment suit followed" (*New York Times,* 11 March
1925, 1) on the basis that Alice had supposedly lied about her race and passed as
white. This case threatened social mores and categories pertaining to class,
sexual and gendered protocols, and, perhaps most forcefully, expectations re-

garding racial behavior. In this chapter, I look to Alice Rhinelander in order to demonstrate (a) how the liminal subject complicates performative demands of race; (b) how racial 'truth' and corporeality are viewed as—and are made to seem—commensurate; and (c) how law is used as a modality of racial discipline to punish and 'correct' the recalcitrant subject who fails to ratify discursive racial classification and accompanying performative demands.

Even though interracial marriage had never been prohibited under law within the State of New York, the discursive capital of anti-miscegenation rhetoric and taboos were, nevertheless, ever present and underscored the entire *Rhinelander* case. The public exposure of Alice's possible blackness and the attendant exposure of Leonard Rhinelander's transgression in entering into a miscegenous union was an undeniable social infraction, one that challenged Leonard's white masculine subject position. Performative demands attendant to this subject position require that the white individual maintain white purity by reproducing *within* the racial group. In entering into a miscegenous union, Leonard defied this demand; he symbolizes transgressive breach in his performative failure of white masculinity, in that he (potentially) 'invites' the strain of 'black blood' into the body of whiteness and, in so doing, threatens pollution. It is the potential threat of miscegenous procreativity that signals Leonard's abrogation of the discursive injunctions of whiteness; he derogates from the performative decrees of normative white masculinity, positioning himself as the agent through which whiteness becomes vulnerable. Leonard poses a threat *from within* the very ranks of whiteness, rendering him the aberrant 'internal other.' The trial, thereby, served as his effort to recuperate his status in white masculinity. It is in the trial that Leonard Rhinelander attempted to disavow his own culpability in what this union represented, through claiming that Alice had deceived him.

During this era, New York State law only permitted divorce on the grounds of adultery, but annulments could be (and still are) granted if one party's consent to a marriage is obtained through force or by fraud. It was to fraud that Leonard made recourse when he claimed that he had been 'duped.' But how could such a claim be proven? And was race grounds upon which fraud could be established? Explaining the basis for matrimonial fraud, Edgar M. Grey, writing for the *New York Amsterdam News* (9 December 1925, Editorial and Feature page; my emphasis), stated:

> The law specifically makes a difference between the marriage contract and all other contracts and declares that, while in the ordinary contract any misrepresentation would be fraud sufficient to void a contract, in the marriage contract the misrepresentation must be of such a nature as to *reach the essence of the agreement* before any fraud will be allowed.[2]

In the first decades of the twentieth century, racial mixing was widely denounced within both black and white communities.[3] And this generalized anti-miscegenation sentiment was reflected in the belief that belonging to the same race was of critical importance in the decision to enter into matrimony.[4] That one party should misrepresent the 'truth' of their racial origins was, then, a factor that was perceived as corrupting the 'essence' of the marriage. And Leonard claimed that Alice had misrepresented her race: she had perpetrated this fraud by refusing the performative demands to which she was subject, that is, performing her (supposedly) 'true' black racial identity.

Interestingly, Alice Rhinelander presented an ambiguous racial identity. Preceding the trial, her attorney, Lee Parsons Davis, stated that Alice "would deny she had any Negro blood . . . [and would prove] that she was white" (*New York Times*, 29 November 1924, 15).[5] By the following day, her counsel claimed to neither affirm nor deny that Alice was black,[6] but by the time the trial began, Davis admitted "for the purposes of [the] trial that she has some colored blood in her veins" (*CR*, 1106). Davis made clear, however, that this admission was not a "concession that she is a negress" (*CR*, 1181). Thus, her attorney drew a distinction between having 'black blood' and *being* black, a curious delineation, especially given the widely accepted rhetorics of the one-drop rule and his own subsequent mode of argumentation that relied on a definitive designation of Alice as corporeally black.[7] The ambiguity of Alice Rhinelander's race was only compounded by the racial classification of other members of the Jones family. Her mother, Elizabeth Jones, was 'pure' white of English origin. Alice's father, George, had emigrated with his wife from England, and was designated in his naturalization papers as 'colored.' Alice's sister's, Emily and Grace, were respectively listed as mulatto and black ('Negro') on their birth certificates.[8] Yet, while Emily and her husband were listed on their marriage license as black, Grace, who married an Italian, was listed as white. Further confusion arose in the press when the *New York Evening Journal* (15 November 1924, 3) reported that the family had been designated as white in the 1915 New York State Census. Neighbors and members of the community seemed similarly unable to decide whether the Jones family was black or white; they attended a prestigious white church and Sunday school, they were reputed to not associate with blacks, but at one and the same time, members of the family, and Alice herself, were unquestionably accepted by some as black. Accordingly, no one could decide definitively how to define Alice. As the *Daily News* (15 November 1924, 1) succinctly pronounced: "Some thought her colored. Some did not." It seemed that the members of the family occupied a space somewhere between black and white communities, neither denouncing nor claiming membership to either. Perhaps the most telling indication of how Alice herself might have identified is to be found in a newspaper article written in the *New Rochelle Standard Star* (5 January 1927) just over a year after the trial (cited in Wacks 2000, 164 n. 6). The paper reported that Alice intended to begin legal proceedings in order to clear the allegation that she had Negro blood. Albeit, the case for annulment was tried on the basis that Alice was indeed black, that Alice was 'other' than what she purported to be. Integral to this allegation was the contention that Alice had misrepresented the inherent racial 'truth' of her body.

As Amy Robinson (1996, 249) remarks, "[t]he preconditions for the pass always concern its proximity to a model of identity: a social taxonomy of designation which, since Plato, has been dominated by the vocabulary of the visual subject." Alice's misrepresentation, consequently, was a product of two inter-related operations; her liminal corporeality evaded the visually reliant social taxonomy of racial demarcation, and her enactment of racial identity (*afforded* by her liminal body) together produced the possibility of passing. The court proceedings took issue here and, in order to buttress the economy of visually based racial logic, implicitly placed the phenomenon of 'passing' on trial.

The subject who has formulated a racial identity that counters their discursive designation executes a breach of racial 'law' and 'logic.' In doing so, they demonstrate that the body and the subject cannot always be made to behave in a manner that is acceptable to discursive power; they illuminate that the power of discourse and the power exercised through multiple technologies and institutions does not always function in accordance to its aims. A liminal subject who has been read as 'white,' yet is discursively demarcated as 'black' (through supposedly quantifiable fractions of blood), challenges discursive power through the (mis)reading that facilitates the assumption of a white racial identity. And this breach, then, exposes that power is not unidirectional, and that the power that is exercised through mechanisms of racial discipline cannot always predict the outcomes of its prohibitory (and productive) rhetoric.

When such a breach is detected, however, the workings of *corrective* disciplinary punishment become evident. For if a liminal subject is identified as having attempted to pass-as-white, they are categorically *reinserted* back within the logic of binary understandings of race. It is for this reason that the phenomenon of passing cannot be viewed as a liberatory or subversive enterprise. It is important to stress that liminality is itself *produced* by dominant cultural norms; the binarism of black and white as oppositional categories *creates* the idea of a subject who can be said to exist *between* these two realms. What I mean here is that the very possibility of 'racial mixing'—which creates the supposedly liminal subject—is contingent on the *construction* of putatively distinct categories that can or have been breached. And while this subject may (momentarily) disrupt or displace racial logic and power/knowledge relations, they also effect or are utilized to effect the *resecuring* of hegemonic racial norms and relations of power. Liminality cannot and will not be tolerated within hegemonic white racial logic. It is discursively unrecognizable and untenable. It is for this reason that passing is delimited in its transgressive potential: if the pass is suspected, the subject is recuperated back into oppositional logic through being validated as white or reprimanded through a definitive designation as black. And while it is inviting to assume that the undetected passing figure engages in a liberatory practice, by passing-as-white and being read as white this subject, again, is reabsorbed into the binarism of black/white. In being read as 'not-black' they are read as white and, accordingly, no threat to racial hegemony is identified.

By considering a material instance in which racial liminality is encountered—in the *Rhinelander* trial—it is possible to analyze specific operations of racial discipline within the legal arena. What becomes particularly evident is the regulation of the individual within the 'truth' claims of racial ontology, a regulation that refuses to permit liminality. The breach is inevitably received or responded to in ways that accord to the various power/knowledge relations that proclaim a racial essence that can definitively only/ever be *either* black or white. And it is this very insistence on interior substance that is the *foundational premise* upon which the reenactment (the performativity) of race *relies*.

Ontology is what is called forth, cited, and insisted upon in the performative recitation of race. And it is through the never-ending discursive recourse to and reiteration of race as ontologically secure that race, as a performative phenomenon, is consolidated. Yet the passing figure engages in a 'shadow-play' that is interpreted as betraying supposed racial innerness.[9] When detected, ontology must be reasserted, but this is a 'truth' that is reestablished within racial purity rhetoric through seemingly paradoxical modes of argumentation; the 'rightful' racial status of the subject before the Court has concomitantly been conceptualized as that which is in plain sight (corporeally announced) and, yet, potentially hidden in a manner that belies racial 'truth.' Always, and inevitably, however, these apparently disparate arguments are grounded in the same epistemological premise; they both insist on race as a static prediscursive substance. Accordingly, the adoption of either of these positions requires that racial 'innerness' *must be* reasserted, that the subject be brought back in line with racial norms. Thus, the performative disobedience that has been exercised by the willful subject before the Court is domesticated. This subject is disciplined or corrected according to the performative dictates or norms of the racial position to which they are assigned. And this takes place through various legal mechanisms (whether they be findings of 'fact,' arguments adopted by counsel, or judgments of the Court) that operate to 'expose' that the body and the subject does, indeed, reflect the norms of the supposed 'true' racial identity; the body and the subject *must be made* to be seen to articulate racial 'truth.' It is to this particular operation that I want to turn attention by analyzing *Rhinelander.* Exploring the ways in which Alice Rhinelander is assessed and constructed by the counsels, the witnesses, the jury, and the final judgment elucidate the laborious task of racial reconstitution involved in the inevitable reassertion of binarized racial logic.

THE BODY AS RACIAL EVIDENCE

In the initial claim brought forth by the plaintiff, Leonard Rhinelander, affirmative fraud was charged on the basis that Alice had told Leonard that she was white. The argument here was, then, that passing was indeed (provisionally) possible. The defense refuted with the argument that Alice did more than simply *not* pass—rather, she *could not* pass by virtue of her body. For Lee Parsons Davis, Alice's attorney, the issue at hand was whether or not Leonard could establish that Alice had said to him "by word of mouth, affirmatively, in substance, 'I am pure white and not colored?'" (*CR*, 1183). But in a confusing maneuver, the plaintiff amended the initial complaint during the trial to argue instead for negative fraud. Thus, Alice was accused of having concealed her race through silence—now on trial for having failed to tell Leonard that she had colored blood.

It is impossible to know whether or not Alice Rhinelander intentionally executed a pass-for-white. What is evident is that at times, in certain situations, and by particular individuals both she and other members of the Jones family were read—were *passed*—as white. The motivations and rewards of passing are clear; implied in much of the press coverage and explicitly articulated in Leonard's attorney's (Judge Isaac Mills) trial rhetoric was the idea that, for Alice, passing-for-white meant escaping the strictures of her class and racial origins and gaining access to the Rhinelander name, money, and of course, status in whiteness.

In order to rule out the possibility that Alice had duped Leonard, her counsel argued that race is clearly manifest 'on' the body, that the corporeal inevitably marks, contains, and enunciates the race of the subject. In executing this line of argument, Davis effectively rendered Alice an exhibit by entering her into evidence *as a body*—a body that definitively reflected corporeal norms of black racial status. Alice never took the stand to give her own account of the relationship and her actions. It was only through her personal letters to Leonard (eighty-six of which were entered into evidence by Mills), her representation by counsel, and the depiction of her by opposing counsel and various witnesses that Alice was given voice.[10] She was essentially only externally animated, but was ultimately reduced to her body, as it was this that was offered as the most potent 'proof' in the trial.

Davis carefully laid the groundwork for the jury to view and find Alice's body as unmistakably black. One of the initial ways through which he executed this was to demonstrate that certain enunciations of Alice's subjectivity should have signaled to Leonard that his wife had colored blood running through her veins. Early in his cross-examination of Leonard, Davis asked if he had ever heard Alice use the expression, "You all going to a strutting party" (CR, 486). Learning that Leonard had, Davis followed by questioning Leonard as to how, if he had heard this "typically negro expression" (CR, 487) issue from Alice's lips and combined that with her appearance, he could have "no idea that there was any colored blood in her make-up" (CR, 486). Davis's argument suggested that certain manners or patterns of speech were inherently black—were performances of blackness—that unequivocally articulated racial innerness. Indeed, the *New York Times* reflected the sentiment that Alice's speech unquestionably announced her class and racial origins when it was reported that her letters to Leonard were "illiterate and crude" (12 November 1925, 1)[11] and at times displayed "a truly negro rhythm" (13 November 1925, 1).[12] Another method Davis used to ensure that the jury would be inclined to definitively 'see' Alice as black was to call upon various members of the Jones family and point out physical traits that supposedly indicated that they had colored blood; George Jones, Alice's sisters, Emily and Grace, and Emily's husband, Robert Brooks, were each called forth in order to show the 'darkness' of the Jones family.[13] Davis insisted that this weight of evidence verified that Leonard had to have been aware of Alice's race; Leonard knew (he had spent considerable time in the Jones household), Leonard liked it, and Leonard was the pursuer and abuser of this innocent victim.[14] In Davis's words, Leonard was the "wrongdoer" who had been "leading this girl on." According to the defense, Leonard was only making the claim of racial fraud and seeking an annulment because the miscegenous transgression had been detected and the family name threatened. Leonard was now "besmirch[ing] her name" (CR, 1245) such that Alice would "walk out of [the] courtroom shunned by those of the colored race [and] . . . by the white race" (CR, 1271). Davis, thus, made an appeal to gendered mores, and requested that the white male jury view her beyond the confines of race, view her instead as a *woman* who had been deceived by a wealthy cad. Alice might have lied about her age (stating on her marriage certificate that she was younger than her years), but this Davis attributed to the "human nature in women" (CR, 1177). It could, then, in no way be taken as an indication that Alice may have lied about her race, rather, it was a deceit shared by all women. This strategy, as Jamie Wacks (2000, 170) notes, "was risky because it challenged a popular notion that white women were a group apart from and better than black women by suggesting a sisterhood stemming from common behavior toward men." Yet while Davis employed this rhetoric seemingly to have the jurors empathize with Alice, the threat that may have been presented by this argument was assuaged by the 'proof' that he offered in order to argue that Leonard could not have been an unwitting victim of fraud.

Having established for the jury the undeniable racial 'truth' of the Jones family, Davis made his most compelling strategic maneuver by moving onto Alice herself. He had Alice expose her hair (CR, 300), exhibit her hands (CR, 511), and then, in the words of the New York Times (24 November 1925, 3), "Mr. Davis dramatically called on Justice Morschauser to clear the courtroom of all men not having business there so that he might have Mrs. Rhinelander partially disrobe and show the jury how dark her skin was. He [Davis] contends that Rhinelander could not have known her as well as her did without knowing that she was colored."[15] The Court espoused that Alice's facial appearance could in no way be taken as an indicator for her race. Alice's body, however, could be and, consequently, "for that limited purpose it may be received" (CR, 695, my emphasis).[16] By referring to her in this capacity, it becomes evident, as Lewis and Ardizzone (2001, 158) note, that for the Court "Alice had quickly ceased to be an individual person . . . and had become a body, an 'it,' not a 'she' ": a body that configures and bears the limits of subjectivity.

"The Court, Mr. Mills, Mr. Davis, Mr. Swinburne, the [all white and male] jury, the plaintiff, the defendant, her mother, Mrs. George Jones, and the stenographer left the courtroom and entered the jury room" (CR, 696) where Davis had Alice parade before them with her breasts, back, and legs exposed. The intent here was to demonstrate to the jury the 'obvious blackness' of Alice's naked body. Davis stated:

> I let you gentlemen look at a portion of what he saw. He saw all of her body.
> And you are going to tell me that he never suspected that she had colored
> blood! That is what he testifies to. You saw that with your own eyes. A boy of
> twelve would have known that colored blood was coursing through her veins.
> (CR, 1242)

With this rhetoric Davis challenged the jury as to their ability to verify racial 'truth,' the presumption being that the common man should be able to ascertain whether an individual before them was white or had the mark of black ancestry (if they possessed all their faculties and were racially literate). The jurymen were utilized in this capacity as racial 'experts.' If they found in Alice's favor, declaring that her body did indeed announce its supposed racial ontology, they would invalidate the claim of racial fraud by supporting the notion that Leonard must have been aware of his wife's race. In this way the fear that race could be that which an individual could hide would be dispelled. The notion of race as a perceptible and secure corporeal ontology that is always/already apparent would be resecured and the ability to pass for an identity from which one is discursively prohibited would be rendered a futile venture before the law.[17]

CORPOREAL AMBIGUITY AND THE EVIDENCE OF RACE

In contradistinction, Leonard's counsel, Mills, claimed that Alice had indeed been able to mask this racial ontology. He claimed that both Alice's ambiguous physical features and performance of whiteness enabled her to pass, to beguile, and to defraud. For Mills, Alice's pass was enabled by the fact that she had physical features similar to her father, George Jones. However, while "every feature of [George Jones'] face [was] distinctly Caucasian [this was with the exception of] . . . the color" (*CR*, 1429). Unlike her father, Alice possessed the epidermal signifier of whiteness that, when coupled with her father's features, confounded the ability to tell Alice's 'true' race. Mills claimed:

> To look at her she [Alice] inherits from her father. She has got the same fea-
> tures largely that her father has. Long face. Aquiline nose. The other features
> of the Caucasian. Her lips are not different to her father's lips. The father's
> lips are as thin as my lips. That is her facial appearance. You have seen her
> color. (*CR,* 1431)

Mills posited, therefore, that because Alice had both the facial traits and skin that facilitated her ability to pass, Leonard could not have been aware of, and should not be held accountable for the deception that had taken place. Alice's corporeal ambiguity belied the notion that race is that which is visibly guaranteed. For not only was Leonard unable to 'tell the truth' of her race, others, Mills claimed, had had similar difficulty with both Alice and other members of her family. The plaintiff called as a primary witness one such individual who had believed Alice and the extended Jones family to be white. Miriam Rich and her husband had socialized with the young Rhinelanders, and initially Mrs. Rich was to be a witness for the defense, as she had believed that "Alice was a white girl . . . a good white girl" (*Philadelphia Inquirer,* 25 November 1925, 4). She and her husband had been to the Joneses for dinner, had "met there twenty refined white people" (*New York Times,* 25 November 1925, 3) and accepted the family as white.[18] Upon learning in the press, however, that Alice's birth certificate designated her as black, Mrs. Rich became a witness for Leonard. She claimed that Alice had explicitly told her that she was white—the implication being that Alice had deceptively fabricated an inauthentic racial identity. Miriam Rich now felt

betrayed, as her association with the duplicitous Alice Rhinelander had ruined
her socially; she stated that as a consequence of the publicity of the case, "The
whole of Mt Vernon had a good laugh at me" (*New York Times*, 25 November
1925, 3).

Thus, Mills's rhetorical strategy was to claim that, in addition to the phenotypic markers that enabled her to pass-for-white, Alice also actively fostered a
white identity. He stated that "years of efforts of the Jones family" (*CR*, 1333) and
the "vaulting ambition" (*CR*, 1302) of Alice's white mother, encouraged Alice
and her sisters performance of whiteness. According to Mills:

> there came into the mother's heart the ambition to have her two younger
> daughters marry white men. They went to the white church, they went to the
> white Sunday School, they cultivated white acquaintances, and the two
> daughters went out upon the sidewalks of New Rochelle and sought white
> men and brought them home, unnamed and unaccounted for, and this
> mother, in her great ambition, received them. (*CR*, 1290)

That Alice was received as white by hoteliers, that men she wrote to believed she
was white and, tellingly, that her own counsel accepted as true her initial affi-
davit that denied 'Negro blood,' meant, Mills insisted, that Alice's race *was* that
which could be disguised (*CR*, 1433–1434). Therefore, Leonard's failure to detect
it did not render him culpable. Alice was the reprehensible party as she had
defied the disciplinary decrees of her discursive positionality.

While Mills may have proclaimed that Alice *sought* successful racial trans-
figuration, both his and the defense's arguments were fundamentally grounded
in the same epistemological premise: race is ontologically secure in that it is
either apparent or can become so. Mills argued that although Alice may have
been able to pass, it was a contingent pass that, *upon close inspection,* divulged
the 'truth' of her racial status. This line of attack that was put forth by the
plaintiff was curiously paradoxical; on the one hand Mills was insisting that
Alice's blackness (in the family members, Alice's actions, and 'on' Alice's body)
was hidden to plain sight—that the visual had, indeed, faltered on this occasion.
Yet at the same time he relied on what he depicted as the very tangible presence
of Alice's blackness in order to make his case against her and to reinstate her
within the discursive norms of black femininity.

Mills represented Alice as a 'vamp' and 'wily mulatto,' whose hypersexuality
and cunning, which supposedly signified her blackness, seduced Leonard and
rendered him helpless against her.[19] Beyond the ontology of her body, Davis
depicted Alice as a demure and abused woman who had been wronged. But
Mills firmly entrenched Alice within the dominant discursive imagery of 'black

womanhood' that has persistently positioned black femininity as marked by the traits of sexual aggressiveness, potency, and promiscuity.[20] In constructing Alice in this capacity, Mills effectively argued that it was precisely her 'black' racial traits (that he went on to systematically 'illuminate') that facilitated her ability to successfully keep this blackness hidden, to 'deceive' Leonard, and to pass-for-white. Ultimately, Mills linked Alice's racial and class origins through depicting her as a scheming money-hungry jezebel, desperate and determined to access what he labeled the "white material" (*CR*, 1291) of the Rhinelander name and a place among the elite of New York society.[21]

Mills insisted that Alice was the aggressor in the relationship. He argued that she had waged a campaign with various stages, had a "diabolical plan" (*CR*, 1409) to ensnare Leonard, and was successful; she became Leonard's mistress, she secured an engagement, and finally "the campaign had been won" (*CR*, 1418) in having Leonard marry her secretly. Through her various ministrations Leonard became Alice's "slave, body and soul" (*CR*, 1101) (an image that inverted the black/white racial paradigm) such that "he did not know black from white" and "did not know or have control of himself" (*CR*, 1350). But Alice was not merely depicted as sexually aggressive in Mills's rendering; she was also cast as sexually loose. Mills outlined that Alice had engaged in premarital sex, not only with Leonard but also with an earlier lover. He claimed that in her letters Alice continually referred to the attention she received from other men in order to make Leonard jealous and constantly reminded him of the relations they had in a manner so relentless as to ultimately bedevil Leonard. A letter, introduced into evidence by Mills that suggested that Alice had had an abortion, only compounded her allegedly loose sexual morals.[22] In the climate of the early twentieth century, one of these transgressions of gendered and sexual mores alone would have been damaging; together they pointed toward a wayward, impure feminine subject deserving of social censure. That Alice was sexually aggressive, manipulative, unchaste, and wanton, all suggested for Mills that Alice was undeniably stained by black blood. Yet it was this very blood, so Mills claimed, that enabled Alice to manufacture or perform white femininity—these traits of 'true' black femininity enabling her, at one and the same time, to veil her blackness.[23]

By conducting this mode of argumentation, Mills highlights the notion of the inevitable performative disclosure of racial 'truth,' a truth that always ultimately 'shows itself.' His demonstration of the ability to detect the acts and behaviors that 'gave away' her blackness *recovered* and evacuated the fear generated by his earlier proposition that the body may become a site of alchemy or a vehicle of duplicity. One simply needed to be racially literate and ever vigilant.

LEGAL IMPRIMATURS AND THE
RITUAL OF RACIAL TRUTH PRODUCTION

In a reassertion that race is ultimately both detectable and definable, the jury did find in Alice Rhinelander's favor, declaring not only that she *did not,* but also that she *could not* have defrauded Leonard. While on the surface the finding might seem like a vindication of Alice, such a reading would be simplistic. Alice may not have identified herself as black and, thus, finding in her favor was a reprimand: it meant that the jury were forcibly reinscribing Alice as black, were stipulating that she could not lay claim to a white or liminal identity, and were reasserting that any attempt to do so was a performative disobedience and failure to abide by the disciplinary decrees of race. The very fact that the case even came before the Court meant that Alice's race was under question, an ambiguity that the law cannot permit. Thus in order to reestablish racial logic, the jury must configure Alice's body as 'black' and claim that this blackness is evident. This disciplinary decree is an instantiation of power that demonstrates the productive capacity of law, in that this injunction sought to delimit Alice's performative racial possibilities in the demarcation of her raced corporeality. By finding in Alice's favor, the legal judgment in *Rhinelander* demonstrates an instance in which the individual is instructed as to how racial subjectivity can be lived or performed. This normalizing judgment reprimands the failure of efficacious self-discipline (where the subject has failed to unquestionably enact norms associated with designation) and stands as an attempt to domesticate and correct the behavior that is perceived to have betrayed somatic truth. The rhetoric of racial purity required that Alice heed and ratify the maxim that one-drop of black blood marked an individual as black. She should, thereby, have embraced and proclaimed a black identity. To recall Foucault (2000c, 331),

> This form of power that applies itself to immediate everyday life categorizes the individual, marks him by his own individuality, attaches him to his own identity, imposes a law of truth in him that he must recognize and others have to recognize in him. It is a form of power that makes individuals subjects.

If Alice herself would not embrace and clearly articulate a black identity then the law would claim one for her. In designating Alice as black, the Court augmented the ritual of truth production that decrees that black racial status is based on the supposedly quantifiable presence of 'black blood'; it sought to impose a law of 'racial truth' that marked the territory of her identity and the enunciative possibilities of her subjectivity. Both the jury and the Court establish through this finding that ontology is secure and is always perceptible. Thus, racial 'essence' is deemed as that which cannot be hidden; rather, it is in plain sight and racial passing is ruled out as a duplicity that can remain undetected. The finding in this case endeavored to attach Alice to a 'black identity' and, in so doing the Court invalidated her performance of whiteness and censured her performative disobedience in the attempted interlope into whiteness. The legal actors in this case can be seen here to actively pursue the molding of conduct and behavior and to foreclose certain articulations of identity. In short, the apparent desire of the finding in *Rhinelander* was to *reconstitute* Alice and her performance of race *as incontestably black.*

As seen through this analysis of Alice, the performative constitution of racial subjects (and the performative 'nature' of 'race' itself) operates through the perpetual recourse to ontology; the expression of race is perceived as natural, inherent, corporeally determined, and ultimately inescapable. Thus, the act of passing (for white, for an-other) can only ever be interpreted as a performance of racial identity that is seen to be incommensurate with the 'truth' of the individual. This individual betrays discursive designation and trouble arises.

The passing subject evades the visual, the primary realm through which racial discipline (or the performative dictates of race) operates. Moreover, in terms of dominant racial logic, this subject fails to self-regulate in accordance to the racial position they are assigned within discourse. Instead, they generate an identity and are read as 'belonging' to a race from which they are discursively prohibited. The 'ability' to engender this 'shadow-play' is inevitably perceived as a failure or refusal to heed the 'truth' of identity and supposed corporeal ontology. The act is viewed as one of negligence, a betrayal, and an insubstantiality. Effectively, then, this subject has not been 'coerced' by disciplinary observation that demands that the 'truth' of corporeality act as the foundational mechanism in the resolute regulation and constitution of subjectivity. What occurs simultaneously to the event of visibility faltering is the possibility of breaching discipline, of perhaps only momentarily eluding the political anatomy of panopticism—a possibility that is only availed through corporeal ambiguity. Yet when faced with this act, the 'failure' of self-discipline, the disciplinary apparatus of law *must* respond through efforts to *normalize* the subject. The necessity here arises from the ever-present imperative to sustain the naturalized effect of race. This foundation of the performative *affect* that *is* race (and here it is important to note that I am casting race as the effect of an affect) is resecured through the never-ending recitation of 'racial truth.' This analysis has outlined that this process is achieved, and noticeably so in *Rhinelander,* through legal actors endeavoring to 'uncover' ways in which the body/subject before the Court does, indeed, express and conform to the norms of the identity position to which they are perceived to 'belong.'

Thus, Alice Rhinelander may not 'look' black, but she is *made* to do so; her body is read as unequivocally reflecting supposed 'black' corporeal norms. Likewise, Alice may not 'act' black—her capacity to pass signaling this possibility—but she is represented in such a way that her actions, manners, and comportment become perceived as those which definitively articulate a 'true black racial essence.' The semblance of one racial identity is reassembled in such a way that both the internal and external markers of race are seen to *come to* enunciate the discursive truth that is sanctioned by power/knowledge relations. The liminal or ambiguous subject is, thereby, recuperated back into the rhetorics of dominant racial logic (in this case by legal authorities) such that the body and subjectivity *becomes* commensurate with racial norms that are supposedly determined by color and blood.

What cannot escape notice here is that the passing figure is always and inevitably imbricated within the very same dynamics of power that they hope to transgress; as Robinson (1996, 237) states, "[a]s a strategy of entrance into a field of representation, the social practice of passing is thoroughly invested in the logic of the system that it attempts to subvert." While this may be the case—while on a macro-structural level passing-for-white will ultimately concretize and ratify the binarized system of race—the very possibility of passing for another offers a point of departure for thinking about the potential and limitations present in efforts of resistance to the performative imperatives of identity. Much can be learnt from the passing figure in regards to the significance of their acts of performative disobedience; while they may indeed be recuperated or reinstated within the very same system that their actions defy, the defiance, in and of itself, points to ways in which subjects can renegotiate their subjectivity *within* the productive constraints through which they are constituted.

5

Passing Phantasms

RHINELANDER AND ONTOLOGICAL INSECURITY

Within the rhetoric of dominant racial logic, the signifying power of white skin has always required the concomitant verification of a subcutaneous claim to whiteness—'pure' white lineage. And, while 'looking white' might have granted one possession of whiteness *without* legal title, in order to possess fair legal title, one had to *be* white (Saks 2000, 74). As the progeny of a 'blue blooded' Huguenot family, Leonard Rhinelander's genealogy remained unquestioned. His possession of fair legal title, as 'white,' was unequivocally accepted. Once in the Court, however, the gaze of law did not rest solely on his wife, Alice, whom he had accused of racial fraud. During the course of the trial, Leonard's own approximation of whiteness—more specifically, *white masculine* subjectivity—did not escape scrutiny. It was uncontested that Leonard Rhinelander possessed the phenotypic markers of whiteness that invited the social sanctioning of white subjectivity. And as a white subject, he was presumed to have performed certain 'acts' in accordance both with his white corporeality and with white 'ideals' to ensure that he be viewed as white. In this chapter, I explore the idea that just as Alice Rhinelander assumed the image of whiteness (albeit, in an allegedly fraudulent capacity), so, too, did Leonard. Both subjects exemplify *the phantasm of identity,* for this case elucidates that *all* identity is a form of passing and is, as such, ontologically insecure.

As Sara Ahmed (1999, 92) has argued, identity "involves assuming an image that has no proper 'fit' with the structure of the subject; [instead], it is the act of assuming an image that constitutes the subject."[1] Here, Ahmed extends Carole-Anne Tyler's (1994, 221) contention that "[t]he subject of the enunciation must pass through the statement in which his [or her] 'I' is uttered." All subjects can be said to *pass through* an image of identity that they desperately seek to inhabit, because it is through this image that one is discursively placed and co-extensively operates within the world. As I've discussed, there is no ontological 'essence' to subjectivity. Discursive assignment and disciplinary regulation operate to compel individuals to attach themselves to a subject position stipulated by power/knowledge relations. This position—let us say white femininity or masculinity—can only exist as an *idealized image without intrinsic content*. As a consequence, it is possible to see that beyond Alice's pass-for-white an additional form of passing is visible: Leonard was also 'passing,' because as a discursively positioned white masculine subject he attempted to occupy the space, the image of white masculinity.[2] Ahmed complicates any seemingly unilateral assertion that all identity is an ever-repeated act of passing, insisting instead that there are different kinds of passing, that these various forms of passing are incommensurable, and that there are explicit distinctions that mark the politics of different forms of passing. The way that passing-for-another is socially viewed and theorized inevitably marks this act as discrete from the assumption of an identity (and here I mean the 'taking-up' of an identity) that is discursively validated. These two forms of passing are separated by a *structural* (rather than essential) distinction, as they have a differing relation to the imaginary space of whiteness. In the first form of passing, the passing-for-an-other (such as that produced by Alice passing for white), there exists a disjunction in the image assumed in social encounters. There is the initial image assumed (for example, being read as 'white'), but also the threat of the detection of an additional image that, as Ahmed (1999, 93) argues, is "*always yet to be assumed.*" There is the ever-present knowledge of being positioned as *outside belonging*. In this way, the passer who passes through an image from which they are discursively prohibited is always aware of the disciplinary gaze that may, at any point, identify the 'deceptive' refusal of supposed 'ontological truth.'[3]

The second form of passing, that is, the assumption and constitution of a discursively legitimated white subjectivity is distinct because, in comparison, it is a passing through *into* belonging. While this passing is still and only-ever *an assumption that cannot contain the subject*, a belonging is produced through a prior history of self-identification and identification by social structures and institutions that constitute the subject as white and sanction their belonging. Both forms of passing, however, foreclose on the possibility of the subject stopping and *occupying* the space of whiteness.[4] The pass can only ever engender a *becoming* that is an endless yearning process that can never assume the fixed status of *being*. The image of whiteness is just that, an image that is impossible to *fully* inhabit.[5] The subject seeks exhaustively, to no avail, to master its illusory ideals. It is a phantasm. As Ahmed (1999, 94) insists, "[p]assing, by definition, is a movement through and across. [I]t is the literal act of moving through space (in which there is no moment of departure or arrival)."

As a process of becoming, the production of white masculinity by the discursively identified white male subject, such as Leonard, is always a *performative pass*. The attempt to assume an image—the act of passing—is inevitably the embodied recitation of signifiers that project a particular bodily image. This image that is generated is performative because the *effect* of the projected bodily image—identity—is an *action* that is a relentless endeavor, a perpetual passing, through striving to completely inhabit an image of an identity. However, the always-constrained ritualized production of identity that seeks to acquire the ideal image is marked by the inevitability of failure. Speaking about heterosexual gender, Butler reminds us that:

> Insofar as heterosexual gender norms produce inapproximable ideals, het-
> erosexuality can be said to operate through the regulated production of
> hyperbolic versions of "man" and "woman." . . . [T]he compulsory character
> of these norms does not always make them efficacious. Such norms are con-
> tinually haunted by their own inefficacy; hence, the anxiously repeated effort
> to install and augment their jurisdiction. (1993, 237)

For Butler, the attempt to *occupy* the norms of gender (or in the terms of the present analysis, gendered race) in any stable sense will always be impossible. The norms themselves are hyperbolic fictions that cannot be 'acquired.' Thus, any effort to repeat the norm will always be a repetition with a difference—a reiteration—precisely because the hyperbolic norm is uninhabitable. As I discussed in chapter 3, the subject endlessly executes a dissimulated simulation (a concealed and disavowed rendition) of a fictional ideal, and this simulation will always inherently be a failure to occupy—or a slippage from—the ideal. Yet the subject continues to approximate the norm. This is not a matter of choice. As already established, the subject is compelled to negotiate compulsory performances in order to survive as a social being. And as the final portion of the abovementioned excerpt from Butler states, norms are perpetually recited due to the fact that they are not innate, and it is precisely this continual recitation that resecures the force of the norm.

It is this *action* that *is itself* the embodied practice or performance of performative dictates and is that which *functions* to constitute identity.[6] But identification is a phantasm that exists only in the enactment. There is no 'essence,' only fabrication. Acts might produce the effect of an essence, but they "produce this on the surface of the body, through the play of signifying absences that suggest, but never reveal, the organizing principle of identity as a cause" (Butler 1999,

173). To enact identity is thus to *pass through performative utterances* that signify (and labor to consolidate) a specific subjectivity. Rather than being an enunciation of internality, identity is always a doing. Employing the turn of phrase marked by Elin Diamond (1996), this doing is always, however, a "thing done." For what is enacted is always a retracing and recitation of prior conventions (actions, speech forms, stylings). But the 'doing' of any performance (in the present moment) cannot be recognized (and exist as discursively tenable) without accumulated citational force (the thing 'done' must have already *been* done over and over again in the broader discursive terrain). The belonging that marks the pass as white attempted by the white subject, consequently, can be ensured only through the *successful* legally, socially, discursively validated performance of prior conventions. The subject position of white masculinity can only be designated as such through the continual recitation of normative 'acts' that *constitute* the subject as 'white' and 'male.' To reconfigure Butler (1997b, 99), "a [white male] subject only remains a [white male] subject through a reiteration or rearticulation of itself as a [white male] subject."

It is with these ideas in mind that I return to *Rhinelander* and focus on Leonard. *Rhinelander* highlights the act of performative passing as it applies to *all* subjects and reveals that it is the threat of censure that perpetuates the anxious response to the call for the constant repetition of normative acts. Ahmed (1999, 94) argues: "Through fetishism, identity hides passing, and by hiding passing, identity hides the conflict and antagonism that determines the 'work' needed to be done to reproduce a given sociality." Considering *Rhinelander* in light of this statement enables an analysis that renders whiteness less familiar.[7] Exposed are the disciplinary mechanisms of surveillance immanent within performative reproductions of identity. The depiction of Leonard Rhinelander, by both his own counsel and the defendant, operates to identify not only the obligatory labor involved in reproducing the semblance of a coherent white masculine identity but also Leonard's derogation from enunciating this sociality as a performative accomplishment. Judge Isaac Mills for the plaintiff and Lee Parsons Davis for the defendant employed divergent perspectives on this digression; the former deemed it an unconscious failing, the latter, a conscious failure. This distinction is significant as it was utilized to evaluate the extent of Leonard's responsibility for his performance and, ultimately, was to become instrumental in the jury's finding. Leonard is seen as failing to ratify the norms of white masculinity principally through his mental, social, and sexual behavior. These three points of slippage ultimately locate Leonard as the *internal other who is outside belonging*—outside of the perceived boundaries of white masculine subjectivity.

FALLEN: WHITE MANHOOD UNMANNED

Throughout the trial, Leonard Rhinelander was shown to deviate from the performative demands of white masculinity in terms of both his mental and social behavior. Mills argued that Leonard's lack of mental strength and control was evident in the fact that he stuttered, was shy, was easily influenced by those around him and, most particularly, because he was 'duped' by Alice. Under the normalizing gaze of medical knowledge, Leonard had been identified as having "a great sense of inferiority and incomplete mental development" (*New York Times*, 11 November 1925, 1). It was on the basis of these attributes that Mills leveled an implicit charge of 'unmanliness' against Leonard. However, his inability to 'be a man' and embody the attributes of the white-citizen-subject—individual accountability, rationality, self-reflection, self-control, the exercise of free will—was an *unconscious* failing that resulted from a weak mind.[8] He could not, then, be held accountable for his marriage to Alice.

In her defense, Davis argued that Alice had not perpetrated racial fraud: he sought to demonstrate that Leonard *did* know Alice's race and had only brought the case to trial on the insistence of his father.[9] Consequently, Davis's case was premised on the argument that Leonard's actions were not those of a 'gentleman';[10] it was Leonard who had been deceptive. Davis, thereby, leveled an *explicit* charge of 'unmanliness' against Leonard, a charge that was illustrated not simply by Leonard permitting the initiation of the trial but generally supported by his overall social behavior. Namely, he lied to Alice's parents about being chaperoned on the couple's outings, treated Alice in a way that he would not a girl of his own class, and surrendered intimate and sexually explicit letters into evidence in the trial, showing that he was indiscrete. Through acquiring Leonard's confession of this inappropriate behavior (and awareness of such), Davis positioned Leonard as possessing self-consciousness and self-reflexivity. With full capacity and presence of mind, then, the failure to reproduce the ideals of white masculinity—chivalry, honesty, integrity—was seen as a conscious one. Leonard's failure to embody white masculine norms was the product of *willful neglect*.

Leonard's sexual conduct only compounded these failures, and it became evident that both counsels considered that Leonard's violation of certain sexual mores indelibly threatened his tenuous relationship to white masculine subjectivity. Mills's concentration on the miscegenous nature of the marriage reflected the intricacies of the racial injunctions of whiteness that rely partially on a taboo against miscegenation. In his closing statement, Mills beseeched the jury to relieve Leonard "[f]rom this horrid, unnatural, absurd, terrible union . . . grant him deliverance" (*CR*, 1442). The reproduction of whiteness as a performative

accomplishment demands the perpetuation of perceived 'white purity,' specifically in the context of marriage. The white masculine subject, therefore, is
compelled to ensure the territorial parameters of whiteness through reproducing intra-racially—through "being the progenitor of descendents within the
racial group" (Frankenburg 1993, 83). As Butler (1993, 184) states, the "historically entrenched social power of the white male . . . [is] one whose masculinity is
enacted and guaranteed [through paying homage to this performative decree]."

Anti-miscegenation law can be seen to have existed precisely in order to
discipline racial conduct in general and white racial conduct in particular. It
operated, essentially, as a disciplinary prescription of individual conduct. However, these laws also operated as a form of biopolitics, to regulate the population
as a whole. As seen in chapter 2, the laws that policed and punished interracial
desire were an extension of state authority and surveillance into the bastion of
the private sphere. Marriage law was an arena that generally "championed the
freedom of choice" (Grossberg 1982, 201). When it came to racial hygiene,
however, the panoptic gaze of the state forcefully intervened in order to protect
against this perceived threat to the health and the moral well-being of the
population. The apparent necessity to ensure the protection of future generations guaranteed that state resources would be utilized to separate and regulate
racial subjects. Ultimately, these normalizing practices of racial distinction, surveillance, and regulation render the state a locus of what Saidiya Hartman (1997,
186) has termed "the materiality of racism as a technique of power."

Scaling down to the level of the subject, however, Foucault reminds us that it
is the individual body that is central to disciplinary techniques of power. Where
biopolitics is massifying (targeting the population at large), discipline is individualizing. Thus, in disciplinary power—which exists at the opposite pole to
biopolitics within the overarching 'power over life'—"the body and its forces,
their utility and their docility, their distribution and their submission" is the
focus (Foucault 1991, 25). And the body that is central to the concerns stipulated
within anti-miscegenation legislation, implementation, and rhetoric is the white
body. White bodily integrity is policed so as to guard against the infiltration of
contagion, for the act of miscegenation is seen as that which compromises the
corpus of whiteness, representing a *corpus delicti*—a breach to and of whiteness.
While the state did not deem the Rhinelander marriage a crime, the language
employed specifically by Mills illuminates the very-present (albeit, social) censure that interracial unions called forth—censure that does not merely prohibit
interracial desire but through which this desire is foreclosed. It is a desire that is
deemed unthinkable or unimaginable.

The discursive vernacular of miscegenous terror articulates as one of its
primary concerns the compromise of the familial name. More precisely, as in

Leonard Rhinelander's case, it is the name of the white father that is threatened through the union that co-mingles supposedly discrete racial 'bloods.' If the call to whiteness requires that the white subject reproduce the white self through producing 'ideal' white sons, then not only Leonard, but also Philip Rhinelander, failed to sanctify this decree. Leonard was presented as not simply mentally backward, but in need of constant surveillance and intervention in order to conceal his multiple infractions of a properly (white) racialized masculine subjectivity. Philip Rhinelander institutionalized his son for his supposed mental infirmity, as well as placing him under the constant watchful eye of those in his service. During the course of Leonard's testimony, for instance, he divulged that on one of the occasions that he was absent from Alice's side prior to the marriage, he was accompanied at his father's demand to Havana by one of his father's employees. Furthermore, Leonard testified that he left the Jones's home, following the newspaper release concerning his 'miscegenous marriage,' at the insistence of his father's attorney.[11] It became apparent, also, that during the trial he was not left to his own devices. Instead, during this time Leonard shared not only residence, but also a bedroom, with this same attorney. It would seem, then, that Philip Rhinelander exercised extreme vigilance in attempting to patrol, and suppress from social detection, his son's transgressive behavior.

Davis argued that the Rhinelander money was behind the suit and that Philip Rhinelander initially compelled the action. Despite this, the older Rhinelander failed to comment on the case, let alone show at his son's side during the trial.[12] As long as his son's increasingly enfeebled white manhood remained a private affair, Philip Rhinelander was able to exercise patriarchal control in mitigating Leonard's undesirable behavior. The young couple, however, had eloped without his knowledge. Once this disciplinary breach became public, it was imperative, in order to protect his own status in whiteness, that Philip Rhinelander distance himself from his son's transgression. Instrumental to the discursive capital of hegemonic white masculinity is the consolidation of dominance through the subordination of other forms of masculinity. White masculinity can only assert itself *against* alternative enunciations that are deemed 'inferior.' Faced with Leonard's white racial slippage, the only manner through which Philip Rhinelander could stabilize his own investment in whiteness was to negate his connection and, through silence, convey his refusal to condone his son's performative infraction.

Leonard Rhinelander did not simply compromise whiteness through threatening its purity; he acted in a manner that destabilized the racial economy upon which the power of whiteness is predicated. The maintenance of white dominance requires the concomitant subjugation of racial 'others.' Likewise, heteronormativity functions through discursive relations of power that position masculinity as dominant over femininity. In Mills's depiction, it was under Alice's sway that Leonard confounded both white and masculine power.

For Mills, Alice encapsulated the image of the 'wily mulatto,' a black female who, during slavery, was believed to use her sexuality to seduce the white master in order to access white privilege. The anxiety that was produced by this tropic figure remained within the white American imagining into the twentieth century, embodied within the 'mixed-raced' individual who attempted to interlope into whiteness by passing or who appropriated whiteness through miscegenous reproduction. This fictionalized construct of the 'wily mulatto' built upon the depiction of black women as hypersexual, salacious, and lascivious, adding the traits of cunning and a desire for the *possession* of whiteness.[13] As Wacks (2000, 168) comments, "The wily mulatto was reputed to try to use her sexual hold on white men as leverage to advance the black race as a whole by vying for the inheritance of white male power." Mills fostered the notion that Alice had such intentions, implying that her race predisposed her to sexual manipulation against which Leonard was a hopeless victim.

Mills outlined various "stages" of Alice's "fastening upon" Leonard (*CR*, 1100), suggesting that Alice had premeditated and executed a conscious campaign in order to secure her union with the Rhinelander name. Not only did she seek to be Leonard's mistress, she orchestrated to consolidate her affair through matrimony. Writing for *The Crisis* in 1926, W. E. B. DuBois noted, "if Rhinelander had used this girl as concubine or prostitute, white America would have raised no word of protest . . . It is when he legally and decently marries the girl that all Hell breaks loose and literally tears the pair apart" (quoted in Lewis and Ardizzone 2001, 228). White male desire for a black woman was one matter. During slavery, sexual relations between a white master and a black female slave ensured that the relation of power would be maintained after the sexual act: the white master remained dominant (Wacks 2000, 169). However, according to Mills, the relationship between Alice and Leonard inverted this dynamic. He argued that Alice did not simply seduce Leonard but "got that boy . . . so that he was an utter slave in her hands (*CR*, 1099–1100), and furthermore, "by her ministrations [Leonard] had been reduced to the utter depths of degradation" (*CR*, 1349). By repeatedly referring to Leonard as Alice's slave in both "body and soul" (*CR*, 1101), and depicting him as completely at her mercy, Mills constructed an image of white masculinity as divested of its racial *and* gendered power and prestige at the hands of a black female. Leonard had lost his capacity for exercising self-will, for the agency that he was perceived to possess as both a male and a white subject was subsumed to the will of this wanton jezebel. Utilizing the rhetoric of slavery only functioned to compound the imagery of power inversion, a representation that challenged the foundations upon which the American racial economy is predicated. This threat was mitigated and finally domesticated through the disrobing of Alice, which recreated the performative rituals of the auction block and, thereby, reestablished 'acceptable' schematizations of racial power. Despite this reassertion of white racial dominance, Leonard's slippage from white masculine ideals, in Mills's formulation, was entirely premised on Alice's racialized, gendered predisposition for manipulation. Therefore, the miscegenous threat in which Leonard became complicit was due fundamentally to this 'Delilah' who "had him so . . . that he did not know black from white"—that is, so that "he did not know or have control of himself" (*CR*, 1350).

The primary manner through which Mills sought to establish Alice Rhinelander's 'hold' on Leonard and her 'fraudulent' deception was through the offering into evidence and the reading of her letters to Leonard (eighty-six in total). While represented by Davis, Alice at no time spoke; she had no voice within the trial. She was silenced, so that her letters, her presence in body, and Leonard's, Mills's, Davis's, and the other witnesses' depictions of her were the only capacity through which her identity was enunciated.[14] The letters, Mills implied, spoke for themselves by showing Alice's character, her intentions, and her deviancy. Above all, these letters supposedly demonstrated that Alice had a "diabolical plan which she prosecuted month after month" (*CR*, 1298). With the offering of each letter by the defense, Davis objected, arguing that these were "unnecessarily spreading filth" (*CR*, 197) and were not relevant to the issues in the case. At each junction, the Court overruled Davis's objection and entered the letters into evidence. Davis warned Mills that if he insisted on exposing the personal details of Alice's correspondence, which could result in compromising and denigrating her name, he would be compelled to respond in kind.

True to his threat, on the cross-examination of Leonard, Davis introduced, and subsequently the Court entered into evidence, two of Leonard's letters to Alice that exposed Leonard's defiance of dominant sexual ideologies. These two short letters, written three years prior to the trial, function as the primary evidence of Leonard Rhinelander's aberrant white subjectivity and his failure to achieve the requisite status of 'manliness.' The reading of these letters disclosed four behavioral transgressions that violated the maxims of both the white racial and heteronormative economy. The contents were deemed to be so salacious that the presiding judge, Justice Morschauser, ordered all women and children from the courtroom.

These two letters affirmed Leonard's earlier testimony that the couple had indulged in premarital intercourse. The social decrees of early twentieth-century sensibilities in the United States levied strenuous disapproval against such behavior. Not only was it deemed inappropriate conduct, it destabilized the imperative upon which the heteronormative economy is premised. Reproductive sexuality within marriage ensured legitimate procreativity that, in turn, protected patrimony. It was seen to be the female imperative to protect her status within heteronormativity by ensuring that any potential offspring be born within the contract of marriage; restraint by both parties was solicited. Societal dictates required what Foucault (1998, 37) has referred to as "a sexuality that is economically useful and politically conservative," and continued to promulgate Victorian notions of 'good' and 'bad' behavior and subsequently 'good' and 'bad' men and women (Lewis and Ardizzone 2001, 148).[15] These constructions of a disciplined sexuality compelled men to control their sexual selves "if women submerged theirs" (Lewis and Ardizzone 2001, 148). Davis argued that the exposure of Alice's promiscuity besmirched her character, but he firmly attributed the blame to Leonard. At an earlier point in the trial, Davis demanded of Leonard: "[w]hat is the worse deception, to lead a girl to believe you want to marry her and take that which is most precious to a woman, or for her to say that she is white and not colored?" (*New York Times*, 18 November 1925, 4).[16] Davis insisted that Alice's actions were contingent on her belief of Leonard's intentions of matrimony. By arguing that Leonard had manipulated Alice into a sexual liaison, Davis offered further corroboration of Leonard's inability to respect and carry out the actions required of a 'gentleman' and as indicative of his moral downfall.

In the first of the letters read before the Court (*CR*, Defendant's Exhibit S), Leonard alluded to behavior seen as one of the most self-abasing practices in nineteenth and early twentieth-century medico-sexual discourse. Leonard wrote that after penning a letter to Alice, he "undressed and scrambled into bed, but not to go to sleep" (*CR*, 1073); rather, Leonard took Alice's letter to bed with him. The letter proceeds as follows:

> Oh! blessed sweet-heart of mine . . . my heart seemed as though it would
> bust with joy, and when you mentioned the time we were in bed at the
> "Marie Antoinette," *something* that belonged to me acted the way it usual
> [sic] did when-ever I am with you, darling, and *it* just longed for the touch
> of your passionate little fingers, which have so often made me so very, very
> happy. You know, don't you, old scout, what that "*something*" is and how it
> acted when you began being naughty!! Oh! sweetheart, many, many nights
> when I lay in bed and think about my darling girl *it* acts the very same way,
> and longs for your warm body to crawl upon me . . . God! Alice can you
> imagine me reading your tempting notes in bed last night; and the way that
> "*something*" which belongs to me acted!!

In his cross-examination, Davis elicited from Leonard that it was not his intention to tempt Alice with this letter. Rather, it was "a letter full of smut [written] to satisfy [his] own passion" (*CR*, 682).

The anti-masturbatory strictures of the eighteenth and nineteenth centuries remained firm within early twentieth-century heteronormative discourse.[17] Stokes (2001, 214) comments that phobia against masturbation reached a pinnacle in the mid-nineteenth century with the issuance of numerous pamphlets and guidebooks that warned against the 'evils' of the 'self-abusive' practice. A U.S. cleric wrote in 1887 that masturbation "debilitates the physical constitution by a wasting of the vital power, it impairs the mental faculties, it corrupts moral nature, it sears and petrifies the conscience" (Spence, quoted in Stokes 2001, 115). At issue were notions of sexual integrity and sexual degeneracy, as masturbation was seen to exist outside or, more strenuously, in opposition to the procreative heterosexual economy. Marriage was to be the arena in which pleasure was to be satiated.

Leonard maintained that he was reduced to this practice of satisfying his own passion in order to remain 'true' to Alice (*CR*, 681). Davis, however, used the admission to reinforce his depiction of Leonard as a deficient example of manhood. In *Studies in the Psychology of Sex* (1920), Havelock Ellis outlined the numerous supposed byproducts of masturbation[18] and, as Stokes (2001, 115) notes, the symptoms cataloged "were often conflated under the more general diagnosis of 'degeneration,' which could signify physical, mental, and moral deterioration." Earlier, George Beard (1884) had argued that these "unnatural emissions" would lead to a "loss of manhood."[19] Freud (1894) had also been concerned with the negative effects attributed to masturbatory practices, suggesting that they disposed the individual to various neurotic disorders. Considering Mills's depiction of Leonard as mentally (and hence, to some degree physically) infirm, and Davis's exposure of Leonard's moral weakness, these views on masturbation are particularly poignant. For Davis, Leonard's behavior simply compounded his general moral degeneracy. More broadly conceptualized, however, Leonard's actions can be seen to have wider and more dangerous implications. Inextricable from blood, white semen is the carrier of white civilization. Semen, in white racial ideology, is itself the irreducible 'essence' of whiteness; it is liquid corporeal power—the vehicle of blood—or, as the nineteenth-century physician Homer Bostwick (1848, 81) described it, "the very cream and essence of blood." So, in addition to the threat of the miscegenous union with 'black blood,' Leonard Rhinelander demonstrated an intolerable disregard for the sanctity of whiteness. Not only did he threaten to enervate whiteness through his choice of marriage (illustrating his refusal to abide the injunction-bound procreative mandate), but also through his waste of the 'life-blood' of whiteness;

the behavior was beyond the parameters of necessary procreative practices and further imperiled his ability to lay claim to the subject status of normative white masculinity.

Later in the same letter Leonard wrote:

> Do you remember when we were in bed together and how I used to ask you, dear, for you to do it because I couldn't manage *it* myself? You were always able to make both of us happy . . . I just loved for you to crawl upon me and do it all yourself, because you never failed and you knew how. (*CR*, 1074)

In addition to this excerpt suggesting that Leonard allowed, or even preferred Alice to possess sexual control, the letter intimates that Leonard was afflicted with impotency. Liberal humanist ideology demands male control and female submission, configuring masculinity as active and femininity as passive. Furthermore, within this logic normative white masculinity is marked by the requisite traits of power, authority, virility, and sexual prowess. The masculine ideal also exists as various forms of control, including the demand that men exercise power over their own bodies. The suggestion, then, that Leonard could not "manage *it*" (*CR*, 1074) independently, conjures the image of a tragically wounded masculinity and is indicative of a masculine crisis. Leonard was compelled to relinquish the mantle of control to Alice, further implicating him in the realm of unhealthy or diseased masculinity.

Leonard represented, then, two simultaneous threats to white heteronormativity. First, in his choice of a sexual union (within the context of marriage) with a woman discursively defined as 'black,' Leonard threatened to 'pollute' his white legacy. This threat of interracial procreativity signaled his abrogation from upholding the sanctity of whiteness. Second, and removed from his relationship with Alice, the suggestion of his impotent state signaled a more generalized sexual non-procreativity. Within an economy that is marked by a reproductive imperative, *not* responding to this demand indicates a performative failure. These two points of white masculine slippage exist in tandem, imperiling both the present and future of white masculinity and, hence, 'whiteness' itself.

The second letter that Davis had entered into evidence outlined a behavioral transgression that proved to be unqualified evidence of Leonard Rhinelander's aberrant (and definitively degenerate) white masculine subjectivity (*CR*, Defendant's Exhibit N-1). The *New York Daily News* (quoted in Lewis and Ardizzone 2001, 143) described the letter as "a narration of abnormal practices in the love tryst" between Alice and Leonard. It was upon these 'practices' that Davis's attention was focused.

Leonard's letter to Alice highlighted that the couple had performed oral sex and recalled in detail the manner through which Leonard had brought Alice pleasure. Davis's interrogation of Leonard regarding this behavior centered on the contention that the practice was 'unnatural.' The questioning proceeded as follows:

Q: Do you remember telling this jury that your conduct with
this girl was natural?
A: Yes.
Q: Without mentioning it except as it is mentioned in the letter,
you knew that that was not a natural thing?
A: I did not; no.
Q: You had no suspicion inside of you that to put your head
between her legs was an unnatural thing?
A: No. (*CR*, 688)

Seemingly disturbed that Leonard did not find his actions abhorrent, Davis pursued the point:

Q: You were bringing some kind of sexual delight to this girl
without the use of your own natural organs?
A: Yes.
Q: Using your tongue?
A: Yes.
Q: You hadn't the slightest suspicion . . . that that was an unnatural thing?
A: I did not; no. (*CR* 688–698)

As the supposed bearer of civilization, white masculinity is grounded in the notions of restraint and control, and is primarily opposed to 'savagery.' For the racialized discourse that positions white masculinity as civilized and superior is dependant on the fictionalized construction of 'primitive' masculine 'others,' the quintessential 'other' being the black male. It is upon the visible presence of male 'others'—through the dissemination and consumption of narratives such as black male hypersexuality—that the possibility of 'dangerous'/ 'other' masculinities is contingent. The maintenance of the status of normative white masculinity is, as a consequence, perpetuated through the refusal of behavior that could be seen to compromise this status. As Robinson (2000, 163) states, "Manly self-control for white men . . . is predicated on the ability to control the expression of other, more dangerous masculinities." The act that Leonard Rhinelander outlined was behavior that existed beyond the parameters of early twentieth-century ideas of normative white masculine sexual expression. Oral sex was firmly located within the realm of abnormality; it existed outside of the reproductive imperative and could not be seen as the act of a white man. Indeed, the acts described were viewed as not only unnatural, but criminal. Oral sex was included in the New York Penal Code of 1925, which provided a maximum twenty-year sentence for acts of sodomy: these acts were defined as being those of "a person who carnally knows in any manner any animal or bird; or carnally knows any male or female person by the annus [sic] or by or with the mouth; or voluntarily submits to such knowledge."[20]

Admitting this practice, thereby, signaled a form of sexual depravity, and Davis's implicit designation of the "unnatural" act as an expression of Leonard's "animal desire" (CR, 683) suggested a primitive sexual appetite, an appetite that resided within the dangerous masculine 'other.'[21] Leonard can be seen, therefore, to have again derogated the performative compulsion of white masculine subjectivity, indeed, to have compromised the ideal to such a degree that his *racial* identity could be questioned. For not only could "succumbing to [such acts of] sexual passion . . . sap a man's force, rendering him weak and degenerate" (Bederman 1995, 48), it could also suggest a 'descent into blackness.' Williamson notes that at the turn of the century, particularly in the Southern states, the 'Negro' became an idea. Blackness became a matter of morality and a white individual could be said to display 'Negro-like' behavior. More specifically, "[v]ery often the immorality of [this] 'white nigger' included a suggestion of sexual transgression" (Williamson 1995, 107). The rise of scientific racism and eugenicist ideologies proposed that 'essential' racial identity was expressed in behavioral practices. Blackness was associated with more than traits such as hypersexuality, lasciviousness, and promiscuity: it was also seen as incomplete humanity and, according to Lynne Segal, represented "the colour of the 'dirty' secrets of sex" (1990, 176). It is black masculinity that has been discursively constructed as bestial and as synonymous with unrestrained submission to sexual desire. To 'act like a man,' on the other hand, was not to disavow desire. Rather, the sign of 'true masculinity'—discursively configured as 'white masculinity'—was the possession of a powerful sexual drive met only with an equally powerful capacity for self-restraint.[22] To indulge in the 'darker-side' of sexual desire, articulated in *Rhinelander* as the aberrant practice of oral sex, was to abandon or lose oneself to corporeal desire. In his closing statement, Mills, too, clearly made the connection between this practice and race. Stating that "that was not a white man's act. That was an act of the black and tan" (CR, 1349), Mills concurred with Davis's interpretation and configured the young Rhinelander as *discursively black* (albeit, Mills attributed Leonard's slippage—into blackness—to Alice, by representing her as contagion). During the course of the trial, then, both accounts operated in order to have Leonard undergo a process of becoming discursively colored. Yet as we have seen, Leonard's subjectivity is not only discursively resignified in terms of blackness, but also in terms of femininity; Leonard is systematically positioned as a weakened male hysteric,[23] that is, as 'woman,' at the same moment in which he is racially reconfigured due to his nonobservance of white sexual norms. White masculinity was only able to retain the apparent guise of sexual supremacy over 'virile black masculinity' through the notion that white men governed their bodies by way of sexual discipline or the disciplining of desire. In acting outside of the confines of controlled or restrained normative white masculinity, the oppositional logic of liberal humanism firmly entrenched Leonard within the realm of the 'other.'

The defiance of dominant sexual ideologies through the acts outlined in Leonard Rhinelander's letters—premarital sex, masturbation, impotence, and oral sex—exposed him as having further failed to enunciate the performative pass into white male belonging. As belonging is contingent on the recitation of appropriate 'acts,' Leonard's defilement of white masculine 'norms' jeopardized his subject status as a white male. The plaintiff's letters, thus, consolidated not only his fall from sexual grace, but also his fall from racial and gendered grace.

THE BODY AS SUBJECT TO/OF LAW

Rhinelander highlights that racial and gendered subjectivity, as produced and embodied through the act of social classification, is an axiom violently enunciated within law. For it is the articulation of law—here through the rhetoric of Mills and Davis, and expressed through the instructions of Justice Morschauser to the jury, and ultimately by the jury's finding itself—that functions to survey, assess, and finally, secure regulatory gender and racial performatives. *Rhinelander* also shows that the legal trial cannot be perceived as a self-contained sanctum or text. Rather, it acts as a locus of cultural reproduction wherein discursive meaning is at once interpellated and reinscribed. Legal trials act as a particular form of narrative that connects the governing principles of law to general culture and vice versa. These two arenas condition one another; legal injunctions refashion and reenforce the discursive laws of signification and the performative decrees in and through which social subjects are constituted. Likewise, performative compulsions and existing signifiers of social law form and simultaneously find expression within the legal arena.

The trial can be viewed as Leonard Rhinelander's attempt to "seek the protection of the law against [Alice's] social and legal claims growing out of the relationship" (*New York Amsterdam News,* 9 December 1925, Editorial and Feature page).[24] It can be perceived as his desperate endeavor to secure legal and social verification of *Alice's* disciplinary infraction, to confirm her intrusion into an identity category that she had no claim to under law. In seeking legal reprimand of Alice's deception and a reassertion of her blackness, Leonard, it would seem, was trying to rearticulate his own identity as distinct from the 'truth' of hers—a truth that could only be relationally enforced.

Yet Davis exposed that Leonard knew what he was doing, was aware of Alice's race, and that he socialized with both her family and their black friends. Leonard, thereby, was aware of his transgression but he formulated an aberrant identity regardless. He was careful to keep his union with Alice hidden, imploring her to "remember to keep . . . [their] *secret* locked safely in . . . [her] heart" (*CR*, 1074). Not only their engagement, but also their marriage needed, at Leonard's insistence, to be shielded from public knowledge and from Philip Rhinelander's knowledge in particular.[25]

He was prepared to entertain the risk of censure only as long as the infraction remained undetected and invisible. Once his defiance of the prohibition against miscegenation was exposed, however, Leonard turned to the law in the hope of averting the gaze that carries censure with it and resecuring his imperiled identity. This attempt was executed through turning the surveillance and corrective discipline of law onto Alice. But the eye of the law could not be predicted or controlled. The legal gaze, in interrogating Alice, encapsulated Leonard in its purview. Once placed within the vision of the legal surveying eye, Leonard could not escape, and an initial performative slippage heralded the further exposure of his failure to occupy the hegemonic name he had been assigned.

The rigor that marked the scrutiny to which Leonard Rhinelander was subjected refutes the idea that whiteness enjoys a privileged position of invisibility. Placed before social and legal law in this instance, whiteness *becomes* visible and begins to take shape through the articulations of what it *does not* purport to be, through the designation of 'acts' or 'behaviors' that reside beyond its sanctioned boundaries. Hence, the discursively decreed white subject is divested of the supposed privilege of invisibility based on normativity and, through their performative failure, experiences 'being seen.'

While under law Leonard's white corporeality was validated against the black body of Alice, he was shown to have failed to heed the attendant corporeal commitment; a legally defined *white body* must *perform whiteness* in order to survive. The body must perform the law, must demonstrate that the sanctity of whiteness has been upheld. It is law that functions as a primary assessor of the success of performative recitations through its mapping of the discursive possibilities of bodies and their attendant performances. Law, as conceptualized and articulated by the legal actors in this case, reads Leonard's performance of white masculinity and acts as arbiter and disciplinary enforcer. It is the all-white, all-male jury that stood before Leonard and made the judgment that Alice had not deceived him. The jury had been presented with instructions from Justice

Morschauser regarding the issues that were to govern their finding. There were seven instructions:

1. At the time of the marriage of the parties was the defendant colored and of colored blood?
2. Did the defendant before the marriage by silence conceal from the plaintiff the fact that she was of colored blood?
3. Did the defendant before the marriage represent to the plaintiff that she was not of colored blood?
4. Did the defendant practice said concealment or make said representation with the intent thereby to induce the plaintiff to marry her?
5. Was the plaintiff by said concealment or by said representation, or by both, induced to marry the defendant?
6. If the plaintiff had known that the defendant was of colored blood, would he have married her?
7. Did the plaintiff cohabit with the defendant after he had obtained full knowledge that the defendant was of colored blood? (*CR*, 18–19)

These seven issues explicated the judge's contention that race is unequivocal, and made explicit to the jury the necessity to clarify both Leonard's knowledge of and participation in the interlope. The jury returned, finding in favor of Alice on each count, thereby declaring that Leonard was aware of Alice's racial ancestry. In part, therefore, these findings supported the reading offered by Davis of Leonard as having perpetrated a conscious deception and conscious failure in rearticulating the ideals of white masculine subjectivity. In refusing to grant the annulment, the Court decreed that Leonard Rhinelander had entered into matrimony knowing that he was marrying a woman with 'black blood.' His failure to consecrate the requisite injunctions of whiteness, therefore, must have also been conscious: if he knew that Alice was black, then he must have been aware of his disciplinary infraction.

Law can thereby be perceived as implicitly mandating reflexivity in certain embodied practices of racial and gendered identity. For the jury's findings and the Court ruling establish Leonard as an active participant in the (inadequate) construction of his own white masculinity. Leonard's culpability in the refusal to abide by white maxims has a dual effect under law. Law finds no need to protect Leonard in his claim, due to his disregard for the performative compulsions of white masculinity. His slippage from consecrating the laws of racial and gendered signification facilitates the law's abrogation from any necessity to defend his interests. While it may vindicate his legal title as corporeally white, the attendant rights of the possession of this body do not, on this occasion, demand the protection of legal patronage. Indeed, in this case law expresses the anxieties surrounding the maintenance of boundaries around different selves, for Leonard's derogation from the regulatory decrees of normative white masculinity position him as posing a threat *from within* the very ranks of whiteness. In order to maintain its sanctity and cultural freight, hegemonic white masculinity must be reasserted and augmented through the exposure of infractions and the expropriation of the undesirable/failed subject. The detection of Leonard's refusal to performatively ratify whiteness in accordance with his white corporeality identifies him as the 'internal other' that must be censured.[26] In order to perpetuate the parameters of identity, rather than protect Leonard (due to his body), law must punish him as a transgressive white subject. As Hacker (1992, 217) notes, "the artifact of 'whiteness' . . . sets a floor on how far [whites] can fall." Leonard Rhinelander must then exist as an example of the disciplinary incursions that are resolutely inflicted on the subject who 'falls too far' in defying legal and social performative injunctions.

Leonard's conscious abdication from discursive normativity resulted in a literal and symbolic social death. He was disinherited by his father, excluded from the prestigious New York Social Register (in which he had been on the list of dilatory domiciles), effectively barred from his previous social circle, and exiled to Nevada. It is unclear as to whether this exile was self-imposed or not but, either way, Leonard Rhinelander ended his days divested of his previously privileged identity and class security.[27]

Through interrogating the politics of 'passing through performance,' *Rhinelander* calls into question the stability of 'race' *per se* as an efficacious enunciation of 'internality' and the reproduction of white racial identities in particular. But Alice's and Leonard's passing cannot be viewed in the same light. Nor it is possible to claim that both subjects challenge the hegemony of whiteness—that always appears as 'natural'—in the same capacity. Each of these subjects executes a performative passing (through whiteness) that is generated from different motivations and, as such, each pass presents specific ways to think through the compulsory recitation of race.

In chapter 4, I argued that Alice's passing-for-white challenged the fixity of a white racial identity. Her actions, her intrusion into the realm of whiteness and (possibly) into a white identity, demonstrated that supposed corporeal 'truth' can be reenacted 'differently' and, through this very manipulation, 'truth' is disavowed. Likewise, Leonard also acts against discursive 'truth' that proclaims his 'inherent' whiteness. What we see through the interrogation of Leonard's subjectivity is that a validation of the body is never enough. Rather, diligent labor is involved in the reproductive maintenance of any given sociality—a sociality that is conferred on the subject based on repeated and rearticulated corporeal designation, which contributes, in turn, to forming the subject *as a* subject. For although the whiteness of Leonard's body may not have been called into question and although, inevitably, he could not 'lose,' as it were, the epidermal 'sign' of his whiteness, he is seen to be unable to sustain an 'ideal' status as a white masculine subject. The *Rhinelander* trial rhetoric demonstrates the circumscribed spectrum of possible/passable modes or 'actions' that are sanctioned within the regulatory mechanisms of white masculinity. And the proceedings of the trial establish that even though Leonard Rhinelander had been granted prior validation of a white identity, this was not sufficient. In order to maintain his privileged connection to whiteness it was imperative for him to endlessly continue to perform in accordance to its disciplinary demands.

Two points arise from this analysis. First, the interrogation that Leonard is subjected to by both counsels, by the media, and by various witnesses, exposes the disciplinary mandates or performative injunctions that govern the normalized—and seemingly unmarked—'nature' of white masculinity. In doing so, what become visible are the various techniques of power (specifically, in this case, those exercised through legal and medical discourse) and regulatory efforts that operate to sustain the subjectivating norms of hegemonic conceptualizations of white masculinity. Second, in rendering these mechanisms visible—or marking the strictures and disciplinary control that governs the formation and maintenance of identity—it becomes clear that the subject never safely reaches a point where subject status is absolutely guaranteed. There is no instant that can be identified as marking one's *arrival* into an image, as one can never be said to fully occupy the image of identity. The subject, consequently, can never be validated as having *passed,* as the reproduction of the phantasm of identity is always only ever a *passing:* it is a *becoming,* devoid of the ontological security of *being.* The embodied practice of identity, accordingly, cannot be fixed or resolved; rather, it involves rigorous labor that demands a self-reflexive discipline. For ultimately, the semblance of coherence reflected is simply an illusion, a performative compulsion, passing as 'truth.'

6

Imagining Racial Agency

Rhinelander seems to refuse the possibility that either Leonard or Alice might reimagine themselves, let alone the schematizations of race in early twentieth-century America. Both are ostensibly recuperated in line with normalizing demands of race and the accompanying dictates of racial discipline. Both are discursively identified as having failed in the articulation of their respective racial 'truths.' Leonard failed to reproduce white norms, and Alice failed to adequately self-discipline—to clearly and unambiguously act in accordance with what the law deemed to be her racial designation. The consequence, as it plays out in the course of the trial, is that each of these subjects is instructed as to their failure: the juridical reprimand for Leonard is that he is found to be personally responsible for his failure to performatively enact the imperatives of whiteness; for Alice, the finding is a juridical reprimand stating that she cannot exist as a liminal subject or a white subject but, instead, can only and must be black. Both are cast as aberrant and replaced within the normative injunctions that constitute the respective racial sites of 'whiteness' and 'blackness.'

Alice and Leonard had each attempted a racial rearticulation, it would appear. Alice can be read as endeavoring either to enunciate a white identity or to formulate an identity that is unencumbered by rigid demarcation into the oppositional realms of blackness and whiteness. Leonard, while not forsaking a white racial identity, defies the normative demands of white masculinity in his embodiment of that subjectivity. The identification of these acts, most specifically within the disciplinary realm of law, results in both subjects being reinserted within dominant conceptualizations and imperatives of race. Actions that seek to recite race in new directions appear to be ultimately thwarted.

Racial agency seems foreclosed and normalization incontestable with the apparent inevitability of detection, reprimand, and discipline at work in *Rhinelander*. This chapter explores these limitations. I begin with considering various ways that agency has been understood, specifically focusing on how it has been formulated by Foucault and Butler. I ask: what understanding or form of racial agency is enabled within the theory of performativity? If subjectivity is constrained and discursively constituted, is there any possibility to alter or resignify the compelled recitation of (racial) identity? How can Alice be thought of as a subject who exercises racial agency? Indeed, can she be interpreted in this light at all? And if so, is there resistant potential in her actions? Is this resistance subversive, or is subversion not necessary in order for acts to be resistant?

THE CAPACITY TO ACT

Understood as 'the capacity to act,' agency has commonly been thought about in two incommensurable ways, stemming from two radically different views of 'the subject.' On the one hand, agency has been imagined as something possessed and wielded by the knowing, autonomous subject of liberal humanism.[1] As Susan Hekman notes:

> It has become a commonplace of contemporary philosophy that the epistemology of modernity is rooted in the epistemology of the knowing subject. Modernity's search for absolute, indubitable knowledge has been defined, at least since Descartes, in terms of the knowing, constituting subject.
> (1995, 194)

The constituting subject is seen to be the masterful owner of property *in his own person.* Consequently, this individual (inevitably cast as 'man') has been thought of as self-determining and capable of exercising agency through the rational operation of free will.

On the other hand, however, a radical revision of the essentializing claims of liberal humanism has generated an attack on the subject as origin of meaning, knowledge, action, and free thought. This approach has instead argued that the subject is 'constructed' by discursive power, and insisted that rather than the individual wielding the power to constitute the self, the self is *resolutely constituted,* that is, determined by discourse. In this understanding agency is disavowed. Here the operations of discourse function in terms of sovereign or juridical power, rendering the subject a mere object.

Butler rejects both of these understandings of the subject and their accompanying configurations of agency (or lack thereof) in her account of performativity. However, both she and Foucault, to whom her conceptualization of the subject is at least partially indebted, have often been associated with the latter interpretation of agency. In these readings of Butler and Foucault, the general criticism runs something like this: if discursive power constructs the subject and *all* its relations, then it is impossible to conceive of a subject who would be capable of action that is not determined through and by power. The 'human' as 'agent' is, thus, evacuated. This, however, is a problematic interpretation of discursive power, as it simply reverses the relation between the subject and power. A liberal humanist account establishes that the subject governs discourse while the revision of this notion maintains these two terms but exchanges the order. Critiquing the relationship between subject and discourse through this reversal works to simply shift the metaphysical site that had been occupied by the subject of modernity to Power, Culture, Discourse. These forces are perceived now as monolithic and absolute. They are made to occupy the subject position, and come to substitute for the subject. The troubling result, as Butler points out, is that

> construction is still understood as a unilateral process initiated by a prior subject, fortifying the presumption of the metaphysics of the subject that where there is activity, there lurks behind it an initiating and willful subject. On such a view, discourse or language or the social becomes personified, and in the personification the metaphysics of the subject is reconsolidated. (1993, 9)

To read either Foucault or Butler as proposing agency in these terms is to elide the complex theorizations of power/discourse that they provide. A poststructuralist interrogation of the subject does not pursue a nihilistic rereading of subject formation. Following on from Foucault, Butler poses a question that is premised on ambivalence. She asks: "How can it be that the subject, taken to be the condition for and instrument of agency, is at the same time the effect of subordination, understood as the deprivation of agency?" (1997b, 10). What Butler proposes in answering this query is an account of the subject as neither constituting nor constituted. She insists that the subject is constructed—this is a discursive subject—but this does not mean that agency is impossible. What Butler foregrounds is a rejection of the idea of identity as something that is *imposed* or as something that is absolutely *determined*. But her account of agency does not require, indeed it refuses a return to an autonomous or voluntarist model of the subject. Before exploring the specifics of Butler's formulation of agency within the theory of performativity, I want to retrace Foucault's account of power, as it is often on the basis of these ideas—and Butler's deployment of them—that the possibility for agency and resistance seem foreclosed.

In *Discipline and Punish* and related texts, Foucault was essentially concerned with the fields of *power relations* in which subjects emerge. The subject, for Foucault, is formed *in* power and *power produces subjectivities.* Thus: "One has to dispense with the constituent subject, to rid the subject of itself, that's to say, to arrive at an analysis which can account for the constitution of the subject within a historical framework" (1980d, 117). Adamant that subjectivities do not preexist the networks of power in which they are formed, Foucault insists that subjects cannot be said to control these networks. Power is not owned, is not a property; rather, it is exercised. Power is not an 'entity' and there is no central point to this power. Instead, power is "the moving substrate of force relations which, by virtue of their inequality, constantly engender states of power, but the latter are always local and unstable" (Foucault 1998, 93). Power, then, is produced in every exchange or relation: "Power is everywhere; not because it embraces everything, but because it comes from everywhere . . . [it is] the name that one attributes to a complex strategical situation in a particular society" (Foucault 1998, 93).[2] And it is through relations of power that subjects come to be and operate in the social realm. Because of its diffuse operation, the disciplinary power that Foucault describes in *Discipline and Punish* has, as noted above, often been received as one that totalizes power (subjects can't escape) and as one wherein power is *simply* domination.[3] Moreover, it has been interpreted as an account of power that is based on a notion of violence, punishment, and perpetual threat that produces power as a monolithic force over an army of docile and inert bodies.

Yet Foucault explicitly argues that power is not absolute and that resistance is immanent in each relation of power. For instance, in *Discipline and Punish*, he states:

> power is not exercised simply as an obligation or prohibition on those who "do not have it" . . . it exerts pressure on them *just as they themselves, in their struggle against it, resist the grip it has on them.* [These relations] are not univocal; they define innumerable points of confrontation, focuses of instability, each of which has its own risks of conflict, of struggles, and of an at least temporary inversion of the power relations. (1991, 27; my emphasis)

Foucault stresses the *active role* that the subject plays in the process of their own formation. When considering *technologies of power,* however, he shifts analytic registers. Now, as McWhorter explains, "we are focusing our attention on the relations of power that exist between subjects who have already been constituted historically" (1999, 212). Technologies of power operate through what Foucault terms *governmentality*. These are the practices, techniques, and devices by and through which control is exercised over people. But these exercises of control—or government—are, as Han (2002, 193) states, understood by Foucault "polemically—in the etymological sense of *polemos* (combat)." They are constantly in tension and thus marked by a state of *agonism*. For they can only be exercised *as an action* (*exist* in *action*) over subjects who are 'free'—free in the sense that these subjects are faced with a field of possibilities in the way that they respond to the coercive attempts to control their conduct.[4] Technologies of power (that is, any form of technique that attempts to determine the conduct of others) are always practiced in tandem with technologies of the self (how the subject relates to themselves). In relations of power, agonistic exchange exists *between* individuals who can exercise power: historically constituted, subjectified agents themselves *develop* and *deploy* power. Subjects/agents comprise the system of governmentality, and it is within these relations that they can utilize their freedom.[5] This operation is perhaps most succinctly outlined by Foucault in his essay, "The Ethics of Concern for the Self as a Practice of Freedom," where he states:

> I intend this concept of "governmentality" to cover the whole range of practices that constitute, define, organize, and instrumentalize the strategies that individuals in their freedom can use in dealing with each other . . . [Thus] governmentality makes it possible to bring out the freedom of the subject and its relationship to others. (2000a, 300)

Precisely because power is not owned but exercised or deployed from multiple and contesting sites, and because of its contingency (it is reliant on bodies, locations, specific institutions, discursive avenues), *the very exercise of power* always (and necessarily) *produces unintended effects*. That subjects are immanent *within* power networks, and transmit power, means that they can and do effect *resistances* that work to reverse, displace, contest, and revise the objectives of power. Thus again we see the productivity of the Foucauldian notion of power. In this formulation, power is neither absolute nor unidirectional and, while subjects might be formed in power, they are never *reduced to power*. Instead, power is that which can be exercised by subjects in their relations with others and their relations with self, in ways that potentially create spaces that allow for practices of freedom.

Butler's account of agency relies on Foucault's claim that being an agent is a product of being subject to power. Taking this idea and thus reframing the dualist debate that sees the subject as the condition of or impasse to agency, Butler argues that the subject is a site of *ambivalence*. In *The Psychic Life of Power* she states: "the subject emerges as the *effect* of a prior power and as the *condition of possibility* for a radically conditioned form of agency" (1997b, 14–15). Thus, Butler rejects the idea that the subject can somehow wield power voluntarily and determine the conditions of their existence. Power, instead, at once 'acts on' the subject and is 'acted by' the subject.[6] Formed in power, the subject enacts the 'requirements' of power.[7] It is these requirements that constitute the subject, but the reenactments of this power operate in such a way as to conceal the prior working(s) of power. The subject appears, then, as if they were the origin of power, for these acts are seen as the subject's 'own' power.

To be formed in and subject to the prior workings of power is not, however, to be reducible to this power: agency, that which is 'acted by' the subject, "exceeds the power by which it is enabled" (Butler 1997b, 15). Again calling forth her indebtedness to Foucault, Butler insists that the way power is reiterated may go beyond, or be done in ways that are *unintended* by power. It is in the recitation of performative imperatives that Butler locates the possibilities for this 'radically conditioned form of agency' referred to above. For while the subject is compelled to repeat the constraining norms through which their subjectivity is formed, "[a]gency is to be found," Butler states, "in the possibilities opened up in and by the constrained appropriation of the regulatory law, by the materialization of that law, the compulsory appropriation and identification with those normative demands" (1993, 15).

This necessity to endlessly repeat actions that are enabled *by* the law does not mean, then, that these actions are limited *to* the law. Norms, as I have argued, are uninhabitable and because of this the subject's resignifications of these same norms generate agential possibilities. This agency is not exercised by a 'choosing' subject (a formulation that would simply echo the liberal humanist account of agency). But this is not to say that 'choice,' in a revised sense, does not exist. A *form* of will is exercised in the 'act' of recitation. This is, however, always necessarily a recitation of an existing convention and, as such, that which is enacted or exercised *cannot be said to originate with the subject.*[8] The option, according to Butler, is then not "whether to repeat, but how to repeat or, indeed, to repeat and, through a radical proliferation of gender [or ways of 'doing' race], to displace the very norms that enable the repetition itself." In enacting norms, social, discursive, and symbolic structures are reproduced. But because these norms are enacted by agents, they are always altered (and potentially, partially transcended) in the very practice of reiteration.[9] Agency resides, then, in the necessary slippage between the discursive command and the reiteration— the *enacted effect* of that command (Butler 1993, 122).[10] So, between maxim (the performative decree) and the inevitable difference produced in the interpretation (the performance) lies critical possibility. And importantly, as Elin Diamond notes, "As soon as performativity comes to rest on a performance, questions of embodiment, of social relations, of ideological interpellations, of emotional and political effects, all become discussible" (1996, 5). It is the manner in which performance relates to performativity that must be interrogated, and the question that must be asked is this: can performance make a difference?

Lois McNay has argued that, because the formation of subjectivities within performative theory "appears to be primarily a capacity of structures rather than of individuals, Butler's idea of agency lacks social and historical specificity" (1999, 178). Context inevitably determines the capacity for agency, and the structures within which an agent comes into being and operates will all influence the kinds of agency that become available. In order to provide social and historical specificity to the question of how racial agency might work it is essential that racial performativity be mapped in terms of lived and embodied experience—in terms of these *performances of identity.* Only then is it possible to consider the potentials for agency that arise or are seized and the agential practices that are enacted.

Butler, as we know, is concerned with the heteronormative reproduction of gendered identities that operate to retroactively construct sex as that which appears 'natural.' While this is Butler's primary focus, in *Bodies That Matter* she does set herself several questions pertaining to racial performativity that are particularly important for this analysis. She asks: "How is race lived in the modality of sexuality? How is gender lived in the modality of race? How do colonial and neo-colonial nation-states rehearse gender relations in the consolidation of power?" (1993, 117). While she recognizes that gender, sexuality, and race exist inseparably, then, "as part of a dynamic map of power" (Butler 1993, 117) in the formation of the subject, a theorization of racial performativity and, hence, the possibilities for racial agency are not fleshed out in Butler's analysis. If we accept that gendering is always already racialized, that the racing of a subject is always gendered, and that sexualities are raced,[11] how might race be brought to the foreground so as to map the possibilities for racial agency?

I begin to unpack this question by returning to *Rhinelander v. Rhinelander,* in order to consider how agency operates in terms of the two primary subjects within the case. *Rhinelander* proves to be productive for such an analysis because there are multiple points at which a discussion of agency can be entered; that is, there are different levels and different capacities through which agency can be discussed and in which both Alice and Leonard can be seen as agents. At this point, however, I want to explore the most apparent formulation of these two subjects as agents through a consideration of how they are constituted or positioned by disciplinary power as ever-constrained agents.

DOCILE RACIAL AGENTS?

The form of agency most evident in *Rhinelander* immediately begins to look nothing like agency at all, for it is a form of agency evacuated by what is traditionally meant by the term. This, in and of itself, is not a problem. What is a problem, however, is that the agency identified in this kind of a reading of the case discounts the potential for any form of productive or subversive agency.

Both Alice and Leonard are positioned by discursive forces as agents. They appear before the Court as subjects in their own right and are dealt with as such by the respective counsels, by the judge, the jury, and the media. Yet they are positioned and constituted as individual and accountable agents *in order to be maintained* in line with disciplinary power. As Foucault explains, "Discipline 'makes' individuals; it is the specific technique of a power that regards individuals as both objects and instruments of its exercise" (1991, 170). Subjects must be seen as 'individuals' and, hence, as culpable agents in order to be regulated. But, as individual 'cases' to be assessed, monitored, and judged, they are products of power/knowledge relations and objectified subjection. By this I refer to Foucault's insistence that disciplinary power is an "*epistemological power,* the power to extract from the individuals a knowledge [*savoir*] and to extract a knowledge from these individuals submitted to the gaze and already controlled by different powers" (quoted in Han 2002, 119). Subjection and objectification work within disciplinary power so that they are mutually conditioning. One becomes a subject through being objectified, such that objectification and subjection become the possibility for one another. Thus, they are circularly reinforced. This operation becomes particularly noticeable in what Foucault refers to as 'the examination.' As one of the key instruments of discipline, the examination visibilizes and objectifies the subject. The legal trial can clearly be seen as a series of examinations, and both Alice and Leonard are irrefutably *subject to* this ritual of power which functions in a double capacity. In *Rhinelander,* this examination can be seen in the first instance to discipline Alice and Leonard by normalizing their behaviors in accordance to their discursive positioning—both are *subjected* through this process. Additionally, the examination functions to extract a knowledge from the individual that enables this control to be augmented. Thus, Alice and Leonard are objectivized as *racialized* subjects. Through achieving these ends the legal examination in general, and *Rhinelander* in particular, can be seen as a primary mechanism that "maintains the disciplined individual in his subjection" (Foucault 1991, 187). As a consequence of individualizing practices of discipline, these subjects appear to be agents, but as 'malleable material,' they are docile.

To be maintained within disciplinary power, the subject who strays—who enacts performative anti-discipline if you will—must be assessed as an agent in order for a desirable form of docility to be reestablished. Leaving aside a consideration of Leonard's agency, I want to focus attention here on Alice's. Alice is undeniably judged as an agent who has failed in her capacity to enunciate the 'truth' of her racial ontology. Yet she is judged on 'law's' terms, not her own. She is interrogated within the rhetoric(s) of the trial based on the agency that law is seen to exercise in its reassertion of racial 'truth.' Without intending to personify law, we can see that the structural functionings of law in the trial only ordain to see Alice in accordance to the terms that are established through prior legislation and legal judgment pertaining to race.

Thus, the construction of Alice's agency can be seen as tactical and cynical. She can *have* agency—she has acted as an agent in a prohibited capacity—but she cannot *be* an agent. In a formal sense, then, agency is given or attributed to the subject in that the individual must appear as responsible. This becomes particularly pronounced when we consider that the primary issue under interrogation in the case was Alice's agency. What was being assessed was whether or not Alice had intentionally and willfully disregarded racial discipline by appropriating a white identity. And essential to this was the question of what Alice was thinking. But while this may have been the foundation of the case, Alice's agency was *not allowed to appear*—she was effectively silenced through not being brought to the stand to testify on her own behalf. She had strenuously denied fraud, and in answer to the amended complaint her lawyer had stipulated that "[s]he denies that she has any knowledge or information sufficient to form a belief as to any of the allegations contained in the paragraphs or subdivisions of said complaint" (*CR,* 11).[12] Not being permitted the power to speak, however, it is her half-naked body that is presumably seen to speak for her. She may have denied Leonard's charges—both in the trial documents and in the press—but in the Court of law she was denied a voice, denied the right of active *self-representation* and, consequently, Alice was reduced to the position of docile object.[13]

DEFYING DOCILITY THROUGH
PERFORMATIVE DISOBEDIENCE

While this may be one manner through which to interpret the agency in operation in *Rhinelander,* to do so would be to underestimate the potential ways of thinking about agency as offered by Foucault and Butler. It would be to delimit the subject and to render them simply inert targets of power—power that cannot be contested or refashioned. As we have seen, this is a view that both Foucault and Butler adamantly reject. Alice may have been constructed *within* the trial as a docile figure, but she can in no way be considered as a subject devoid of agential *potential* before, during, or after the court proceedings. As I argued earlier, the subject is constituted in and by relations of power, but they cannot be said to be formed in purely repressive or dominating terms. Rather, as we have seen, power is productive and always open to radical and innovative potentials. When *Rhinelander* is reconfigured in light of this argument the following questions arise: what possibilities for exercising individual power can be seized in the practice of race? How might we consider Alice's ability to evade the absolute domination of racializing power that decrees an unequivocal delineation between 'whiteness' and 'blackness' and demands that the individual be attached to one of these racial categories in accordance with discursive designation? What types of acts can be identified that signal Alice's ability to defy the workings of juridical racialization? And how might she be interpreted as reiterating race in ways that are unintended by power? Through investigating these questions I ultimately ask: what possibilities are opened up in a subject's refusal to assume their assigned racial status? I wonder: may resistant potential be identified in Alice's enactments of (racial) struggle? Moreover, this inevitably raises the question as to how it is possible to determine whether certain racial reenactments are resistant or if they merely consolidate racializing power. These are all pressing questions and I don't presume to be able to generalize the answers that might be identified. Yet in localizing or contextualizing the concept of racial performativity within *Rhinelander,* a concrete example is provided as to what Butler might mean when she argues that there may be ways in which "[t]he law might not only be refused, but might also be . . . forced into a rearticulation that calls into question the monotheistic force of its own unilateral operation" (1993, 122). In what follows, the labor involved in the formation of racial subjects is shown to be ever-tenuous, and ruptures and dissonances can be seen to generate the possibility for a defiance of the regulatory power of race.

Butler suggests that a form of agency is to be found in the *critical appropriation* of the normativizing demands of race or the normalizing process(es) of foreclosure.[14] Alice Rhinelander defied such foreclosure, for in passing-for-white she staged what Messer-Davidow (1995) would refer to as an "acting otherwise." Alice challenged the performative injunction that demanded she recite the conventions of the position that she had been assigned within discourse. During the course of the trial, it was established that members of her family were black, that at times she had been socially accepted as black, and that her birth certificate designated her as black. Yet Alice was seen to have refused this positioning, as she had performatively reproduced a white identity to the extent that it confounded detection. Before the Court, and within early twentieth-century racial rhetoric, racial ambiguity could not and would not be sanctioned. Racial logic demands, rather, that the subject be forcibly located within one or the other dichotomous classificatory realms of 'blackness' or 'whiteness.' Despite the trial functioning as the arena within which her performance was assessed and her 'blackness' ultimately proclaimed, Alice shows that a form of critical agency is possible in the performative recitation of race. If, to be discursively constituted *as* black, one must inhabit the 'norms' of black subjectivity but, instead, one acts *otherwise* to these conventions to reproduce the semblance of a white identity, it follows that a performative restaging through agential practices is possible.

While *embedded* within discourse, Alice can redeploy the call to inhabit normative ideals of racial subjectivity by *defying those assigned to her* as a discursively decreed black subject and acting otherwise—acting white. In making this claim, I am not framing acting otherwise as a practice that simply 'acts against' normative strictures. To claim that Alice 'acted otherwise' to the call to race (or the imprimatur that insisted that she enunciate a black racial identity) risks interpreting her actions as simply substituting one set of normative demands for another. In this rendering Alice would be merely reinscribing the binarism between blackness and whiteness—refusing blackness through acting white. This is not the form of 'resistance' that I would identify Alice as exercising. Moreover, this kind of reenactment of race can only be seen as nominally resistant, in that it simply secures dominant formulations of race as that which signifies complete and fixed realms of identity. Thus, Alice would be moving from the domain of blackness into whiteness. But Alice never simply refused blackness in order to embrace and proclaim a white racial identity. Instead, she slipped between identifying and being identified as a white and a black racial subject. Recall that at times Alice was designated by others as alternately black or white. And Alice herself changed how she (was) identified, oscillating between blackness and whiteness. It is here, in the non-space of definitive self-identification that Alice's resistant potential is located. Saying that Alice acted-otherwise, then, calls attention to the power of the *refusal of fixity*.[15]

Alice's 'acting-white' is a redeployment of power facilitated by her ambiguous body, a body that enables her to pass.[16] But sustained and successful passing must be seen as more than simply an *ability*. It is a *tactic*, or what Ahmed insists is a technique that requires more than simply (mis)recognition. Ahmed explains:

> this technique is exclusive and exclusionary—it is not available to all subjects—as it depends on the relation between subjects and structures of identification where the subject sees itself, or is seen by others, as not quite fitting . . . The ability to pass for white involves *a technique of the self: the production of a bodily image . . .* which is seen to be conflatable with whiteness. (1999, 101)

To *continue* passing, the subject must labor to have that pass recognized and validated. Alice, therefore, had to be aware of which acts would enable her to be viewed as a viable white subject. She had to choose how she would act, with whom she would align herself, and within which social situations she would place herself. In doing so, Alice evaded the regulatory mechanisms of hegemonic racialization (and, consequently, the borders enforced between black and white subjects) insofar as she reoriented her position in relation to the border—reorienting her racial status under both performative and juridical injunctions. This tactical evasion is executed through her practices of performative disobedience that enable her to occupy a discursive blind-spot or loophole.[17] This is a loophole that is engendered because when within it, when inhabiting it, one cannot be detected because it so resembles that which it opposes.[18] *It is hidden in plain sight.*

In chapter 3, I explored the paradoxical argument upon which racial purity rhetoric was, and continues to be, premised. Within this conceptual framework, race is presumed to be corporeally announced—in plain sight—and is simultaneously a 'truth' that is seen to be (and is feared as capable of being rendered) potentially hidden. In these concomitant beliefs, what remains constant is the insistence on race as an essentialized 'innerness' that will, ultimately, be exposed. In occupying a loophole that enables the passer to be hidden in plain sight, visibility falters in the very same moment that the subject is visibly verified as 'belonging' within the discursive bounds of whiteness. If panoptic power is ever-present, diffuse, and pervasive, and functions to perpetually "coerce by means of observation" (Foucault 1991, 170), it is imagined as totalizing. As Foucault (1991, 200) tells us, within the structure of panoptic power, visibility "is a trap." All structures, however, have potential loopholes, and the structure of race and its disciplinary surveillance is no exception.[19] To speak of a 'loophole' is to call forth imagery of retreat, hiding, and evasion. Indeed, it is defined in the *Concise Oxford Dictionary* as an "outlet" or "means of evading a rule"; the *New Oxford* defines this term as "an ambiguity in the law or set of rules." If the discursive laws of racial purity demand an observance of the rule of hypodescent, then the very nature of the rule occasions its defiance. For if it only takes 'one drop of black blood' to be designated as black, then there is all likelihood that this 'racial truth' will be *imperceptible*. Moreover, the very prohibition on claiming a white racial identity functions (inadvertently) to point out, indeed to map the path of resistance, to highlight the possibility of the loophole.[20]

Panoptic racial power flounders when meeting the passer. Passers evade the totalizing gaze of power because in the successful (undetected) pass the gaze does not even hesitate on the passing figure. They are simply *passed-over* as white. A loophole becomes, then, a space of concealment, a space in which racial 'truth' need not be confessed.[21] Thus, the regulatory gaze fails to detect 'racial truth' in the same instance in which it visually validates a 'racial truth'—the 'truth of whiteness'—a verified belonging that brings with it its own set of regulatory demands. This is not to say, however, that this agential practice of racial rearticulation can be attributed to the subject. Rather, a slippage occurs *between* the structure that demands racial designation and the manner in which the subject takes up this command. And as Michelle Burnham (1992, 62) argues, it is *in this site between structure and subject* that a form of agency is possible, an agency that works within the "very architecture of the structure."

Alice cannot be seen to be a *non*-viable racial subject precisely because she has so successfully occupied a viable (white) racial subject position. Alice defies performative demands precisely through repeating them so diligently. The beauty is that she answers *prohibited* performative demands. In doing so she "escapes reigning discourses and structures [of race, but does so] only in the very process of affirming them" (Burnham 1992, 64). Alice's *liminality* resists racial purity laws (and their legacy) that discursively demand the existence of only oppositional 'blackness' *or* 'whiteness.' In Butler's (1993, 124) terms, she is seen to occupy one of the ambivalent sites generated at the margins or limits of discursive intelligibility and legitimacy. Yet in refusing a *fixed racial position* (which is read as a refusal of blackness), Alice is seen to approximate whiteness. As such, she reinscribes the notion of absolute division between these two realms—she can only be one or the other. Alice, therefore, "inscribes that which [she] simultaneously transgresses" (Burnham 1992, 67).

The detection of Alice's pass-for-white and the manner through which she was reinstated within the dominant binarized logic of race exposes the contingency of the refusal of the law. The subject may adamantly object to the interpellation within discourse (consider Alice's denial of a black identity), but interpellation 'works' as Butler claims, without the subject necessarily recognizing themselves within, or even *hearing* the interpellation. Interpellation, Butler explains, "is an address that regularly misses its mark . . . It seeks to introduce a reality rather than report on an existing one" (1997a, 33–34).[22] Hailed persistently as 'black,' Alice may fail to recognize herself in the interpellation or she may interpret the interpellation as an inadequate and incomplete address. But no matter what Alice's protestations, the militant discursive adherence to the law of hypodescent continues to interpellate her in a manner that falls short of describing what may be her own complex experience of identity. As I have argued throughout the foregoing analysis, this law operates to *produce* a racial reality rather than reflect one: but the subject cannot refuse this production. Racial subjects are perpetually formed within the regulatory call to identity even as they struggle against it. The categorization that is opposed is referenced and hence reiterated in the act of questioning or rejecting that same categorization. Thus discourse continues to construct a social position for Alice that, by virtue of the call, she is compelled to respond to, even if only to protest it.[23]

While Alice's performative disobedience reinstates the dominant binarism of racial epistemology, and while she is recuperated back into this binarism in the legal imposition of black racial subject status, her defiance does have critical force. Predominantly, Alice functions in a critical capacity to expose the inability of racial purity law(s) and their discursive legacy to *resolutely* police the *formation, classification,* and *enunciation* of racial subjectivities. The cumulative effect of the practice of racial purity laws has operated to form the racial subject by way of the regulatory mechanisms that are instituted. At the same time, these laws regulated how subjectivities can be articulated; by defining to which race a subject 'belongs,' judicial decree mandates how that racial subject can operate in the social realm and, consequently, what privileges are accorded to the subject in that operation.

The ability to execute this technology of discipline in the fashioning of racial subjectivity requires, however, that the corporeal clearly signify and, thereby, pronounce a racial truth that is recognized within discourse. The body must announce itself as transparently and manifestly 'black' or 'white,' and be detectable as such in order for it to be discursively positioned as a particular raced body. It is this raced body that then circumscribes the supervision, constraints, shaping of behavior and so forth that is, in turn, productive of racial subjectivity. Race must be in plain sight.

In defiance of this necessity, Alice attests to the inefficacy of crediting an epistemological guarantee to the visible: you can't 'believe' what you 'see.' While, as Cutter (1996, 99 n. 12) claims, "[r]ace is determined by an association with individuals who have been socially coded as 'black,' rather than by physical markings," it is these physical markers that act as prompts in intersubjective exchanges to discursively 'race' subjects. It is when this absence of physical markers of racial status is coupled with a 'concealment' through silence (which does not proclaim an association with 'blackness') that the passing figure wittingly defies racial injunctions. Alice is not simply (mis)taken for being white, nor does she pass only by virtue of her light skin. Rather, we could presume (as Butler does in relation to another case) that she "refuses to introduce her blackness into conversation, and so withholds the conversational marker which would counter the hegemonic presumption that she is white" (Butler 1993, 171). Her racial status does not announce or 'show itself' and she does not 'claim it.' Alice thereby disavows loyalty to that which has supposedly called her into being.

It is this disavowal that signals Alice's opposition to and defiance of regimes of racial discipline and normalization, augmented in law, that function to *con-*

stitute racial subjectivity. Through this disavowal, *Alice refuses to be constituted as black*. Indeed, Alice's actions can be seen as representing a form of counter-power. This counter-power is a *resistance* that thwarts the possibility of a totalizing power that would render the subject completely docile to disciplinary control, a docility that would see the subject recognize and surrender to the imposition of a law of racial 'truth' (Foucault 2000c, 331). However, within a Foucauldian understanding of relations of power, the subject upon whom power is exercised is a *participant* who can "adopt strategies [that] modify . . . them" (Foucault 2000, 283), for "[w]here there is power, there is resistance" (Foucault 1998, 95). Alice resists the force of racial purity laws, and the discursive capital these produce, highlighting that power functions within these legislative measures to *elide complete or totalizing control*. While she cannot refuse the power of normalizing racialization in a 'pure' sense, Alice can and does engage in these disciplinary practices "carefully, deliberately, but with modifications that militate against standardized outcomes" (McWhorter 1999, 181), thereby demonstrating that the performative labor of race can be reenacted otherwise. In this capacity, Alice shows that race is devoid of ontological security and, as performative imperatives, racial injunctions can be refused and reworked (Butler 1993, 122). Alice's very defiance of performative dictates is resistant in that she represents a defiance of regulatory maxims; she acts otherwise to her socially and legally assigned subject status. It is this performative disobedience in acting otherwise that must be seen as an agential counter-practice. It is not the event of (mis)recognition that produces this disobedience. Rather, Alice *actively articulates* a racial identity that complicates classification.

Called before the Court, she is compelled to 'confess' the 'truth' of her race, to put to rest the complication that she represents. In this way, Alice's attempt at concealment is subjected to interrogation, highlighting the critical relationship between concealment and confession that is so important to Foucault's project. *Discipline and Punish*, which analyzes the normalizing practices of the disciplinary economy that at once confines and renders the subject exposed to continual surveillance, and *The History of Sexuality: The Will to Knowledge*, which argues that confession produces truths (that is, discourses of sexuality) rather than repressing them, explicate that confession and concealment operate as necessary corollaries. Together they comprise a power relation that at once produces and reveals the (produced) 'truth.' Institutional and discursive arrangements expose the body and its conduct to the ever-watchful eye of disciplinary power, and the confessional economy operates to expose 'the soul'—the 'truth' of the individual—and to fix them within this confessed truth. The confession is thus established "as one of the main rituals we rely on for the production of truth" (Foucault 1998, 58).

As we have seen, the body is constituted through disciplinary practices in order to reveal or confess racial truth. And it is for this reason that Alice is paraded in a state of undress before the Court—the trial ritual becomes yet another space in which the production of racial ontology is augmented. In this arena, "One confesses—or is forced to confess. When it is not spontaneous or dictated by some internal imperative, the confession is wrung from a person by violence or threat; it is driven from its hiding place in the soul or extracted from the body" (Foucault 1998, 59). Yet Alice does not take the stand. Instead of viewing this as simply a sign of Alice's *lack* of agency, as passivity in the face of power, it can be reinscribed as a refusal that functions as a form of *agency in defiance.* In remaining silent, Alice can be viewed as willfully abstaining from the imperative to confess. In her silence, Alice exercises a localized tactic of resistance to power. She rejects the occasion that could wrench from her a confession and 'withholds' the truth that power (or the regime of race) would have her claim. For this would be tantamount to a self-proclaimed performative instantiation of black subjectivity—the performative dynamic of confession *producing that which is confessed.* Instead, Alice is able to retain a degree of ambiguity or complication through her refusal to speak and, in doing so, she 'troubles' the political technology of the body, that is, the knowledge and mastery of the body or the hold that power has on her body.

Yet we know that this confession was obtained by other means; recalcitrant in her silence, Alice's body is made to speak for her, by way of a perceived *corporeal confession to racial truth.* It is, as Foucault points out, extracted from the body. She may have been able to performatively reproduce a contingent white identity—but this reenactment was not completely efficacious. Thus the legal arena was able to function in a recuperative and corrective capacity in order to reinscribe the boundaries of whiteness. In doing so, what the legal practitioners in this case implicitly *seek* is to maintain the (ineluctable) notion of a 'whiteness' that is 'pure.' But this is a futile gesture. For in the moment that the subject stands before the Court and is inserted into a subject position decreed by the Court several factors become evident.

Alice signals the threat of rupturing the boundaries of whiteness as she highlights the *constructedness* of whiteness through her ability to reproduce it in her attempted interloping. This is precisely the significance of Alice's ability to be (potentially) hidden in plain sight; this practice reflects what Butler would call "the imitative structure" by which race is produced. That she does so is not to suggest that Alice represents subversive power for, as I have argued, her actions are interpreted as simply reenforcing the binarized logic of racial possibilities. Her actions do, however, have critical and resistant force. They may not subvert the broader structural power of race and the discursive workings of this regime, but at a local level they do resist racial strictures. And it is this resistance that (a) challenges the construction of racial classifications, (b) exposes the arbitrariness of the classification, and (c) highlights the *regularized* and *normalized* disciplinary system of race. (Here I point to the various operations of discipline that compel subjects to enter into agreement—through processes of subjection—on the descriptive validity of the system and the moral consequences of racial ascription and deviation from this.) The success of this regularized system is contingent on the maintenance of subject's commitment to and participation in the tacit collective agreement to sustain this system.[24] Alice abdicates loyalty and so calls into question the integrity of the system. Thus she signals that classification *per se* is invalid, ever-contingent, and ultimately, incapable of effortless functioning. Moreover, Alice compromises the illusion of a whiteness that is able to protect itself against interlopers: only *detected* 'assaults' enable the parameters of whiteness to be protected. Alice was detected in her interloping and so could be defined as residing outside of the white racial category—the boundaries reenforced and the phantasy of a whiteness that *can* be conceived of as 'pure' (before the law) refixed in that *moment* of the reinscription of its periphery. The premise of the disciplinary regime produced through racial purity laws (and their discursive legacy) is that race is an ontology that *is* or *will become* self-evident. If, then, it cannot be *seen,* or if there is the possibility that it *may not be detected,* this poses a danger to whiteness. For if hegemonic whiteness is ensured through vigilant border protection, the possibility that there may be those that slip through the check-points—past the guards—compromises the integrity of whiteness. As such, Alice acts as an agent who represents not only the tenuous foundations upon which hegemonic discursive racial decrees rely, but she additionally functions as a figure who suggests the possibility that there may be those who *do* successfully evade the regulatory mechanisms of racial foreclosure and *are* hidden in plain sight.

Rhinelander v. Rhinelander attests to the meticulous methods of racial reinscription that diligently and anxiously labor to orient and enforce borders between racial subjects. The arguments of both counsels in the case and the findings of the Court demonstrate the efforts of legal discourse to maintain racial division, to constitute racial subjectivity, and to assail instances of disjunction between the body (as racially determined under law) and the expression of raced subjectivity in relation to that material body. Alice highlights, however, that racial purity law and rhetoric perpetually rewrites and reinscribes a notion of race that *exists only in fabrication.* More poignantly, Alice's modification of racial reinscription shows the impossibility of such endeavors, the loyalty to discursive decrees upon which these rely, and the possibilities that may arise to challenge these mandates; Alice stages a critical refusal along the fault-lines of racial subjectivity and in 'acting otherwise' reenacts resistant racial possibilities. Her capacity to execute this demonstrates that, as an 'idea' that must be perpetually reasserted and guarded from performative reproduction by those not sanctioned, 'whiteness,' as a 'pure' and ontologically secure axiom, cannot be sustained. Ultimately, 'whiteness' is seen to be not simply permeable, but a phantasm—one that is exposed in the very moment of crisis before the Court, that is, the moment in which a subject must be discursively replaced. It is the effort of militating against acts of performative defiance and manipulation of discursive and legal mandates that ruptures the supposed integrity of whiteness. Inevitably, in attempting to refix whiteness, this movement simultaneously unfixes, for in endeavoring to fortify its boundaries, law unmasks whiteness for what it is—an intricate disciplinary illusion and legally invoked ideology requiring the exhaustive aid of judicial attention in order to survive.

7

Practicing Problematization

RESIGNIFYING RACE

> Performativity describes this relation of being impli-
> cated in that which one opposes, this turning of power
> against itself to produce alternative modalities of power,
> to establish a kind of political contestation that is not a
> 'pure' opposition, a 'transcendence' of contemporary
> relations of power, but a difficult labor of forging a
> future from resources inevitably impure.
>
> —Judith Butler, *Bodies That Matter*

Racial passing 'unsettles' because it challenges accepted beliefs that race is stable
and fixed, transparent and visually embodied. The act of passing represents a
dissonance between the external racial signification of skin and the supposed
internal racial truth that is made to inhere in blood. To pass-as-white is to
tactically redeploy power, an action facilitated by an ambiguous body or a body
that can be visually verified as white; it is to defy racial ascription and prescriptions. Eddie Murphy's *Saturday Night Live* sketch, "White Like Me," parodies
race and seems to suggest that passing—this embodied defiance—might be the
answer to America's race problems.[1] First aired in 1984, the sketch shows African
American Murphy conducting a mock-serious experiment where he transforms
himself (with the help of "the best makeup people in the business") into Mr.
White in order to "go underground and actually experience America" on the
streets of New York, "as a white man." The audience sees him prepare for his role
backstage and hears that he learned the tropes of whiteness by watching "lots of

Dynasty," reading Hallmark cards, and studying how white people walk ("their butts are real tight"). Ready to enact whiteness, he enters the white world: he goes into a convenience store where the white owner tells him to take a paper for free; we see him on a bus with other whites who, after the last black passenger has disembarked, celebrate by breaking out into the song "Life is a Cabaret" and, finally, he enters the Equity National Bank where the white loan officer gives him a huge sum of money despite his having no collateral, no credit, and no identification, and tells him: "Pay us back any time. Or don't. We don't care." Murphy highlights here both what George Lipsitz (1998) has called a "possessive investment in whiteness"—where white people secure their stakes in an advantaging system—and what Cheryl Harris (1993) has marked as the social and economic benefits that accrue to white skin and status. Murphy ends the sketch, however, with a warning:

> I'll tell you something. [Pan to Eddie's black buddies applying white makeup.] I've got a lot of friends, and we've got a lot of makeup. So, the next time you're huggin' up with some really super, groovy white guy, or you met [*sic*] a really great, super keen white chick, don't be too sure. They might be black.

This "don't be too sure" resonates as a threat to notions of whiteness as pure and impenetrable and, as seen in previous chapters, it declares that whiteness is not an essential possession or expression of internality but an enactment that can be appropriated by those discursively defined as being 'outside' its parameters. But while passing may undercut systems of inequality through granting the individual access to white racial privilege, it also works to undercut itself. It is predicated on the imperative to *not* be detected and, as such, the threat it represents cannot be registered. Murphy's sketch may indeed hold more radical potential for unsettling race than undetected acts of racial passing, for the excessive or hyperbolic production of white identity holds the potential to expose race as artifice. Then again, the sketch can simply be read *as* an excessive *visible* performance and, as a consequence, be discursively discounted as a farce. Due to these reasons, passing does little to disturb dominant economies of race: it generally reinscribes the black/white binary, meaning that it does not rework racial categories.

The limited potential in passing-for-white is also evident in the fact that not everyone can do it. As this is the case, this chapter asks: if you can't pass-for-another and if passing itself has such circumscribed possibilities, how might race be reworked? How can racial agency be conceived beyond that form provided by a disjunction between the body and the enactment of race? For the purposes of this chapter more broadly, I am interested in the question of how *all* racial subjects—regardless of designation—might trouble the representational, disciplinary authority of race and contest the imperatives of racial performativity.

Butler's answer to this question would seem to lie in the fact that performativity is compulsory but always unstable, and it is this instability that creates space for reworkings. It is compulsory because viable social existence is contingent on the reiteration of recognizable norms, and failure to adequately do so results in disciplinary reprimand or punishment. But performativity is unstable, Penelope Deutscher notes, "because of the perpetual need for reiteration and reenactment and because parody lies at the heart of 'natural' [identity]" (1999, 178). The parody referred to here *is the very enactment of identity*, that is, the enactment of hyperbolic norms that are always and irrevocably copies of a copy and never, as they would seem, original enunciations. The performative imperatives of race must be recited—racial norms must be copied—but due to the instability of these imperatives or norms of racial identity, they are inevitably open to alteration. The hegemonic norms of race can be and are opposed precisely because agency and alteration are immanent in recitation. Importantly, though, these norms that are opposed are those (same ones) upon which ones identity is predicated. This means, as Butler makes clear in the quote I open with above, that one is always "implicated in that which one opposes." Escaping the system of race is not possible because we are formed as subjects within it: transcendence or 'pure' opposition is foreclosed. Instead, "[s]ubversion must take place from within existing discourse, since that is all there is" (Salih 2002, 59). One is *in* power even as one contests it, formed *by* power even while reworking it.[2] As Foucault famously remarked in his *History Of Sexuality: The Will to Knowledge* (1998, 95), there is "no single locus of Great Refusal." So instead of 'revolution' or absolute evasion, subjects might labor to forge "a future from resources inevitably impure," attempting to reenact race from within and in relation to the norms through which they themselves are formed. In doing so, subjects must "repeat those injuries [that call them into being] without precisely reenacting them" (Butler 1997, 41).

Injuries that call subjects into being, however, are *not* normatively equivalent, nor are all forms of power to resist equal. Within the context of the white racist episteme, black subjects have borne the weight of excessive injury and the capacities for black subjects to exercise agency is obviously different from that of white subjects, precisely because they are not situated similarly in relations of power. It is a historical reality that the black body/self was and continues to be torn asunder by the brutal legacy of institutional whiteness. Captivity and forced labor, Jim Crow and ghettoization, the crack epidemic and chronic unemployment, HIV/AIDS, the prison-industrial complex and Hurricane Katrina represent an incomplete arc of trauma that has been lived by the black body/self within anti-black, racist strategies in North America. This is, as Hartman (1997, 51) states, a "history that hurts," and it is this "still-unfolding narrative of captivity, dispossession, and domination . . . [that] engenders the black subject in the Americas."[3] Given this reality, black agential practices are limited, constrained within what can be thought of as the non-autonomy of the field of action. But the black body/self's history is one of resistance: this history, as George Yancy has insisted, is one where "to resist is to re-story one's identity, even if that story is fragmented and replete with tensions and is only short lived and the systemic material conditions of oppression have not been completely removed" (2008, 113).

How resistance or the reenactment against the injury of identity might be pursued is left largely decontextualized in Butler's account of performativity, and questions remain as to how to distinguish between the inevitable alteration that inheres in general performative reproductions of identity and those critical alterations that labor to forge new social realities. What are specific ways that race can be critically recited so as to destabilize hegemonic norms? In what follows, I consider the African American vernacular practice of signifying as a grounded empirical example of this kind of labor against injury or effort to 're-story' identity.[4] Representing a cogent illustration of agential racial resignification, signifying highlights the radical politics upon which the critical construction of self within intolerable regimes has been contingent. More than this, though, the practice shows deliberate racial recitation against terms of injury or domination and points to how all racial identity might be rethought. Building on the ideas that arise through looking at this practice, I then return to Foucault for a more optimistic understanding of social transformation than that provided by Butler's immanent politics. Analyzing Foucault's later work on 'technologies of the self' provides the opportunity to trace the relation between resignification and active embodied resistance a little more fully and to consider how, through critique, it might be possible to embrace new modes of racial becoming.

INTERROGATING TERMS OF RACIAL SUBJECTION: SIGNIFYING PRACTICES

I was not hunting for my liberty, but also hunting for a name.
—William Wells Brown

The African American renaming ritual of signifying is possibly one of the most powerful examples of the resistant performative reenactment of race. As theorized by Henry Louis Gates, Jr. (1987; 1988), this black speech tradition is comprised of the reflexive and figurative use of formal language. Often thought of as the use of rhyming and troping expressions made within specific black speech communities in order to gain the upper hand in verbal encounters, it is a practice that is difficult to define and incredibly intricate in its operations. Above all else, signifying—or "Signifyin(g)," the term Gates employs for his theorization of the black vernacular practice so as to differentiate it from the conventional understanding of signification—is a method of reading, a rereading that functions as a formal revision of meaning.[5] Dominant linguistic structures and content are repeated but reversed such that a revision of the received meaning takes place. According to Gates (1988, xxii–xxiii), "black formal repetition always repeats with a difference, a black difference that manifests itself in specific language use."

The dominant language may be recited but this is coupled with a distinct and unique 'black language,' resulting in a form of double-voice; talking involves talking back—talking from but *in response to* and *through* traditional verbal signifiers. Signifying operates, as such, as a device through which the dominant tropes and performatives—of language, the injury of identity, of the 'truth' of 'race'—are always reworked. While the same signifiers may be used in black vernacular as in 'standard' English, that which is signified is distinct. Classic examples of this would the African American reuse of "*down, nigger, baby* [or] *cool*" (Gates 1988, 47). While terms such as these, and other forms of signifying, have often been dismissed as simply slang, Gates challenges this assumption and argues that they need to be rethought. For Gates, such signifying operations do more than merely act as dialect or a passive misuse of dominant meaning: they critique "the nature of (white) meaning itself, [and] challenge through a literal critique of the sign the meaning of meaning" (1988, 47).

Signifying is conscious and self-reflexive. Using various rhetorical tropes—such as synecdoche, irony, metaphor, metonymy, satire, chiasmus, catechesis, aporia, and metalepsis—signifying plays with language. This is 'achieved' through trickery,[6] manipulation, and counter-interpretation, and can be seen in such 'games' as loud-talking,[7] shouting, sounding, rapping, calling out one's name, and playing the dozens.[8] Signifying can be regarded as a black hermeneutic in which lexical signification is reworked and meaning obfuscated for those who do not understand the 'play.' Confusion is produced through the unsettling and ultimate displacement of the relation between the signifier and the signified. This acts, then, as a method or device of encoding (for unity or for resistance) and can result in the inversion or transfiguring of racial relations of power. To 'signify' is a response to and attitude toward attempts at control and domination. But the ability to engage in linguistic manipulation and revision highlights the ultimate impossibility of totalizing domination. White and black meanings may be interrelated in this operation—the same signifiers may be employed—but two distinct and incommensurable *orders of meaning* are produced. Thus, such signifying cannot be said to be reliant on or merely a parody of dominant structures of language. As a practice of resistance, signifying becomes the "exchange of given meanings for denoted meanings peculiar to the worldview and context of 'black' life" (Jones 1993, 508).[9]

Signifying is most importantly characterized by how it is distinguishable from the conventional operation of signification; rather than relaying information or signifying something directly through the use of a signifier, the black vernacular game is to signify *upon* something. It is a *doing,* a style or practice in which meaning is conveyed through indirection or circumlocution.[10] This indirect discourse might resemble that which would usually be signified by the signifier, but this same signifier is disassembled during the process of the evocation or repetition.[11] This characteristic is central to signifying and it is this disassembly that enables the revision and critique at work within the practice.

Because the trickery involved is so slippery or allusive, the most productive way to demonstrate the subversive potential of this practice is through example. And possibly one of the best-known examples of signifying as a mechanism of critique is to be found in Ralph Ellison's prologue to *Invisible Man* (1995, 9–10). Here, Ellison tells of his protagonist who, "under the spell of the reefer . . . discovered a new analytic way of listening" (1995, 8). And he heard someone shout a sermon entitled "The Blackness of Blackness." In this piece, Ellison has the preacher sermonize on what 'black' *is:* the normalized descriptor and utterance 'black' is referenced and repeated; however, this is done in such a way as to review and critique its supposed fixity. In order to appreciate the complexity and force of Ellison's prose, full citation is required:

> "Brother and sisters, my text this morning is the 'Blackness of
> Blackness.' "
> "And the congregation of voices answered: 'The blackness is most black,
> brother, most black . . .' "
> "In the beginning . . ."
> "At the very start," they cried.
> ". . . there was blackness . . ."
> "Preach it . . ."
> ". . . and the sun . . ."
> "The sun, Lawd . . ."
> ". . . was bloody red . . ."
> "Red . . ."
> "Now black is . . ." the preacher shouted.

"Bloody . . ."

"I said black is . . ."

"Preach it, brother . . ."

". . . an' black ain't . . ."

"Red, Lawd, red: He said it's red!"

"Amen, brother . . ."

"Black will git you . . ."

"Yes it will . . ."

". . . an' black won't!"

"Naw, it won't!"

"It do . . ."

"It do, Lawd . . ."

". . . an' it don't."

"Halleluiah . . ."

". . . It'll put you, glory, glory, Oh my Lawd, in the WHALE'S BELLY."

"Preach it, dear brother . . ."

". . . an' make you tempt . . ."

"Good God a-mighty!"

"Old Aunt Nelly!"

"Black will make you . . ."

"Black . . ."

". . . or black will unmake you."

"Ain't it the truth, Lawd?"

While Ellison's signifying 'sermon' may appear elliptical, it calls forth racial norms by invoking the 'essence' of blackness. At the same moment, he highlights that this 'essence' is a production that is called into being through the cumulative performative utterances of 'black.' He satirizes the very concept of ontology in order to disassemble the naturalness of the relation between the signifier and signified. In doing so, he throws ontology into crisis. "The Blackness of Blackness" stages a radical interruption of fixity and of the social order. Ellison achieves this by demonstrating the ambiguity and arbitrariness of the sign 'black.' As the sermon states: "black is" and "black ain't"; "black will" and "black won't"; "it won't" and "it do"; "it do" and "it don't"; and finally—with possibly the most direct reference to the force of the performative—the signifier "black will *make* you," that is, the signifier will *produce* you as "Black." Ellison thus refuses the disciplinary decrees that insist that there is a racial 'truth' and that this truth be ratified in the performance of identity. This refusal is an anti-hegemonic practice that destabilizes the terms of subjection through which subjects are constituted. Working within discursive constraints this practice calls on the normalized 'name.' It is, however, an artful and challenging approximation; the name is reiterated precisely in order to point out the artificiality of this production. In the process, this act poses counter-histories, counter-identities, and imagines a new sociality by insisting that meanings of blackness, black life, and black subjectivity cannot be captured within the confines of the white racist episteme.[12]

The second example of signifying that I want to draw attention to demonstrates an explicit critical appraisal of racial injunctions and efforts of domination. It also highlights the way signifying can function as an *intertextual* tool of response.[13] Here, T. Thomas Fortune stages a *signifying upon* Kipling's "White Man's Burden":

> What is the Black Man's Burden,
> Ye hypocrites and vile,
> Ye white sepulchers
> From th' Amazon Nile?
> What is the Black Man's Burden,
> Ye Gentile parasites,
> Who crush and rob your brother
> Of his manhood and his rights? (quoted in Gates 1988, 103)

This text operates as a form of satire produced through the critical deployment of intertextual references. In the process of making these references, the rhetorical trope not only challenges received meanings of race to be rethought; it also reframes the terms upon which Kipling's text is dependent, thereby achieving a certain rewriting of the discourse of blackness (and, necessarily, whiteness). Whiteness and blackness are reinvested by Fortune in a manner that foregrounds a nonnormative or nondominant perspective. What this piece signals, as a consequence, is that signifying is doubled-voiced (black and white meanings intertwine) while simultaneously being delivered in a unique style generated and practiced by certain black speech communities.

The theorization of signifying is important beyond the scope of literary criticism—the frame through which Gates investigates the practice. As a grouping of performances, signifying is a form of speech. It is a mechanism of narration, a strategy of interaction, and it operates as a tool employed in relations of power. As Wahneema Lubiano (1995, 96) cogently argues: "Signifying redefines racial differences as cultural difference, with all the complexities entailed in such a recategorization, and puts our notions of reality up for grabs." But, more than this, signifying performances challenge subjection and alter the terms upon and through which subjectivity is constituted; they generate a radical negotiation of the ways that (racial, behavioral or linguistic) norms are reiterated and *lived*.

Due to the ability of signifying to operate in this capacity, it can be viewed as an effort of decolonization through the recolonization of the sign. The sign is 'liberated,' in a sense, through the play of ambiguity and becomes a-new in the critical reuse of language. As conceptualized by Samia Nehrez (quoted in hooks 1992, 1), 'decolonization' is "an act of confrontation with a hegemonic system of thought; it is hence a process of considerable historical and cultural liberation. As such, decolonization becomes the contestation of all dominant forms and structures, whether they be linguistic, discursive, or ideological."

While signifying takes place within the linguistic realm, similar practices—ones that challenge hegemonic meanings and resignify dominant configurations of racial subjectivity—can be registered on multiple levels of social practice. This might be seen, for instance, when racial performative demands and enunciations are reenacted through *critical* performances of clothing style, leisure interests, formations of community, culinary preferences, and bodily comportment or stylization. In making this claim I am suggesting that the *necessary resignifications* involved in the articulation of the norms of a given identity site can, when reflexively approached, become embodied instantiations of resistance. Such reworkings in material practices can be seen in the innovative ways in which slaves, working within the confines of dominant power, reinvested terms of subjection so as to refute injurious power/knowledge relations that cast them as will-less, abject, and insentient.[14] Also, the way that the Civil Rights and Black Power movements reinvested the term 'black' with a new set of (positive) meanings stands as a key example of how this linguistic reworking was inseparable from (a) the accompanying behavioral practices that were generated in order to contest dominant (white) understandings of blackness and (b) the altered material conditions that followed for blacks (such as desegregation) from these contestations.

It is essential, however, to note the distinctions that are being made here between the various forms of resignification that I have raised. I am making three claims. First, all enunciation and, indeed, the constitution of identity is reliant on the subject resignifying (or reciting) the existing signifiers of a given racial site in order to ward against the crisis of *not being:* we must recite/resignify in order to *exist* as viable and recognizable subjects. These signifiers, however, will always be repeated with a difference due the fact that every enunciation will inevitably 'slip' from the idealized norm. At the same time, this exposes the crisis of instability upon which racial identity is predicated. Second, the black vernacular practice of signifying also resignifies existing signifiers—with a difference that Gates (1988, 66) has called a "black difference."[15] This slippage from the norm is, though, an intentional one.[16] Finally, I want to suggest that within the more generalized practice of signifying identity a similar interruption might be staged—a resignification of hegemonic norms that, while referencing the norm, does so critically and in the spirit of challenge. Needless to say, resignification always takes place within specific social, political, economic, historical, and spatial contexts that work to constrain and enable subjects to varying degrees. As such, that which one contests and the way in which one contests will radically alter depending on the positioning of the subject.[17] What I want to illuminate, however, is that a discursive space is opened-up in the act of resignification, notwithstanding the specifics of the material conditions.

Critical resignifications can be analyzed in terms of Michel de Certeau's (1988) account of 'practice.' Practice marks those 'ways of operating' whereby dominated subjects exercise *tactics* that politicize and rework subject positions and terms of oppression. These tactics—or what be could considered acts of anti-discipline or performative disobedience—are never complete, assured or secure. Instead, a tactic for de Certeau (1988, xix) is:

> [A] calculus which cannot count on a "proper" (a spatial or institutional localization), nor thus on a borderline distinguishing the other as a visible totality . . . A tactic insinuates itself into the other's place, fragmentarily, without taking it over in its entirety, without being able to keep it at a distance . . . because it does not have a place, a tactic depends on time—it is always on the watch for opportunities that must be seized "on the wing." Whatever it wins, it does not keep. It must constantly manipulate events in order to turn them into "opportunities."

When framed in terms of 'practice,' the resistance staged by the dominated becomes visible as fleeting, fragmentary, and always transient, but the character of resistance is altered, such that in order to 'be resistant' an action need not be imagined as that which can 'win over' the system upon which subordination is premised. What it 'achieves' is the (perhaps only momentary) 'freedom' of exceeding the constraints of domination. Various performances (of identity, norms, and meaning) would be viewed in this understanding as linguistic and behavioral tactics or motivated repetitions through which subjects *create* and *make* new imaginings and new enunciations from the received language and its structure. "The 'making' in question," de Certeau (1988, xii) states, "is a production, a *poiesis*." Reframed again, in a Foucauldian conceptualization that will be elaborated below, this is a poetry or artistry (a technology of self) that functions as a form of 'care for the self'—the refashioning of self in relation to (but always within) discursive structures and norms. For de Certeau, the dominated are able to deflect the power of the received order by reappropriating (or recolonizing) language within the field of the linguistic system. They thus *escape* the dominance of the structure *without leaving it*. As such, it is possible to witness the capacity in which "users make (*bricolent*) innumerable and infinitesimal trans-formations of and within the dominant economy in order to adapt it to their own interests and rules" (de Certeau 1988, xiii–xiv).

Through this analysis, signifying becomes visible as the agential use and creation of language, gesture, and meaning that, while implicated within domi-nant structures, is not reducible to them. The 'practice' enables an extension beyond the confines of dominant discourse. And through manipulation, perfor-mative racial injunctions are altered: blackness is reframed and the law is resig-nified. But these tactical maneuverings show that resignification is not simply an individualized practice, rather, subjects and communities can be and have been intimately linked through shared efforts of racial performance; thus, a powerful collective political dimension is articulated as integral to the practice of (black) racial resistance in reiteration. This analysis also guides an understanding of the possibilities or contexts within which radically divergent forms of subjectivity might be inaugurated—as refusals of the discursive norms through which sub-jects are called into being—and highlights that black subjects have systematically rallied against dominant strictures that have demanded the performative recita-tion of passive subordination and abjection or ideals associated with whiteness. Signifying demonstrates the potential that is initiated and the agency that is possible (indeed inevitable) in the resignification immanent within reiteration. More than this, though, these acts highlight how race is transformed in practice and the critical and intentional dimensions of such labor.

REARTICULATING RACIAL BEING:
FOUCAULT'S ETHICS AND "PROBLEMATIZATION"

Even if we accept that there are incalculable effects to all (or most) statements or activities, this does not mean that we need to concede that there are no calculable effects. Without this possibility, political intervention may be construed as either totally meaningless (why bother) or entirely spontaneous (it just happens). Critical reflection on past, present, or future practices is essential to the exploitation of the gaps within hegemonic norms that allow for potential transformation of social relations.

—Moya Lloyd, "Performativity, Parody, Politics"

Critical practices of resignification are not guaranteed to successfully subvert the injurious norms through which hegemonic forms of identity are fashioned but, as Moya Lloyd emphasizes in the above quote, this does not rule out the pos-sibility that there are aims and ends that might be gauged or anticipated. Any form of political intervention, whether it interrogates terms of injury, states of oppression or constraints of subjection is contingent on this possibility. It is the final clause of Lloyd's quote that I want to take as a point of departure for this concluding discussion. This idea of the *critical reflection* on the norms and practices that constitute us as subjects is, as I have argued, the modality through which any form of intervention is to take place. Foucault's later work provides ways for thinking more tangibly about these possibilities, particularly in terms of *how* the critical resignification of racial identity might be pursued in an active way, how such practices can have aims and intentions, and how such activity might in turn refashion concepts of self in relation to others and networks of power/knowledge.

For Foucault, the activity of critical reflection on the normative terms through which subjectivity is constituted would be identified as 'struggles against subjection,' or efforts to wrestle "against the submission of subjectivity" (2000c, 332). This kind of work comprises what Foucault calls ethics.[18] Ethical activity, in this understanding, "has to do with actions and choices, not with mindless behavior" (McWhorter 1999, 195). It is the practice of fashioning freedom from the normative forms of subjectivity within which we are formed and form ourselves, and bringing out freedom in our relations with others. In this activity what is essentially asked is: who are we? By this, Foucault (2000a, 290) refers to the notion that the subject "is not a substance. It is a form, and this form is not primarily or always identical to itself." The subject constitutes themselves differently in different moments in relation to different norms and power/knowledge networks. For example, how the subject constitutes themselves as a political subject or as a sexual subject will be distinct; in each case, one has a different relation to the self despite the fact that these modes of being coexist. These ways of being (the self), however, are not formed in isolation. Rather, the individual uses "models that he finds in his culture, his society, his social group" (Foucault 2000a, 291). Precisely because the subject is a form and not identical to itself—that is, there is no 'true interiority'—the self can be transformed or practiced in different capacities.

The subject practices the self in new ways through posing a different relation to 'truth'; in any given moment, what is the truth that I constitute myself in relation to? Is this truth that which determines me? Or, can I pose a divergent or oppositional truth that may counter or contradict the truth through which my subjectivity is formed?[19] Reframing the experiences of slavery in light of this notion, it could be asked: does the enslaved recognize themselves (even partially) in the hegemonic truth which claims that they are insentient, passive, and abject beings?[20] Or does this subject challenge this truth through posing *another*, a truth that asserts a complexity of subjectivity not defined within dominant paradigms?[21] It is through posing a different relation to truth that people are able to modify their own and other peoples' behavior; as Clare O'Farrrell (2005, 109) remarks, this "happens through a complex interplay of choice, action and constraint." While subjects exist and operate in a nonautonomous field, there are ways to modify these constraints, always margins of what Foucault calls freedom; that is, the ability to choose from a range of possibilities, to choose one kind of action, not another.[22] Importantly, however, not everyone has the same ability to modify their conduct and that of others because not everyone exists in the *same* field of possibilities: indeed some have a very limited range. Yet as Saidiya Hartman (1997, 50) reminds us, even within the routinized terror of slavery, "[w]ithin the confines of surveillance and nonautonomy, the resistance to subjugation proceeded . . . [and] the enslaved seized any and every opportunity to slip off the yoke." Possibilities, then, are seized in practice, but these possibilities are always marked out in advance—though not determined—by the form of domination.

Any questioning of self and subjectivity—the critical reflection on self—is executed, according to Foucault, through what he terms *the practices of self* or *technologies of the self* that come to represent a care for the self.[23] For Foucault (1988, 2), this care for self—also referred to as 'self-government'—is "an exercise of self upon self by which one tries to work out, to transform one's self and to attain a certain mode of being." By this he means that subjects are able, within the limits of their historical and social situations, to resist the self that is a product of power relations and modify their behavior in relation to the kind of person that they want to become. Care for self is a means through which to stylize the self in new ways, to work on or to engage in an artistry of the self as a form of *poesis*.[24] This can be thought about in terms of envisioning and seeking a new sociality or a new way of experiencing the body/self as raced. Thus, care for the self can exist in agonistic relation to efforts of hegemonic power to mold the conduct of racial subjects; as I have explored, subjects reenact racial subjectivity in ways that might refuse, rework or evade the normative demands exercised through discipline, governmentality, and performative compulsions.

The subject pursues this 'exercise of self upon self' through a practice of freedom that Foucault terms *problematization*. Understood as a form of critique, the subject interrogates their status, actions, conduct, and the meaning(s) of their identity. According to Foucault (1984, 46), this critique or problematization is:

> [A] *historical investigation into the events that have led us to constitute our-*
> *selves and recognize ourselves as subjects* of what we are doing, thinking, say-
> ing. In that sense, this criticism is not transcendental, and its goal is not that
> of making a metaphysics possible: it is genealogical in its designs and archae-
> ological in its method . . . [I]t will separate out, from the contingency that
> has made us what we are, the possibility of no longer being, doing, or think-
> ing what we are, do, or think . . . it is seeking to give new impetus, as far and
> as wide as possible, to the undefined work of freedom. (My emphasis)

What is most important here is the idea of historical investigation, where the individual might conduct a genealogical analysis of their identity and reflect upon themselves as a *contingently* formed racial subject. In this "critical ontology of ourselves" (Foucault 2007b, 118), the subject would ask: in which ways is my raced identity *not* a given but a product of power/knowledge relations? What are the racializing practices, technologies, and discourses through which I am formed? And how do I exercise or submit to power relations that construct and maintain racial demarcations and notions of 'truth'? By locating the contingency of existence as racial subjects—that is, acknowledging that identities are not fixed—and locating the spaces of liberty that are available, such a historico-critical attitude (the practice of freedom) engenders new ways of being raced. It requires that one ask the question: "In what is given to us as universal, necessary, obligatory, what place is occupied by whatever is singular, contingent, and the product of arbitrary constraints?" (Foucault 1984, 45). Within the confines of these constraints—where there might be loopholes or points where resistance is possible—race and the meanings it claims can be (and are) challenged. What can be produced, as Foucault (2000d, 315) states, is a space where "the critique conducted in the form of a necessary limitation" of identity would be transformed "into a practical critique that takes the form of a possible crossing-over" the boundaries of pre-demarcated identity.[25] This might alternatively be thought about as a 'self-overcoming,' where critique facilitates the testing of our limits, such that we might—to reiterate Foucault's point—"separate out, from the contingency that has made us what we are, the possibility of no longer being, doing, or thinking what we are, do, or think" (Foucault 1984, 46).

For such a critique to *be* practical—in the sense that it 'achieves' anything in the concrete reality of one's life—a genealogical investigation of identity must be coupled with an endeavor to craft a new *embodied* reality. George Yancy has noted that historically, black subjects have labored to envisage and realize new pleasures and new bodies, new ways of being in the flesh that refuse configurations of blackness as they have been imagined in the white racist episteme. This labor has been enabled through the fact that *critique has necessarily been accompanied by acts of affirmation,* ones that "explore new . . . ways of emoting, feeling, striving, being . . . [of posing a narrative that] accents and valorizes (in non-essentialist terms) the ever historically shifting positive modes of what it means to be black" (Yancy 2004a, 137). Through affirmation of value, a different kind of body has been constructed, one that is not reducible to white racist knowledge of this body. For white subjects, this kind of work might mean crafting an embodied reality that is actively conscious of racial contingency, and engaging in practices that destabilize the supposed 'fixedness' of the category of whiteness. Any ethical relation of self to self in terms of race must engage in such exploration to seek out and enact embodied practices that increase behavioral possibilities; these practices will be/are ones that enable subjects to live the racialized body in ways that question dominant power/knowledge relations and refuse disciplinary aims of racial docility. They will be practices that increase embodied capacities for pleasure (they are the exercise of freedom) and ones that support and validate the embodied pleasure of others in ways that are disconnected from the intensification of power relations.

To this point, I've establish that for Foucault the following possibilities exist for how subjects might ethically relate to themselves and others: they can pose a different relation to truth; change their actions and others; have goals about the kind of person they want to become; and they can cross-over or practice what can be thought about as a 'self-overcoming.' These possibilities exist because, as already historically constituted (within specific cultural constraints), subjects have the capacity to wrestle with technologies of power, to choose from a range of existing options, and can act against (though always in relation to) attempts to control their conduct. Foucault thus provides an optimistic philosophy and politics through which to think about the *how* of racial reworking, a way of thinking that both allows room for definite aims in the resignification of racial performatives and the potential for calculable effects of social change.

My sense is that critical practices of racial resignifications are initiated from within the terms of Foucault's normalization, those networks of power/knowledge within which the self *emerges* and is recognized as developmental—always placed and seen as developing in relation to a norm. This self, as Ladelle McWhorter (2004, 155) has noted, is always already then "'essentially' a phenomenon of becoming rather than being." Various technologies of race—law, science, community prescriptions—attempt to control the direction of this developmental energy, bringing the subject in line with standardized racial norms. However, as a developmental being, the self is never identical to itself; as a form not a substance, it is always changing. Moreover, the individual will always slip away from and exceed the confines of any identity category, precisely because these are always ultimately uninhabitable; the subject, rather, approximates the normalized category through a performative passing-into an image of identity. "If I can find ways to affirm and care for *that* self," McWhorter encourages, "that developmental self who, 'by nature' defies final categorization, I can resist the oppressive aspects of normalizing networks of power" (2004, 155). The imperative, then, is to foster development—but not in ways that narrow behavioral possibilities; to be aware of disciplinary practices—but to harness discipline to develop the self in new directions.

Another way to think of this ethical work of problematization is in terms of a self-distancing, or what might be understood as a disassembly of self.[26] To disassemble the self is to engage in the self-critique and self-overcoming that I have been exploring, in order to question the 'obviousness' of embodied identity: it is to challenge the norms that maintain us and that we maintain ourselves within. But the 'aim' of disassembly is not to disinvest, to relinquish or abandon identity. As seen through the preceding analysis of 'signifying,' the practice of disassembly is not enough—nor is it an end in itself. Rather, disassembly must be coupled with reassembly: it is the reinvestment in and reconstruction of the self in new and non-normative ways. More than this, though, to disassemble would be to *shift the terms of investment* from the supposed *substance* of identity (understood in the Foucauldian sense as essential nature or abstract ideal) to *practice,* those protean ways of 'doing' race. This might mean refusing to consolidate the black/white binary and race itself as self-evident and necessary, and to instead claim and live the racial self as a conscious process: as unfixed, non-authentic, or as a project. The claiming of shared histories of oppression and pain, similar experiences or affirmative enunciations of racial selves are not, then, foreclosed.[27] However, in Foucauldian terms, ethical ways of 'doing' race must cultivate an open future of becoming a-new and they must militate against the danger of reifying these practices of race into a perceived substance. This might then entail a continual process of disassembly and reassembly of self. To stipulate a direction or to aim for one single modality of embodied subjectivity (an arrival point) would be to pursue substance: a static identity or fixed reality. In terms of performative passing, it would be to attempt to *arrive* at a 'self.' Rather than placing parameters on what we could potentially become, the stylization or what could be thought of as the *poesis* of racial subjectivity would ideally be open to a continual self-cultivating process. Race might then be seen not as an enclosed limit but as a site of creativity, of continual reassessment, formation, expansion, and *possibility.* Through such work, it might be possible to think of 'black' and 'white,' then, not as categories or fixed identities, but as names for particular positions that can be sites of creative formation.[28] Where schematizations and technologies of race require that the subject recognize, abide by, and thus affirm the supposed finality of racial categorization as truth, this rejection of a normalized racial self would necessarily rework race.

The potential to engender such change is not, however, to suggest the re-instatement of the voluntarist subject of liberalism that Foucault and Butler adamantly disavow. Two primary considerations preclude this. First, Foucault argues that power and freedom are inextricable. Moreover, in Foucault's formulation, freedom is never attained, rather it must be continually practiced—we must perpetually labor for the capacity to increase our behavioral options in the rearticulation of subjectivity. This cannot be 'won.' Second, as I've insisted, the subject is not able to freely fashion or liberate themselves and gain unencumbered freedom. Critique, instead, will be a labor of self upon the self, a seeking to extend beyond the historical limits that call this self into being, all the while working *within* these same constraints. Thus, in practicing problematization, race cannot be directly opposed because these terms cannot be escaped. I could not, for instance, decide to renounce my race, to simply refuse to maintain loyalty to the racial terms through which I operate within the world. For not only is my racial identity formed relationally—always performatively reasserted in my intersubjective encounters—but a reality cannot be imagined outside of this demarcation. And to return to where the present discussion began, in resignifying race there can be no absolute predictable outcomes. As Butler (1993, 241) states, "the reach of [the] signifiability [of performatives] cannot be controlled by the one who utters or writes, since such productions are not owned by the one who utters them. They continue to signify in spite of their authors, and sometimes against their authors' most precious intentions."[29] In light of the above analysis on signifying, this impossibility of 'control' might be witnessed when an act of signifying is read literally, rather than figuratively, and the inference is lost through (mis)interpretation. Resignifications of any racialized identity are always open to 'failure,' whether it be through the (mis)reading, recuperation, or expropriation of the sign.

How will it be possible, then, to know which critical alterations might work or count? And "[h]ow can the growth of capabilities," that is, innovative racial significations, "be disconnected from the intensification of power relations [that result in punishment]?" (Foucault 2007b, 116). There will be no clear answers. However, these ambivalent implications do not mean that there is no form available or no need for planned political action. But what becomes particularly important in attempting to *gauge* the effect of our actions—what practices or tactics should be employed and how the signs we seek to generate might be read—is *context*. Reflecting on the genealogies of our identities—how specific racial subjectivities have been formed—and on past practices of resistance will aid in pointing out certain actions that could prove favorable or successful. While we cannot *determine* the efficacy of these practices, we can judge to some degree which practices will be more efficacious in particular contexts.

Only a commitment to rejecting social injustice will guide against nominalism or purely self-interested resignifications of race. For Foucault, these injustices are any crystallization or freezing of power relations "to the profit of some and the detriment of others" (quoted in O'Farrell 2005, 116). In questioning one's relation to power/knowledge networks such injustices might be mitigated but, importantly, this would also require that individuals tease out their own investments in racial identifications and the affirmations of truth and authenticity that these generally demand. Only then is there an openness to new connections, intimacies, and critical embodied encounters.

But considering what racial resignification—through problematization or disassembly—might mean and entail for black and for white subjects requires that a necessary distinction be made. A white subject critiquing their relations to the norms of whiteness cannot be compared to the critique of black racial positioning that is exercised by black subjects. Black practices of racial resignification are ones that seek redress—and pursue pleasure—through reinvesting or counter-investing the body and the performative enunciations of blackness in ways that challenge the violence that has been staged through hegemonic racial logic. The white body has been the beneficiary of these discursive formulations of knowledge and is in no need of redress. Thus the white subject, privileged through and by their bodies, has discursive power that enables a form of pleasure—in the body, in social practice—that has historically been denied to black subjects. As a consequence, there is little incentive for white subjects to challenge racial power; their power (in discursive practice, in visual economies and so forth) is reestablished in almost every performative enactment. But challenging racial power and normalizing regimes is an ethical imperative if the white body/self is to become *other* than what it is. If white pleasure—in mobility, advantage, access, a sense of embodied freedom—has been enabled through the denigration of racial others, it would seem that how pleasure is understood is precisely the problem. What might be entailed for the rearticulation of whiteness, then, would be a reworking or reconfiguring of *what constitutes*, what is meant by *pleasure*. Could pleasure instead be defined as that which is enabled by the ethico-political work of pursuing the expansion of possibilities for self and others? This ethical practice—the struggle against subjection that is based on relations of domination—would take place through prodding, extending, resignifying, ultimately through 'doing' the performance(s) of whiteness differently. And only then—when these kinds of efforts take place *alongside* the transformative racial praxis waged by black subjects—can a critical revision of the disciplinary authority of race be realized.

Such refusals of fixity or practices of racial problematization will necessarily mean that subjects risk themselves, their very sense of self and how they operate in the world. For this work would involve realizing and responding ethically to the fact that our racial selves are not natural but socially formed, that the denigration of certain racialized bodies is only ever *culturally* maintained through social practices, and that complex investments in racial identity are the product of contingent histories. This is not, however, to suggest that race can be done away with, as if reworking racial disciplines and performative injunctions would lead to redefining race *beyond* categorization. This is not to advocate color-blindness. Nor is it to say that racial reworking(s) would be an esoteric endeavor. Rather, my analysis here has charted the disciplinary and performative aspects of race in order to call the subject of race into question, to elucidate the intricacies and inescapable conditions of racial subject constitution, but also to point to possibilities for destabilization within the very terms of categorization. The question here is one of how subjects might reflexively and critically approach the production of themselves and others as raced—within existing realities—and how such productions might be inventively enacted in the day-to-day so as to invite a minimum of domination. Interrogating the discourses, knowledges, and power relations that form us as racial subjects might challenge the injustices engendered in the name of race. But efforts of racial resignification —where race is recited in new directions—will necessitate diligence and persistence, ultimately demanding that we "work on our limits, that is, a patient labor [of] giving form to our liberty" (Foucault 2007b, 119). The responsibility to engage in such ethico-political work will be ongoing, as new systems of discipline emerge. Race continues to be rehearsed in ways that bind. However, precisely because race must be reenacted in order to survive, "we are always in the position of beginning again" (Foucault 2000d, 317).

NOTES

INTRODUCTION

1. *Rhinelander v. Rhinelander,* 219 N.Y.S. 548 (N.Y App. Div. 1927). A copy of the trial transcript can be found at the Association of the Bar of the City of New York. The almost two-week long trial was held in New York's highest court, the Court of Appeals. All references to the trial transcripts are hereafter supplied in the contracted form *CR* (Court Record).

2. In 1927, a survey of state laws banning interracial marriages showed a complex range of definitions for 'Negro' and found that marriages were prohibited between:

> white persons and persons of African descent (Georgia, Oklahoma, Texas), or between white persons and persons of negro blood to the third generation (Alabama, Maryland, North Carolina, Tennessee), or between white persons and persons of more than one-fourth (Oregon, West Virginia), or one-eighth (Florida, Indiana, Mississippi, Nebraska, North Dakota), or one-sixteenth (Virginia) negro-blood; other statutes in more general terms prohibit marriages between white persons and Negroes or mulattoes (Arkansas, Colorado, Delaware, Idaho, Kentucky, Louisiana, Missouri, Montana, Nevada, South Carolina, South Dakota, Utah, Wyoming). (Cited in Smith-Pryor 2009, 95)

Prohibitions against interracial marriages were only deemed unconstitutional in 1967 in the case of *Loving v. Virginia.* 388 U.S. 1 (1967).

3. "Lays Son's Plight to Rhinelander SR."

4. Bernauer and Mahon (1994, 148) have argued that Foucault waged a "campaign [against] the psychoanalytic vision of the person." And indeed, in much of his work, Foucault subjects psychoanalysis (taken generally as an *assemblage* of many heterogeneous elements) to a rigorous critique (see, for instance, 1965; 1970; 1973; 1989; 1998). He argues that it has functioned as yet another normative discipline (on analyses of this argument, see Whitebook 1999 and Deleuze 1988). Jana Sawicki (1991, 54–55) notes: "From a Foucauldian perspective, no discourse is inherently liberating or oppressive. This includes psychoanalytic discourses." I do not presume to homogenize psychoanalytic approaches, but follow Sawicki's interpretation of Foucauldian thought. She states: "[W]e can only conclude that for Foucault, the status of psychoanalytic theory is ambiguous, a matter that must be judged by looking at specific instances, and not by

setting up general criteria." This is a detailed investigation, requiring a specific and nuanced analysis that cannot be encompassed within this study.

5. Two excellent cultural histories of *Rhinelander* are Smith-Pryor's *Property Rites: The Rhinelander Trial, Passing, and the Protection of Whiteness* (2009) and Lewis and Ardizzone's *Love on Trial: An American Scandal in Black and White* (2001).

6. See, for instance, George Lipsitz (1998), Michael Omi and Howard Winant (1986), Cheryl Harris (1993), Richard Dyer (1997), and Sander Gilman (1985).

7. I use *black* in the capacity that it has been rendered a conceptually oppositional term to *white,* and to denote subjects of African descent. When referring specifically to the American black community, I utilize the terms *black* and *African American* interchangeably.

8. Importantly, that all non-blacks exist as masters is, for Wilderson (2009, 10), with the exception of Indians who, he argues, came into being only (and paradoxically) through genocide.

9. Here I am thinking most broadly of Orlando Patterson's *Slavery and Social Death: A Comparative Study* (1982), Giorgio Agamben's *Homo Sacer: Sovereign Power and Bare Life* (1998), and Achille Mbembe's "Necropolitics" (2003), and the uptake of these scholars' work in, for instance, Stuart Murray's "Thanatopolitics: On the Use of Death for Mobilizing Political Life" (2006) and "Thanatopolitics: Reading in Agamben a Rejoinder to Biopolitical Life" (2008), and Russ Castronovo's *Necro Citizenship: Death, Eroticism, and the Public Sphere in the Nineteenth Century United States* (2001).

10. On race and biopolitics, see David Macey's "Rethinking Biopolitics, Race, and Power in the Wake of Foucault" (2009). According to Foucault, "in the biopower system . . . killing or the imperative to kill is acceptable only if it results not in a victory over political adversaries, but in the elimination of a biological threat to and the improvement of the species or race." He is quick to add: "When I say 'killing,' I obviously do not mean simply murder as such, but every other form of indirect murder: the fact of exposing someone to death, increasing the risk of death for some people, or, quite simply, political death, expulsion, rejection and so on" (2003b, 256).

11. But even in making these claims, Hartman (1997, 72) continues to focus on slavery as social death: "the quotidian articulates the wounds of history and the enormity of the breach instituted by the transatlantic crossing of black captives and the consequent processes of enslavement: violent domination, dishonor, natal alienation, and chattel status." I am making several claims here. First, power is incoherent and subjects rework hegemonic terms of identity within relations of domination. Second, these reworkings can and do exceed the constraints of domination. But third, it is the very system of constraint that both produces forms of subjectivity *and* the politics that wrestle against dominant terms of subjectivity.

12. Hartman (1997, 54–55) importantly adds the following:

> Although it has become commonplace in Foucauldian approaches to power relations to conceptualize agency as an enabling constraint or an enabling violation, the problem with this approach is that it assumes that all forms of power are normatively equivalent, without distinguishing between violence, domination, force, legitimation, hegemony, et cetera. Slavery is characterized by direct and simple forms of domination, the brutal asymmetry of power, the regular exercise of violence, and the denial of liberty.

But slavery was not solely marked by the exercise of sovereign power. Instead, Hartman (1997, 228 n. 20) goes on to argue that this was a form of *sovereign biopolitics:* "The modality of power that was operative on the enslaved combined features of modern and premodern power. It was a combination of the 'menace to life' that characterizes sovereign power as well as the management of life in the case of the enslaved population." My argument here is that both within the antebellum period and beyond, sovereign, disciplinary, and biopolitical forms of power are *all* operative. They simply work on different registers. In this study, I am principally concerned with disciplinary power.

13. It is important to note that within the context of Hartman's study (1997), the slave is not constructed as a subject.

14. Historian Vincent Brown, in his "Social Death and Political Life in the Study of Slavery" (2009), has examined a number of scholars who seemingly take up such a viewpoint, in that they broadly position blackness as a totalizing state that, historically and in the present, renders slavery synonymous with social death and blackness as always already synonymous with slavery. Brown focuses specifically on the academic uptake and what he sees as the problematic distillation and extension of Orlando Patterson's (1982) concept of "slavery as social death," where social death indicates a lack of social being. As a scholar of slavery, Brown is most concerned with examining the limitations of this idea in relation to the enslaved, but he is also interested in how the idea is used in relation to the present. For Brown, Patterson's "slavery as social death," and contemporary usages of this concept to account for the present, advance a troubling transhistorical characterization of slavery. He argues in line with Herman Bennett (quoted in Brown 2009, 1233), who has observed:

> As the narrative of the slave experience, social death assumes a uniform African, slave, and ultimately black subject rooted in a static New World history whose logic originated in being property and remains confined to slavery. It absorbs and renders exceptional evidence that underscores the contingent nature of experience and consciousness. Thus, normative assumptions about the experiences of peoples of African descent assert a timeless, ahistorical, epiphenomenal "black" cultural experience.

15. On scholarship that uses Foucault's later work to think about refashioning sexual subjectivity, see, for instance, Heyes 2007; Taylor and Vintges 2004; McWhorter 2009, 1999; and Butler 2004b.

1. RACIAL DISCIPLINARITY

1. 39 Ga. Rep. 321, 324 (1869).

2. 71 Va. (30 Gratt.) 858, 869 (1878).

3. *Scott v. Georgia* 39 Ga. Rep. 321, 324 (1869).

4. See Zuberi (2001). Also see Gossett (1964, 47), who quotes Dr. Charles White's claim in 1799: "From man down to the smallest reptile . . . Nature exhibits to our view an immense chain of beings, endued with various degrees of intelligence and active powers suited to their stations in the general system."

5. I refer generally to her earlier major works: *Bodies That Matter: On the Discursive Limits of Sex* (1993); *The Psychic Life of Power: Theories in Subjection* (1997b); and *Gender Trouble: Feminism and the Subversion of Identity* (1999). I specifically do not want to

suggest that race and sex operate in the same capacity in the formation of the subject. Rather, I simply want to sketch which ideas might be helpful from Butler's analysis of sexed and gendered formation for the purposes of analyzing race. I go into the interrelation of gendered, sexual, and racial performativity in chapter 3. Ann Laura Stoler (1995) provides one of the most notable and rigorous studies of how race and sexuality worked together as disciplinary regimes. Also see Ladelle McWhorter (1999), who offers a nuanced reading of how Foucault's account of sexuality can be redirected, in a more general sense, in order to think about race.

6. In *Society Must Be Defended: Lectures at the Collège de France, 1975–1976*, Foucault (2003b, 242) makes a distinction between two inter-articulated forms of power. *Disciplinary* power, or anatomo-politics, he explains, included a range of "techniques of power that were essentially centered on the body, on the individual body." In distinction (but also intersecting with disciplinary power) was the rise of a new technology of power toward the end of the eighteenth century, biopolitics, which was *regulatory* and "applied not to man-as-body but to the living man, to man-as-living-being . . . man-as-species." In chapter 2, I explore these forms of power in relation to the intersection of race and law.

7. Race, gender, and class, among many other identificatory markers, create a site of ambivalence (or a complex and incoherent matrix) that *is* the subject. The subject is necessarily the composite of multiple discursive forces and is, then, the *inter-articulation* of these forces. Thus, a subject cannot be formed as raced and live this racial subjectivity in a way that is not conditioned by their gendered assignment. At the same time, gendered subjectivity cannot be generated or realized separately from racial subjectivity—among other markers of identity—that operate together to construct the subject. I propose to focus this analysis on race simply in order to facilitate thinking about a generalized account of the construction of race and for analytic convenience, not as a suggestion that race can be thought about as a singular force in determining understandings of subjectivity.

8. For a particularly concise examination of the notion and functioning of discourse, see Stuart Hall (1996b, 201–202).

9. Foucault addresses the concept of the norm and normalization in his published works, *Discipline and Punish* and volume 1 of *The History of Sexuality*, and in his Collège de France courses: *Psychiatric Power* (1974/2006); *Abnormal* (1975/2003a); *Society Must Be Defended* (1976/2003b); and *Security, Territory, Population* (1978/2007a). Under disciplinary power, "The norm's function is not to exclude and reject. Rather, it is always linked to a positive technique of intervention and transformation, to a sort of normative project" (Foucault 2003a, 50). There is, Foucault writes, "an originally prescriptive character of the norm," in that the norm determines what is viewed as normal. Subjects form themselves in relation to and are produced by techniques of power that take the norm as the ideal. In *Security, Territory, Population*, Foucault distinguishes between this idea of the norm as it works in disciplinary power, and the norm as it operates biopolitically. Here Taylor (2009, 50) tells us, "the norm is established from several 'normals,' as represented specifically by 'curves of normality'; statistical analysis . . . constitutes a key technique for regulating and managing populations. From these normals, the 'most normal' or the 'optimal normal'—i.e., the norm—for a particular population is established." A norm is normalizing under disciplinary power in that subjects are

formed and form themselves in relation to it. On the specifics of the norm in relation to biopolitics, see Taylor (2009).

10. Needless to say, within a system of 'normal' and peripheral bodies and subjectivities it is the white subject that is discursively constructed as the norm while black subjects are cast as aberrant. What I point out here, however, is that although figured as deviant to normalized hegemonic whiteness, blackness itself is still discursively normalized as the binary term upon which whiteness relies in order to exist. As such, in relation to normalized blackness, those that exist at the margins of blackness—those that phenotypically appear and genotypically exist as liminal—become more highly marked and more rigorously regulated (that is, they are more vigilantly scrutinized) than readily identifiable black subjects.

11. I explore this idea further in subsequent chapters. An example of the constraint to which I refer can be seen in the legal contribution to broader discursive demarcations of race. In imposing statutory definitions of race, for instance, law augments discursive decrees that mandate the existence of only certain racial positions that can be occupied. Consequently, the historically specific decree that stipulated that a subject supposedly possessing 'one-half black blood' was a mulatto, saw law contributing to the interpellation of this individual *as* a mulatto subject. Moreover, in formulating the civil liberties (such as the right to own property, to testify in court, etc.) to which mulattoes have historically been entitled, law has contributed to this subject's manner of being-in-the-world. This can be seen, for example, in a law enacted in Pennsylvania (1725–1726) that generated the ultimate constraint on subjectivity by issuing a decree condemning mulatto children born of white women to thirty-one years of servitude. See Joel Williamson (1995, 11).

12. In the same way that the identification 'girl' does not exist as a founding moment, the imposition of a racial term cannot be said to operate as a purely juridical command and unilateral enracing of a subject. As Foucault argues throughout his work, it is, instead, the intricate workings of discourse that operate to form the subject—both through external and self-disciplinary mechanisms. For further discussion, see Judith Butler (1997b, 5–6).

13. Note that I use the term *Negro* only when I reproduce quotations or cite historical documents in which the term has been used, or when I respond to the use of this term in the aforementioned cases.

14. In chapter 6, I complicate this framing of racial interpellation and this reading of Fanon.

15. See Butler (1993, 97) who, in regards to gendered constitution, claims " 'sex' is that which marks the body prior to its mark, staging in advance which symbolic position will mark it, and it is this later 'mark' which appears to postdate the body, retroactively attributing a sexual position to a body."

16. The first legislative decree that established this particular definition of black racial subject status was the statute entitled "An Act declaring what persons shall be deemed mulattoes" (chap. LXXVIII, 12 Laws of Va. 184, 184 [Hening 1823] [enacted 1785; effective 1787]). While this definition was altered in 1848 so as to render an individual with one black great-grandparent as black, the statutory definition as of 1785 was reestablished in 1865 (Act of Feb 27, 1866, chap. 17, sec. 1, 1865–1866 Va. Acts 84). For further information, see Lombardo (1988, 444).

17. In chapter 2, I look at one component of this diffuse technology—the legal system—and consider how racial knowledge has been formulated within law, how these knowledges invest bodies, and how they come to define subjects as raced.

18. For a detailed examination of the role of skin (color) in racial practice, see Claudia Benthien (2002). She states: "the white skin is understood as a kind of color-neutral canvas or blank sheet, a tabula rasa, and the dark skin as its colored or written-on counterpart. 'Colored' as opposed to light skin is thus interpreted as a marked epidermis; it becomes a skin that departs from the neutral norm" (2002, 148).

19. See Neil Gotanda (1991).

20. This view was particularly prevalent among Social Darwinists and eugenicists of the late nineteenth and early twentieth centuries. The eugenicist Charles Davenport (1913, 148), for instance, argued against any form of 'interracial mixing' due to the fact that a "hybridized people are a badly put together people and a dissatisfied, restless, ineffective people."

2. RACIAL KNOWLEDGES

1. W. E. B. DuBois notes that during this era, "[t]he word 'Negro' was used for the first time in the world's history to tie color to race and blackness to slavery and degradation" (quoted in Harris 1993, n. 3).

2. Act XII, 2 Laws of Va. 170 (Hening 1823) (enacted 1662). Hening, *Statutes at Large . . . of Virginia*, vol. II, 170.

3. Act XII, 2 Laws of Va. 283 (Hening 1823) (enacted 1670). The purpose of this act was to establish whether Indians, bought as captives of war from other Indians, could be held as slaves. The act decreed that they could not. Instead, if caught as children, Indians would be in service until the age of thirty and, if caught as adults, would be required to provide service for twelve years.

4. U.S. Const. art. I. § 2, cl. 3.

5. For instance, in *State v. Mann* (13 N.C. 263 [Dec. 1, 1829]), Judge Thomas Ruffin sanctioned the complete control of the slave master. In this case a slave named Lydia had run away from her master (the man who had hired her from her actual master/owner for a term of one year), John Mann. Mann shot her in her back as she fled. This action was endorsed by Ruffin who held that "the power of the master must be absolute, to render the submission of the slave perfect" (at 266).

6. On the discrete sexual categories that were produced in terms of race, see also Aliyyah I. Abdur-Rahman (2006).

7. The male and female were together taken as verification that blacks represented a separate species who occupied an intermediary position between Europeans and the highest order of apes, the orangutan (Wiegman 1995, 57). Winthrop Jordan (1968, 227) cites John Ovington's account of the Hottentot in his *Voyage to Suratt in the Year 1689*. Ovington states: "of all the People they are the most Bestial and sordid . . . [they are] the very Reverse of Human kind . . . so that if there's any medium between a Rational Animal and a Beast, the *Hotantot* lays the Claim to that Species." Jordan identifies the origins of black masculinity as symbolized within and through the specter of a mythologized excessive penis to the similarly timed European 'discovery' of both Africa and the baboon. Jordan (1968, 29) explains that this "tragic happenstance" created a link in the European mind between the African "and the animal which in appearance most resem-

ble[d] man." This baboon's "genital member was [seen to be] greater than might match the quantity of his other parts" (Topsell [1607], quoted in Jordan 1968, 29) and this viewpoint came to mark the manner through which black masculinity was to be conceptualized in the following centuries.

8. Fanon (1967, 165) states that "the Negro is fixated at the genital." Remarking on the prevalence of this idea, he cites a 1948 account written by Michel Cournot who states:

> The black man's sword is a sword. When he has thrust it into your wife, she has really felt something. It is a revelation. In the chasm that it has left, your little toy is lost. Pump away until the room is awash with your sweat, you might as well be singing. This is *good-by* (*sic*) . . . Four Negroes with their penises exposed would fill a cathedral. They would be unable to leave the building until their erections had subsided; and in such close quarters that would not be a simple matter. (quoted in Fanon, 1967, 169)

9. The fundamental aim of anti-miscegenation law and discourse was the protection of whiteness. Many of the early statutes focused on preserving whiteness by attempting to prevent sexual relations between white women and black men. While this rhetoric might have been framed through the language of 'protecting' white female virtue, a tacit fear existed that white women might be seduced by the alleged potency of the black male. White females who did willingly engage in sexual relations with black men were often perceived to possess "lascivious and lustful desires" (Maryland statute of 1681 cited in Getman 1984, 117) that were usually associated with blacks.

10. See Golder and Fitzpatrick (2009), chap. 2.

11. I want to stress that law contributes in various capacities (not simply the ones analyzed in this study) to the fabrication of racial identities, by way of initiating and enforcing authorized behaviors. As Ian F. Haney López (1996, 121) argues, "naturalization laws governed who was and was not welcome to join the polity, antimiscegenation laws regulated sexual relations, and segregation laws told people where they could and could not live and work." Together, these laws fashioned race—what racial subjects look like, the meanings that are attached to these looks, and the material conditions/realities that supposedly 'affirm' these meanings (Haney López 1996, 113).

12. The notion of race as performative is central to later chapters.

13. I utilize the qualifier 'came to' because, although anti-miscegenation laws were in place within the earliest period of the colonies, it was only after emancipation—in the period of Reconstruction and through to the twentieth century—indeed, until laws prohibiting miscegenation were finally deemed unconstitutional in *Loving v. Virginia* (388 U.S. 1 [1967])—that these laws were employed as devices to maintain prewar racial divisions. Once slavery had been abolished, anti-miscegenation laws escalated. This can be seen as a reflection of the need to reassert white dominance in the absence of the previous division between black and white subjects that had been ensured through the system of slavery. See Peggy Pascoe (1996) and Eva Saks (2000). This notion will be explored in further detail below. For a comprehensive overview of the history of anti-miscegenation law, see Pascoe's *What Comes Naturally: Miscegenation Law and the Making of Race in America* (2009).

14. Other means, such as interrogations of a subject's reputation, witnesses' accounts, scientific 'evidence,' and the assessment of (racial) performance were employed in order

to ascertain 'racial truth' if it was not evident in appearance. However, each of these methods was, ultimately, the endeavor to ascertain the 'truth' of blood, that is, the locale of race that could not be 'washed out.' I discuss these ideas in later chapters.

15. See Sidney Kaplan (2000).

16. 1 Laws of Va. 146 (Hening 1823). For further discussion, see Karen A. Getman (1984).

17. Godbeer (2002) has speculated that the 'negro' in question was a man and, hence, Hugh was punished for sodomy. Higginbotham has read the case as centering on questions of bestiality (cited in Mumford 1999, 280).

18. See Godbeer (2002, 202) and Mumford (1999, 280).

19. Act XII, 2 Laws of Va. 170, 170 (Hening 1823) (enacted 1662). This provision lasted until 1696 when a new statute repealed the 1662 act.

20. See Act II, 1 Laws of Va. 433, 433 (Hening 1823) (enacted 1657–1658) (which prohibited fornication and adultery), and Act C, 2 Laws of Va. 114, 114–115 (Hening 1823) (enacted 1661–1662) (which prohibited fornication).

21. See Act XII, 2 Laws of Va. 170 (Hening 1823) (enacted 1662). This statute stated:

> *Whereas* some doubts have arisen whether children got by any Englishman upon a Negro woman should be slave or free, *be it therefore enacted and declared by this present Grand Assembly,* that all children born in this country shall be held bond or free only according to the condition of the mother; and that if any Christian shall commit fornication with a Negro man or woman, he or she so offending shall pay double the fines imposed by the former act.

This provision lasted until 1696 when a new statute repealed the 1662 act. This act, thereby, began a confusing legal device of discipline that set apart mulatto children born of free white, free black, and enslaved black mothers. Socially, however, these children were generally homogenized under the classification black.

22. This act, as cited in David H. Fowler (1987, 41), read in part as follows:

> All Negroes or other slaues already within the Prouince And all Negroes and other slaues to bee hereafter imported into the Prouince shall serue Durante Vita And all Children born of any Negro or other slaue shall be Slaues as their ffathers were for the terme of their liues And forasmuch as divers freeborne English women forgetfull of their free Condicion and To the disgrace of our Nation doe intermarry with Negro Slaues by which alsoe diuers suites may arise touching the Issue of such women and a great damage doth befall the Masters of such Negros for preuention whereof for deterring such freeborne women from such shamefull Matches . . . whatsoeuer free borne woman shall inter marry with any slaue . . . shall Serue the master of such slaue dureing the life of her husband And that all the Issues of such freeborne woemen soe marryed shall be Slaues as their father were And . . . all the Issue of English or other freeborne women that haue already marryed Negroes shall serve the Masters of their Parents till they be Thirty yeares of age and noe longer.

23. Act XVI, 3 Laws of Va. 86 (Hening 1823) (enacted 1691).

24. Chap. IV, 3 Laws of Va. 250, 251 (Hening 1823) (enacted 1705). This act also stipulated that the child of a white individual and an Indian was also to be recognized as a mulatto and was, as such, beyond the periphery of whiteness. This act was reenacted in

1753 and 1848 and was established in order to define individuals only for the purposes of holding public office.

25. See Winthrop D. Jordan (1962, 185).

26. The protection of whiteness can be witnessed through the confusing array of demarcations of race. I cite several examples here in order to illuminate this complexity. In 1785, Virginia changed the legal definition of 'mulatto' to an individual with "one-fourth part or more of negro blood" (chap. LXXVIII, 12 Laws of Va. 184, 184 [Hening 1823] [enacted 1785; effective 1787]). While this ruling saw the legislature becoming more lenient in its definition of the category 'black' (remember that mulattoes and Negroes were for all intents and purposes considered as one legal category, that is, black/Negro), all other statutory definitions were stricter (with the exception of an act passed in 1866 [Act of Feb. 27, 1866, chap. 17, sec. 1, 1865–1866 Va. Acts 84] which again enforced that one-fourth black blood made one black). As indicated above (see *supra*, n. 24), the definition of blackness was changed back again to one-eighth in 1848. In 1910 the Virginia legislature deemed an individual with one-sixth 'black blood' as black (Act of March 17, 1910, chap. 357, 1910 Va. Acts 581) and in 1924 embraced the rule that had been in social operation for some time. In this year Virginia passed "An Act to Preserve Racial Integrity" (Act of March 20, 1924, chap. 371, 1924 Va. Acts 534) that stipulated that *any* ascertainable black blood made one black. This definition was further enforced in 1930 (chap. 85, 1930 Va. Acts 96–97). The move toward the acceptance of the 'one-drop' rule of racial classification for blackness will be discussed in more detail below.

27. During this early period of slavery there had not been sufficient interracial mixing for the physical traits of blackness to be "washed-out," so to speak.

28. 11 Va. (1 Hen. and M.) 71, 74 (1806) (J. Roane concurring) (emphasis omitted) (cited in Higginbotham and Kopytoff 1989, 1975). This case was brought before the court by three generations of women within one family who sued for their freedom on the basis that they claimed they were white with an Indian ancestor. Perhaps of primary significance in this case was the decision that decreed who bore the burden of proof in freedom claims. The Virginian Supreme Court of Appeals held here that it was the appearance of the racial subject before the court that was to determine who bore this burden. Those that were visibly black were presumed to be slaves, and it was their burden to prove otherwise. If an individual was visibly white, however, the presumption of freedom was made and it was the responsibility of this individual's adversary to prove otherwise. The intricacies of this case are beyond the scope of the present analysis but are discussed in more detail in Winthrop D. Jordan (1968, 555–560), A. Leon Higginbotham and Barbara K. Kopytoff (1989, 1984–1988), and Ian F. Haney López (1994).

29. For a rigorous analysis of the disciplinary role of vision and the visible realm, see Robyn Wiegman (1995).

30. 11 Va. (Hen. and M.) 134, at 139.

31. One of the best-known studies of the history of the racial sciences is Stephen Gould's classic, *The Mismeasure of Man* (1996). For a recent comprehensive study of this history, see *The Nature of Difference: Sciences of Race in the United States from Jefferson to Genomics,* edited by Evelynn M. Hammonds and Rebecca M. Herzig (2009).

32. Due to the threats against slavery, blood-lines came under stricter surveillance in the Southern states so as to maintain divisions between black and white subjects (and, thus, clearly demarcate slave and free).

33. By these new forms of oppression, I refer to the black codes, and the later legally

endorsed methods of segregation (also known as Jim Crow). Racial segregation, whether implicit or explicit, existed in the North and the South alike.

34. It is important to stress that blacks also demonstrated pronounced antagonism toward miscegenation following the Civil War. In the postbellum period, black women could more forcefully resist white male advances and black men could legally marry and provide for their wives and families. One can presume that for the black community, white/black unions (especially between white men and black women) recalled the pattern of sexual exploitation that was prevalent during the pre-war years. See Joel Williamson (1995, 90–91).

35. See Michael Grossberg (1982, 203).

36. The Civil Rights Act of 1866 (chap. 31, 14, U.S. Stat. 27) had entitled blacks to the right to citizenship. The Fourteenth Amendment further declared that "[a]ll persons born or naturalized in the United States, and subject to the jurisdiction thereof, are citizens of the United States and of the state wherein they reside" (U.S. Const. Amend. XIV—this amendment went into effect on July 9, 1868). The aim of this amendment was to give former slaves full civil rights. Continuing anti-miscegenation laws compromised this intent. Peggy Pascoe (1996, 50 n. 16) provides a list of decisions that upheld and those that struck down the constitutionality of these laws. For further discussion pertaining to the complications (especially in regards to notions of citizenship) that have arisen from the interpretations and implementation of the Fourteenth Amendment, and challenges to its legal interpretations, see Ian F. Haney López (1996).

37. *Bowlin v. Commonwealth*, 2 Bush. 5, 8–9.

38. *Frasher v. State*, 3 Tex. Court of Appeals 263, 276.

39. This was articulated most forcefully in the federal case of *Pace v. Alabama* (106 U.S. 583 [U.S. Supreme Court, 1883]), where the court rejected the argument that barring interracial marriage was unconstitutional and upheld the state law.

40. See David H. Fowler (1987), who chronicles each law pertaining to interracial sex that was passed in each colony and state until 1930. These laws were finally deemed unconstitutional in 1967 (see *supra* n. 13).

41. *Laws*, 1865, chap. 4, sec. 3, 82 (Johnson, cited in Fowler 1987, 391).

42. This law also provided that the individual who performed the ceremony should be issued a fine of not more than $1000, and that the person issuing the marriage license should be fined between $50 and $1000 and receive a prison term of between three months and two years.

43. *Laws*, 1884, chap. 264 (Johnson, cited in Fowler 1987, 386).

44. For an overview of post-Reconstruction statutory definitions of blackness, which functioned as the bedrock upon which anti-miscegenation law rested, see Joel Williamson (1995, 97).

45. Bureau of the Census, U.S. Dept. of Commerce, Negro Population in the United States 1790–1915, at 207 (see Christine B. Hickman 1997, n. 106).

46. I focus on this idea in chapter 4.

47. 163 U.S. 537 (1896).

48. Ibid., at 538.

49. In delivering the opinion of the Court, Justice Brown declared that Homer Plessy "had been deprived of no property, since he is not lawfully entitled to the reputation of being a white man" (ibid., at 544). For a more detailed discussion of the property rights of whiteness that are involved in this case, see Cheryl Harris (1993, 1746–1750).

50. 'Judicial notice,' as listed in *Black's Law Dictionary* (Black, Nolan, and Nolan-Haley 1990, 848), refers to the "act by which a court . . . in framing its decision will . . . without production of evidence, recognize the existence and truth of certain facts . . . which are universally regarded as established by common notoriety."

51. F. James Davis (1998, 5) explains: "This definition reflects the long experience with slavery and later with Jim Crow segregation. In the South it became known as the 'one-drop rule,' meaning that a single drop of 'black blood' makes a person black . . . This definition emerged from the American South to become the nations definition, generally accepted by whites and blacks alike. Blacks had no other choice." By 1920 the notion of hypodescent was strongly embedded in the American psyche, having been recognized by both the federal courts and the U.S. Census Bureau (hypodescent was formally adopted in the 1920 census [see Hickman, 1997]). Within hypodescent, even 'one drop' of black blood is a strong enough pollutant to stain the individual as black. The language of blackness as contaminant is nowhere more clearly articulated than within this ideology.

52. Act of March 20, 1924, chap. 371, 1924 Va. Acts 534.

53. 260 U.S. 178 (1922).

54. For a detailed analysis of *Ozawa v. United States,* see Ian F. Haney López (1996, 79–109).

3. PASSING THROUGH RACIAL PERFORMATIVES

1. For a compelling analysis of the racializing mechanisms and implications of biometric technologies, see Joseph Pugliese (2010).

2. Wiegman (1995, 37) presents this notion in her broader analysis of the role of 'visual modernity' in the construction of the intersections of race and gender relations in the United States.

3. Techniques of power that are exercised cannot be localized. Rather, multiple institutions and apparatuses distribute the exercise of power, operating a complex, diffuse, yet pervasive microphysics of power. This notion requires that power be understood as: a strategy rather than a property; immanent within all relations and enacted through each subject; not simply repressive but productive; not univocal or imposed simply from above, but existing in intricate webs; exercised according to certain aims, but not by the choice or will of an individual subject; always coupled with resistance. See Michel Foucault (1998, 94–95).

4. In "The Ethics of the Concern of Care for the Self as a Practice of Freedom," Foucault (1988) stresses that all subjects are the objects of discourse. The dictates of discipline operate through normalizing discourses and techniques of power to render the subject obedient, compliant, docile or passive. I address the limits of discipline specifically in chapter 7.

5. For a more detailed exploration of the mechanics of panopticism, see C. G. Prado (1995).

6. The Middle Passage instituted a spatialization and disciplining of the black body/self and a regime of truth that worked to teach the black body/self that it was chattel: this body was examined and objectivized on the auction block and, through multiple means, made inferior. This knowledge was confirmed in regimes of discursivity, such as the sciences, that functioned as forms of normalizing biopolitics and

anatamo-politics. The objective of the racial sciences, it would seem, was to discipline black subjects to accept their constitution as abnormal and to confirm white norma-tivity. See Yancy (2004a) and, for a specific analysis of white normativity in the racial sciences, see Julian Carter (2007).

7. Thomas F. Slaughter (quoted in Yancy 2004a, 124) powerfully states:

> Between me and the surrounding world there exists a split of which by lopsided contract my body is the symbol. Blackness embodies the ostracized. Under the duress of domination, I undergo the now familiar two-pronged process of exter-nally imposed inferiorization and subsequent internalization of that inferiority. It is thus probable that in my routine state, I carry white hatred of me within me as my own property.

8. Joel Williamson relays that Charles W. Chesnutt was known to have inadvertently passed-for white. He states that "Chesnutt did not bother to deny his blackness, nor did he advertise it" (1995, 101).

9. See Gregory H. Williams (1995), who relays that at the age of ten he discovered that his father had been passing-for-white. He and his brother had, until this point, believed that they were white and had, as such, been passing without the knowledge that they were doing so.

10. Danzy Senna (1998) illustrates this form of passing in her novel *Caucasia*. When Birdie's mother and father separate, the light-skinned Birdie is taken by her white mother, while Birdie's darker-skinned sister, Cole, goes with their black father. Birdie and her mother decide that Birdie will pass herself off as a Jew. While the two seemingly 'concoct' this plan together, it is implicitly suggested that had Birdie remained with her father the pass would not have taken place. The 'choice' to pass was more or less a mat-ter of surviving at her mother's side. This was her mother's solution: Birdie says, "she explained . . . [that my] body was the key to our going incognito" (Senna 1998, 108–109).

11. I speak of passing here primarily in the past tense. It is, however, not simply a his-torical phenomenon, but continues in the contemporary context as an act through which to resist the imposition of particular racial designations.

12. This is particularly evident in works such as Jessie Redmon Fauset's *Plum Bun* (1990) and Nella Larsen's *Passing*. Hazel V. Carby (1987, 171) has noted that the female mulatto (either in the form of a passer or not) has been "most usefully regarded as a convention of Afro-American literature which enabled the exploration in fiction of rela-tions which were socially proscribed." According to Carby, this figure has embodied the tension between the black and white races.

13. See Henry Louis Gates Jr. (1987, 202), who makes note of this double meaning of passing—that is, to cross a color line and to "pass on" (in death).

14. Ralph Ellison also speaks of this impossibility of being viewed as an individual: "Like the bodiless heads you see sometimes in circus sideshows, it is as though I have been surrounded by mirrors of hard, distorting glass. When they approach me they see only my surroundings, themselves, or figments of their imagination—indeed, every-thing and anything except me" (1995, 3).

15. The notion that whiteness is unmarked is problematic because it assumes that whiteness is not structured through highly regulated acts. This idea is discussed in con-siderable detail in chapter 5.

16. See Derrick Bell (1998) and Cheryl Harris (1993) who discuss the formation of whiteness as property,

17. Both Deborah E. McDowell (1986) and Harryette Mullen (1994) discuss that passing has been figured in these terms. Gunnar Myrdal (quoted in Harris 1993, 1712 n. 5) explicitly frames passing in this way when he states:

> passing means that a Negro becomes a white man, that is, moves from the lower caste to the higher caste. In the American caste order, this can be accomplished only by the deception of the white people with whom the passer comes to associate and by the conspiracy of silence on the part of other Negroes who might know about it.

18. See Sara Ahmed (1999, 101) who, in discussing passing, states that it is a technique that "is exclusive and exclusionary—it is not available to all subjects—as it depends on the relation between subjects and structures of identification where the subject sees itself, or is seen by others, as not quite fitting." This notion of the passer as a subject who experiences a 'not quite fitting' will be explored in chapter 6.

19. The formation of racial subjectivity (more generally) and the formation of a passing identity are structurally dissimilar. This idea is the focus of chapter 5.

20. One of the most recent investigations to consider race as performative is Catherine Rottenberg's *Performing Americanness: Race, Class, and Gender in African-American and Jewish-American Literature* (2008). Rottenberg insists that gendered and racial performativity operate in distinct ways. I do not analyze the nuances of how these two modalities of performativity might work differently precisely because of the difficulty in disentangling their operations. Here I argue that I want to 'suspend' race momentarily, to think about how it can be viewed as performative. However, in practice, racial performativity always works within the modality of gendered performativity and vice versa. I also have serious misgivings about what seems to be one of Rottenberg's central claims on the differences of racial performativity from gendered performativity. She argues that in terms of gendered performativity, the way the subject identifies and what they desire *to-be* are generally conflated (i.e., one identifies as a woman and desires to-be a woman). However, in terms of racial performativity, Rottenberg claims the link between identification and the desire to-be is bifurcated; black racial subjects are compelled to identify as black but aspire to be white or are compelled to desire the attributes associated with whiteness (2008, 43). This framing seemingly ignores the complex operations of racial performativity, where the compulsion to enact race is not simply generated by the workings of white supremacy. For example, black communities also generate performative demands that condition the formation of black identity—such as what it means to be a black woman or man—ones that often reject and rework attributes associated with whiteness. These demands can be just as constraining as those produced within dominant (i.e., white) economies or epistemes of race. Her position also rules out the possibility of positive and enabling black racial performatives and positive investments in black racial identity.

21. The last two conventions cited, so Austin tells us, can be 'sinned against' and the performative would still 'work,' although it would be 'insincere' or an "abuse of the procedure" (Austin 1980, 16). In distinction, the first four rules must be met for the performative to operate efficaciously. Austin (1980, 10–16) discusses his specific ideas on intention in relation to performative speech acts.

22. For instance, to conduct a wedding ceremony in a theatrical performance is not to efficaciously affirm the action of becoming married. When actors, depicting the roles of a bride and groom, utter the statement "I do" on stage, they non-seriously imitate the

performative utterance. The act of marriage being acted on stage is not a 'real' act that is affirmed by subjects that are empowered or authorized to perform the action (whether they be the couple or the individual who oversees and pronounces marriage).

23. The parameters of the following analysis preclude me from presenting Derrida's argument in any degree of complexity. I employ his work here simply in order to demonstrate the lineage of the notion of citationality that Butler positions as foundational in her work on performativity.

24. I use the term 'liberal humanism' to mark the ruling assumptions, values, meanings, and principles regarding 'man,' as they have been formulated in the modern epoch. The common feature of liberal humanism, which I take to validate the use of the single phrase, is a commitment to the human or, more correctly 'man,' whose essence is understood as *autonomy*. Liberal humanism proposes that the subject is the free, unencumbered origin and author of meaning and action: he is unified, knowing, and self-directing.

25. Butler's work is indebted to psychoanalytic theory. In this analysis, however, I have focused on the Foucauldian component of her work.

26. In *The Psychic Life of Power: Theories in Subjection*, Butler stresses that it is insufficient to claim (in Althusserian terms) that the subject is purely a product of the linguistic realm. She argues that as "useful" as Althusser's view is, it "remains implicitly constrained by a notion of a centralized state apparatus, one whose word is deed, modeled on divine authority" (Butler 1997b, 6). To uncritically accept this view would, thus, elide the importance of Foucault's emphasis on the polyvalent exercise of power—a conceptualization that rejects a sovereign or juridical model of power (i.e., one that frames power as that which is only imposed from above). Accordingly, Butler argues that "[t]he notion of discourse emerges in Foucault in part to counter the sovereign model of interpellative speech in theories such as Althusser's, but also to take account of the *efficacy* of discourse apart from its instantiation as the spoken word" (Butler 1997b, 6).

27. In positing this argument Butler draws on, but reframes, the Althusserian notion of interpellation. See Butler (1993, 225; 1997b, 4–6).

28. Here Butler refers to Derrida's notion of *différance,* the play of differences and deferrals that are produced and enabled by the always arbitrary relation between signifier and signified. For Derrida, *différance* generates the 'playing of movement' that is immanent within signification. His primary thesis is that 'presence,' in positive terms, is a production of this play. The attempt, then, to recite or signify gendered norms will always be repeated with a difference. There will always be difference and deferral in the recitation because that which is signified has no prior existence outside of systems of signification. (See Derrida's essay, "Différance," in *Margins of Philosophy* [1982].) As Butler (1999, 186) argues: "The 'real' and the 'sexually factic' are phantasmatic constructions—illusions of substance—that bodies are compelled to approximate, but never can."

29. This is a specifically Foucauldian idea, one that I address in chapter 6.

30. These ideas will be the focus in chapter 6.

31. See, for example, Amy Robinson (1996); Ariela Gross (1998; 2001); Louis. F. Mirón and Jonathon Xavier Inda (2000); and Walter Johnson (2000). For other investigations of the notion of racial performativity, see Dorinne K. Kondo (1997); Lisa Lowe (1996); Vikki Bell (1999a); J. Martin Favor (1999); Catherine Rottenberg (2008); and Saidiya V. Hartman (1997).

32. See chapter 1, where I explain the circularity of this argument. An individual comes, as Butler (1993, 123) states, "to occupy an interpellation by which one is already occupied." The body is read (and as a consequence, discursively occupied) as already raced, and on this basis the subject is discursively called into being as raced.

33. As Butler (1993, 220) states, "regulatory power produces the subject it controls, [and] that power is not only imposed externally, but works as the regulatory and normative means by which subjects are formed."

34. These 'ideals' can be thought of as *images* of a particular identity site that the subject seeks to inhabit. For instance, in enacting femininity, I have a certain image of 'womanness' that I am laboring to embody. I signal the correlation between *ideal* and *image* at this point, as later in the analysis I utilize these terms interchangeably.

35. In regards to gender, Butler (1993, 232) argues: "the term ['female'], or rather, its symbolic power governs the formation of a corporeally enacted femininity." Thinking about this in terms of the classificatory schema of race, it is the imposition of the term 'black' or 'white' that conditions and calls-forth the imperative of a corporeally choreographed (and I do mean this in the sense of theatricality) and enunciated racial manner-of-being.

4. DOMESTICATING LIMINALITY

1. "Mrs. L. Kip Rhinelander in Social Register, Despite Race Assertions in Husband's Suit."

2. "What the Rhinelander Case Means to Negroes."

3. For instance, in remarking on the *Rhinelander* trial, a commentator for the *New York Amsterdam News* ("Rising Above Prejudice," 9 December 1925, Editorial page) wrote, "NEGROES, generally look with as much disfavor upon interracial marriage as white people—possibly more."

4. Reaching back to the 1830s, New York State enacted a statute authorizing annulments for non-age (being legally underage), physical incapacity, bigamy, insanity, and fraud or force. Grounds for fraud often included misrepresentations regarding religion and ancestry, false promise of chastity, and false promise to bear children. That these issues were considered to go to the essence of the institution of marriage reflect the social mores and concerns of the day. In terms of racial misrepresentation, however, it is interesting to note that New York State law did not define precisely *what* a 'Negro' *was* (that is, supposed 'proportions of blood').

5. "Rhinelander Wife Denies She is Negro."

6. "Rhinelander Bride Fears He is Captive," *New York Times,* 30 November 1924, 14.

7. As Wacks (2000, 170) notes, this distinction became important for Davis because it enabled him to argue that while Alice may have had the stain of black blood she was not subject to the traits of black femininity.

8. See *CR,* 24–27.

9. By this, I mean that the passer is perceived to produce or display an unsubstantial, unreal, or counterfeit racial identity.

10. I examine this notion in more detail in chapter 6.

11. "Rhinelander Tells Story of Courtship."

12. "Loved Rhinelander, Wife's Letters Say."

13. The jurors had the opportunity to see George Jones—who was visibly 'colored'—

when Davis had him stand up in court (*CR*, 693). Davis claimed that Emily, Robert, and their daughter, Roberta, were clearly black, as was Grace, both in appearance and voice (in his summation Davis explicitly called on the jury to "listen to her") (*CR*, 1252). Davis's argument was that Leonard had spent considerable time in the Jones household, had socialized with the family (most notably with Robert Brooks, who was 'indisputably' black) and, therefore, had to have been aware that Alice was also black. Another witness was called forth to verify the appearance of Alice's body; Dr. Caesar P. McClendon (who identified himself as colored) testified that Alice had a "dark complexion" (*CR*, 869). He claimed that he had treated Alice, seen her body, and believed it to be "approximately as dark as [his own] face" (*CR*, 869).

14. In his summation, Davis explicitly stated that Leonard "knew it and he like it until the family name intervened" (*CR*, 1253). The implication is, then, that Leonard was all too prepared to deviate from the performative injunctions of white masculinity, but only so long as they remained secret and could not threaten his status in this identity position. This idea is addressed in further detail in chapter 6, in terms of its significance for questions of racial agency.

15. "Rhinelander Wife Cries Under the Ordeal."

16. It is interesting to note this disjunction that is stipulated by the Court. One wonders why Alice's body and not her face was deemed as the corporeal site that would articulate racial 'truth.' Perhaps the face was seen as capable of a manipulation that could disguise this truth. During the 1920s there was an impressive array of 'beauty' products designed specifically to 'enhance' the appearance of black women (read, to enable them to conform to dominant standards of beauty; that is, beauty that is defined in terms of white femininity). In the *New York Amsterdam News* (1924–1925) alone, advertisements for the following products were placed: *Nadine Face Powder* ("Lightens and Refines the Skin"); *Nadinola Bleaching Cream* ("makes your complexion soft [and] fair"); *Rozol* ("A Face Bleach that Really Bleaches"); and *Exelento Skin Soap* (for "facial loveliness"). It was not only black skin that could be altered to appear more 'white.' Hair, too, was targeted as that which needed to be corrected or disciplined, often in order to align with white ideals of feminine beauty. Thus, products existed such as *Suaveline* (for "straight, silky hair"); *Herolin Pomade Hair Dressing* (for "long, soft, glossy" hair); *Pluko Hair Dressing* ("There is no longer need for you to have a scanty growth of short, harsh, wiry hair . . . [make your hair] long, straight, glossy, and beautiful"); and *Exelento Quinine Pomade* ("for soft, pretty hair"). For a detailed discussion of the complexity of these ideas in relation to African American hairstyling politics, see Kobena Mercer (1990).

17. In this way, the power of the visual realm is reasserted. Davis's argument rests on the contention that the scopic veracity of race is inevitably present and, as such, ontology cannot be masked.

18. "Rhinelander Asks to Amend Charges."

19. See Jamie Wacks (2000).

20. Unfortunately, the scope of the present analysis does not enable me to explore the extent of the complex ways in which Alice was represented and constructed by actors in this case (most particularly, by the counsels). I do, however, address this further in chapter 6. For an analysis that focuses solely on the construction of Alice Rhinelander within the case, see Jamie Wacks (2000). Also see Smith-Pryor (2009) and Lewis and Ardizzone (2001). For more general discussions of representations of black femininity, see bell hooks (1981); Patricia Bell Scott (1982); and Patricia Morton (1991).

21. This construction of Alice clearly calls forth the imagery of black femininity discussed in chapter 2. The notion of black femininity as the embodiment of libidinal excess has found particular expression in the stereotype of the 'black jezebel.' Patricia Hill Collins (1990, 77) argues that this stereotype (formulated during slavery, but still maintaining forceful discursive currency) underlies all other stereotypes of black femininity. In this imagery the 'black woman' is cast as a whore (a perceived natural consequence of the corporeal excess first identified in the Hottentot Venus), thereby rendering all black women as essentially possessing the traits of excessive sexual appetite and sexual aggressiveness.

22. In this letter Alice wrote: "how sick I was and how I did suffer . . . So you see, my fun was expence [*sic*] or [*sic*] your fun. But Lenard [*sic*], you can always have me when you want me" (*CR*, 344–345).

23. Mills suggests that Alice fostered a white female identity (with the support of the Jones family) through her attempts to cultivate associations with white people, through attending predominantly white-populated institutions and social gatherings, and through keeping the details of her birth certificate secret.

5. PASSING PHANTASMS

1. Carole-Anne Tyler (1994, 221) argues that "[a]ll subjects are *passing* through the signifiers which represent them for an other, to whom a demand for recognition and a question about being is addressed: (Do you) Hear what I'm saying!? (Do you) See what I am!?"

2. In making this claim I want to stress two important points. Firstly, in identifying 'white masculine subjectivity' I am not suggesting that any form of a unitary and static subject position exists that can be neatly encapsulated within this marker of identity. Nor do I want to suggest that there might be fixed or stable masculine norms. Rather, what I want to mark is a temporally and spatially specific configuration of subjectivity, the normative standards of which are constantly under revision. The particularities of 'white masculinity' to which I refer here are conditioned by locale, by factors of class and social standing, and by early twentieth-century sensibilities. Secondly, Leonard's whiteness and masculinity cannot be read divorced from one another. Norms of both race and gender, along with countless other specificities of identity, work *together* to condition subjectivity. Despite the lived realities of infinite particularities in embodied 'expression,' certain subjectivating norms exist (in any given era) for demarcated 'identities.'

3. See the analysis of passing in chapter 3.

4. As I noted in the introduction, the term 'whiteness' simultaneously encompasses both *the process of being white* and *a discursive systemic social power* supported by practices and beliefs.

5. Here I focus on whiteness; this argument, however, applies to all identity categories.

6. It is this action that obfuscates the performative nature of identity. I make this claim because it is this action that works to cover-over the internal absence precisely through the apparent enunciation of 'innerness.'

7. Also see Ariela Gross (2008) for an analysis of performing whiteness.

8. Any discussion of white masculinity within the U.S. context must, necessarily, note the influence of the religio-political discourses and typologies of Puritanism.

Puritan belief contributed not only to the structuring of the 'American self' (that is, what it meant to *be* American) but, by implication, it also set the standard for norms of white gendered and sexual behavior. The Puritan stress on "Christian piety, moral rectitude, and civic virtue" (Smith 1994, 102) became instrumental in the construction of a very particular vision of white masculinity. Later in this chapter, I consider the specificities of white masculine norms of sexual behavior. These too—that is, the prohibition of certain sexual acts—can be traced to Puritan formulations of subjectivity and citizenship in the New World. The parameters of my investigation, however, limit the possibility of exploring these ideas. For an analysis that does rigorously critique the influence of Puritanism in the construction of North American subjectivities, see Sacvan Bercovitch (1976). For a specific focus on Puritanism and sexuality, see Fessenden, Radel, and Zaborowska (2000). Also see Godbeer (2000), for a close examination of sexuality in early America.

9. Davis established that Leonard's attorney, Mr. Jacobs, was in Philip Rhinelander's employ (*CR*, 412). Leonard, furthermore, conceded that it was not in his power to control his own lawsuit. Taken in conjunction with Philip Rhinelander's efforts to keep the couple apart, public opinion positioned the elder Rhinelander as the party behind the suit. Indeed, in 1929, Alice Rhinelander brought an alienation of affection suit against Philip Rhinelander, blaming him for the destruction of the marriage (Wacks 2000, n. 14).

10. McLaren (1997, 89) defines a 'gentleman' (in late nineteenth to early twentieth-century conceptualizations) as a type of "morality that a man exhibited in his daily dealings." The notion was linked to chivalrous behavior and being bound by honor.

11. In his opening statement, Davis told how Jacobs 'escorted' Leonard (*CR*, 1129) and was constantly by his side after the young Rhinelander left Alice.

12. The *New York Times* (11 November 1925, 4) reported Davis as stating: "I can see only one reason for Justice Mills's remarks . . . and that is that the Rhinelander millions and not young Rhinelander are back of this move to crush a humble family to save an ancient name which is traced back to the Huguenots of New Rochelle."

13. On the various and often conflicting discursive images of black femininity, see the stereotypes outlined by Patricia Hill Collins (1990). hooks (1992, 68) makes particular reference to a specific stereotype of black femininity: "the mythic black female in slavery who supposedly 'vamped' and seduced virtuous white male slave owners."

14. This idea will be discussed in more detail in chapter 6.

15. The particular focus of this analysis precludes an examination of the regulatory mechanisms that operate to constitute normalized sexualities and those that are discursively deemed as pathological. The primary tenets of this argument, however, are predicated on a Foucauldian notion of the discursive regulation of sexuality as articulated in volume 1 of *The History of Sexuality* (1998).

16. "Rhinelander Says He Pursued Girl."

17. Foucault (1998, 104) argues that from the end of the eighteenth century "[p]arents, families, educators, doctors, and eventually psychologists [waged a] war against onanism." Also see his analysis of masturbation in *Abnormal* (Foucault 2003).

18. Among these were "insanity, epilepsy, numerous forms of eye disease, strange sensations at the top of the head, neuralgia, asthma, cardiac murmurs, acne and other forms of cutaneous eruptions, eyes directed upward and sideways, intermittent functional deafness, redness of nose, warts on the hands in women, and hallucinations of smell and hearing" (Ellis 1920, 249–50).

19. On Beard, see Charles Rosenberg (1976).

20. See New York Penal Law, chap. 41, art. 66, sec. 690, in Cahill (1923).

21. See Winthrop D. Jordon (1968, esp. 28, 33–40), who discusses the historical formulations of thought that associated Africans with animals. During the Elizabethan era, the notion that Africans were bestial had definitive sexual connotations. While black masculinity has been associated with sexual excess, it has also been symbolically associated with passivity, as witnessed in the construction of the domesticated, passive slave or 'Uncle Tom' figure. Black masculinity, then, is marked paradoxically as both virile and as metaphorically impotent. Consequently, black masculinity is constructed as feminine— but threatens to be hypermasculine. This threat, however, is recovered, as I discuss below. See Wiegman (1995) for a specific discussion of these ideas, and bell hooks (2003) for a more general discussion of the constructions and experiences of black masculine subjects in the United States.

22. See Dyer (1997, 28), who argues: "the darkness [sexual desire] is a sign of his true masculinity, just as his ability to control it is a sign of his whiteness."

23. For an investigation of masturbation and the male hysteric, see M. David-Ménard (1989).

24. "What the Rhinelander Case Means to Negroes."

25. During the trial, Leonard was disinherited by his father, Philip Rhinelander. The *New York Times* ("Family Disinherits L. K. Rhinelander," 28 October 1925, 27) announced: "Leonard Kip Rhinelander, heir to the fortune of his Knickerbocker forebears, has been disinherited because of his marriage . . . to Mrs. Alice Jones Rhinelander, declared his attorney today." This was surely one of the primary reasons why Leonard had attempted to keep the marriage a secret from his father. He had wanted to wait to marry Alice until after he had turned twenty-one years old, presumably after he had inherited at least a portion of the family money.

26. The manner in which Leonard was depicted during the trial could be interpreted as a form of white masculinity 'in crisis'; that is, he could be viewed simply as an individual who needs to be reprimanded because of his failure. Read in this light, however, Leonard becomes cast as merely aberrant or wayward, and the normative standards of white masculinity only become resecured. What I interrogate later is whether white racial enunciation might be productively resignified in ways that are not simply read as crises that result in disciplinary punishment. Thus, I ask: can identity be rearticulated (in opposition to normative decrees) in ways that do not invite a reading that views them as forms of crises of subjectivity or in ways that do not result in the increased disciplining of the subject? See chapter 7.

27. In 1929, Leonard obtained a divorce in Las Vegas, Nevada, on the grounds of cruelty consisting of humiliation. In 1930, attorneys for Alice and Leonard agreed on a modification of the divorce decree. This provided for a one-time cash payment to Alice of $31,500 and a $3,600 annuity for the rest of her life. Alice, for her part, agreed to relinquish her use of the Rhinelander name. Five years after the trial, Leonard moved back to New York and worked for his father's real estate company. Details are not available but because Leonard was struck off the Social Register, it can be presumed that he did not reenter New York 'society.' Leonard died of pneumonia in 1936, aged thirty-four. See "L. Kip Rhinelander Dead of Pneumonia," *New York Times*, 21 February 1936, 17; and for further details of Alice and Leonard in the years following the trial, see Smith-Pryor (2009) and Lewis and Ardizzone (2001).

6. IMAGINING RACIAL AGENCY

1. See *supra* chap. 3, n. 24, on my use of the term 'liberal humanism' to mark the ruling assumptions, values, meanings, and principles regarding 'man,' as they have been formulated in the modern epoch.

2. A number of scholars have criticized Foucault's formulation of power and the attendant understanding of subject constitution: see, for example, Dews (1987), Walzer (1986), Taylor (1986), and Fraser (1989). Peter Dews (1987), for instance, argues that the Foucauldian model of power is incoherent due to the fact that power is perceived as so diffuse (see Bartky [1995] for an analysis of Dews position). Dews essentially asks: if power is everywhere, then how can it be resisted? As I have advanced (and go on to analyze in further detail), this model of power need not be interpreted as constraining simply because power is omnipresent; it is the very fact that power—as an *event,* a reiterative assertion—is produced in every moment, and that power is immanent in every exchange, that enables subjects themselves to exercise power. See my analysis of *power relations* below.

3. For a discussion of these interpretations, see Lois McNay (1994, 124).

4. These ideas are presented in Foucault's essay, "The Subject and Power" (2000c). In the next chapter, I mark ways in which subjects are not equally 'free' in this sense, and how subjects are not presented with the same field of possibilities, due to their specific positioning within the social realm (based on categorization or racial designation).

5. I explore these ideas more in the next chapter.

6. We see Foucault's legacy clearly here, as the 'acting by the subject' calls forth the Foucauldian insistence on the productivity of power. When the subject is said to enact power, what they are exercising is power that is already/always constituted by points of resistance, contradictions, and by the multiplicity of unintended effects.

7. By 'requirements,' I refer to the compelled repetition of the norms associated with the name—a name that calls forth the subject and works to constitute subjectivity.

8. In *Bodies That Matter,* Butler explains that the name that one enacts (whether it be in line with normative decrees or resignified in a manner that attempts to move beyond the confines of the term) is always limited/constrained by "the historicity of the name itself: by the history of usages that one never controlled, but that constrain the very usage that now emblematizes autonomy" (1993, 228).

9. As Butler (1993, 10) states, "construction . . . is itself a temporal process which operates through the reiteration of norms; sex is both produced and destabilized in the course of this reiteration."

10. 'Necessary' precisely because the idealized norm cannot be reproduced in a truly felicitous manner. A subject will 'slip' from the norm because this norm cannot be 'attained.'

11. For specific focus on the sexualization of race, see Naomi Zack (1997), Julian Carter (2007), Abdul JanMohamed (1992), Mason Stokes (2001), and Aliyyah I. Abdur-Rahman (2006).

12. This statement referred specifically to issues IV and V of the plaintiff's amended complaint (*CR*, 10). These were: "(IV) On information and belief, that in truth and fact the said Alice Jones, also known as Alice Jones Rhinelander, was colored and with colored blood; (V) On information and belief, that the said defendant, Alice Jones, also known as Alice Jones Rhinelander, had colored blood in her veins."

13. I am making a qualitative distinction here between representation by counsel and a subject's right to speak on their own behalf. At issue is not the legal process of representation (which Alice undeniably had) but the notion of marginal subjects having the opportunity to articulate their embodied realities rather than having others/those in positions of discursive power guide and, ultimately, determine their positionality through speaking *for* them. What we don't know is whether Alice made the choice not to take the stand. Regardless, what we are left with is absence—she did not speak.

14. Butler (1993, 137) argues that agency can be gestured toward in acts which are "an appropriation that seeks to make over the terms of domination . . . a power in and as discourse, in and as performance, which repeats in order to remake—and sometimes succeeds."

15. An interesting cross-comparison could be made here between this reading of Alice and Foucault's reading of the French hermaphrodite, Herculine Barbin (1980b). Like Alice, Barbin seemingly actively (and reflectively) resisted disciplinary attempts of normalization by refusing the dualism of male/female. Barbin was able to *appear* as a sexualized subject (that is, be recognized within discourse) but, importantly, Barbin evaded what McWhorter (1999, 206) has called "the finality of categorization." This was enabled due to the fact that Barbin acted in a deviant capacity to the norms of each gender—thus, slipping *between* positions (from one category to another). For a detailed analysis of Barbin, see McWhorter (1999, 199–209).

16. The reality that this form of racial resistance is only available to certain ambiguous subjects is, obviously, a limitation in terms of thinking about racial resistance. If, as I argue, we are to begin to think about ways that race can be rearticulated through acts of agency that refashion the normative structure of racial designation, it essential to be able to identify the kinds of agency that might be available to subjects who do not reside in a liminal space. This idea will be further explored in the next chapter.

17. For this idea I am indebted to Michelle Burnham (1992).

18. This opposition can be seen to operate on two primary levels. Firstly, in my interpretation of Alice's actions, she can be seen to oppose the notion of racial fixity. This, however, is discursively understood as the production of a white identity in defiance of a black identity. Rigid racial demarcation along a binary axis is reestablished. Thus, to see passing as a refusal of racial categorization results in the imposition of yet another racial category ('white') that is just as rigorous in its normativizing demands. Secondly, in refusing the imposition of a black racial identity, Alice opposes the power of whiteness (that is, the power that white supremacist hegemony exercises in the process of racialization). But through what is discursively read as the fashioning of a white identity, Alice merely augments the power of whiteness. She opposes whiteness, then, only through reproducing it.

19. Burnham (1992, 71 n. 20) notes that even Bentham's original design for the Panopticon had a blind-spot. She quotes Alan Liu (1989), who argues, "Bentham discovered after drawing up his plans that a blank space had inadvertently been left in the central tower in the area of the chapel." Unfortunately, Liu's analysis does not consider the potential that this blind-spot may have had for inmates.

20. On this notion, see Butler (1993, 110).

21. This is also a space from which a confession *cannot* be extracted precisely due to the occupation of the loophole. Below I consider the role of confession within the disciplinary economy.

22. Here Butler is challenging the unilateral account of subject formation as proposed by Althusser. See, generally, her essay "On Linguistic Vulnerability," in *Excitable Speech: A Politics of the Performative* (1997a) and "Conscience Doth Make Subjects of Us All: Althusser's Subjection," in *The Psychic Life of Power: Theories of Subjection* (1997b). This account complicates the reading of Fanon that I offered in chapter 1.

23. It is precisely for this reason that it becomes impossible to imagine an agency that is 'outside' of the structure of discourse and located in the subject. The subject, even in resistance, responds to power in which they are immanent.

24. In *Gender Trouble* (1999, 178), Butler argues: "Gender is . . . a construction that regularly conceals its genesis; the tacit collective agreement to perform, produce and sustain discrete and polar genders as cultural fictions is obscured by the credulity of those productions—and the punishments that attend not agreeing to believe in them; the construction 'compels' our belief in its necessity and naturalness."

7. PRACTICING PROBLEMATIZATION

1. All references to this sketch are from http://snltranscripts.jt.org/84/84iwhite likeeddie.phtml. Accessed August 11, 2009. For further discussion of this sketch, see Gayle Wald (2000).

2. This can be thought about as the non-autonomy of the field, where subjects are constrained by the discursive possibilities that bring them into existence and within which they operate. See de Certeau (1988).

3. Within such a reality, it is important to not romanticize resistance. See Hartman (1997).

4. A note on terminology: I have utilized the term 'signifying' to refer here to the colloquial (black vernacular) practice. As I explain below, in certain black communities, the term is utilized to describe a practice of speech—an activity. I employ the term '*Signifin(g)*' only to signal how Gates has attempted to differentiate the black verbal convention (the process of the "repetition and inversion" of discourse) from formal signification. At all other points in this analysis I use 'signifying' to refer both to the black verbal convention and Gates's theorization of this practice.

5. Gates (1988, 46) states: "The bracketed or aurally erased *g*, like the discourse of black English and dialect poetry generally, stands as the trace of black difference in a remarkably sophisticated and fascinating (re)naming ritual . . . The absent *g* is a figure for the Signifyin(g) black difference."

6. Gates (1988) locates the black practice of signifying in the myth of the Signifying Monkey—a trickster figure (often identified as Esu-Elegbara from Yoruba mythology) that can be traced to the oral traditions of slaves. On the genealogy of this figure, see Gates (1987; 1988) and Thompson (1984).

7. See Gates (1988, 82). To loud-talk connotes the antithesis of what the term denotes: "one successfully loud-talks by speaking to a second person remarks in fact directed to a third person, at a level just audible to the third person."

8. 'Playing the dozens' or 'the doubles' refers to the African American ritualistic verbal game in which insult is used in order to gain the upper hand. It is often abusive and sexual in nature. This is a form of signifying in which language is used so as "to stun, stupefy [or] daze" (Gates 1988, 71). The first person to take offense 'loses' the game. An example would be "Your mother is so white, she went to her own wedding naked." (See

Dalton Conley [2000], who provides an interesting autobiographical account of how the doubles or the dozens was played *between* racial groups in his youth.)

9. Roger D. Abrahams (quoted in Gates 1987, 238–239) provides definitions for signifying that also furnish an understanding of some of the primary characteristics of this form of rhetorical play:

> Signifying seems to be a Negro term, in use if not in origin. It can mean any number of things . . . it certainly refers to the trickster's ability to talk with great innuendo, to carp, cajole, needle, and lie. It can mean in other instances the propensity to talk around a subject never quite coming to the point. It can mean making fun of a person or situation, also it can denote speaking with the hands and eyes, and in this respect encompasses a whole complex of expressions and gestures. Thus it is signifying to stir up a fight between neighbors by telling stories; it is signifying to make fun of a policeman behind his back; it is signifying to ask for a piece of cake by saying, "my brother needs a piece of cake."

10. See Gates (1988, 94) for his discussion of Geneva Smitherman's definitions of signifying.

11. In "The Postmodern Rag: Political Identity and the Vernacular in *Song of Solomon*," Wahneema Lubiano (1995, 96) states that signifying or "[v]ernacular language moves along lines of alteration, maintaining contradictory, ironic, oblique stances vis-à-vis experience, narration, or even assumptions about reality."

12. Here I refer to dominant understandings, stereotypes, and markers of blackness that have been discursively generated within and by hegemonic white power/knowledge relations (whether they be legal, scientific, religious, or other mechanisms). As I have stated, these discursive 'truths' are never unilaterally imposed, nor are they passively adopted and internalized by black subjects. Instead, black subjects (and, by extension, *all* racial subjects) always participate in the creation and embodied reality of racialized identity. Racial identity is always a negotiation; it is produced and enabled through (a never completed) agonistic engagement with hegemonic powers which endeavor to constrain the individual.

13. It is important to note that Ellison's text is also directly intertextual in that it responds to and critiques the passage from *Moby-Dick* in which Herman Melville (1967, 18) discusses the "blackness of darkness."

14. For a particularly rigorous examination of slave resistance, see Saidiya Hartman (1997). According to Hartman, blackness within slavery was performatively rearticulated in ways that seemingly only-ever reiterated the abject terms of domination. How, then, she asks, is it possible to conceive of black racial practices that might have destabilized this process of signification? Her response to these questions is to identify the potential for agency in the ambivalent space of slave pleasure. She argues that although enjoyment was often fabricated, and permissible and seemingly innocent pleasures—such as dancing, worshiping, singing—were rigorously patrolled, it was in this realm that resistant opportunities were produced and seized. The direction that this enjoyment took (when it was permitted) could potentially reach beyond the form intended by the master. These times of pleasure, or moments when pleasure was surreptitiously 'taken' in an unauthorized fashion, offered the potential for practices of redress, where the enslaved sought to alleviate the pained state of the captive body. Taking many forms, redress, according to Hartman (1997, 51) included "operating in and against the demands of the

system, negotiating the disciplinary harnessing of the body, and counterinvesting in the body as a site of possibility." Her interpretation of redress clearly demarcates efforts of racial reinscription as those in which slaves were compelled to work within systemic constraints, and with limited possibilities, to redirect the terms of domination so that the body that was marked principally by punishment could be resignified as a positive site of intervention. These actions were an assertion of self in relation to normalized conventions and were ultimately attempts at self-stylized subjectivity. On slave resistances within religion, see Raboteau (1978) and Harding (1969). See also Mirón and Inda (2000, 101–103) for a discussion of how the term 'black,' historically used as a shaming interpellation was, through the Civil Rights and Black Power movements, reworked in order to take on a new set of meanings: "the shaming interpellation black is not simply taken as an order to be obeyed but as the imperative to be cited and refigured" (Mirón and Inda 2000, 102).

15. Gates (1988, 66) states: "The language of blackness encodes [for self-preservation] and names its sense of independence through a rhetorical process that we might think of as the Signifyin(g) black difference." It is important to note, here, that Gates (1988, 46) uses this term—that is, 'signifying' with the bracketed 'g'—to differentiate this black verbal convention from formal signification.

16. On intentionality, see Gates (1988, 51) and Foucault's later work, specifically "The Ethic of Care for the Self as a Practice of Freedom—An Interview with Michel Foucault 1984" (1988). I expand on Foucault's later work below.

17. For instance, I have analyzed *Rhinelander v. Rhinelander* (1925) in order to map the structural distinctions that constrain (and enable) a white male's and a black female's racial identities within this specific case. In particular, I have mapped how each of the subjects in the case were formed (as white male and black female respectively) and how distinct types of subjection (and material conditions) produce alternate forms and paths of resistance.

18 For a sustained analysis of Foucault's ethics, see Timothy O'Leary (2002).

19. I refer to the primary regimes or knowledges of truth (as they are articulated and enforced through multiple technologies of power) through which subjectivity is formed.

20. For an account of the complexities of the question of slave agency, see Walter Johnson's "On Agency" (2003).

21. See Foucault (1988, 11–16). Also see his essay, "Truth and Power" (1980d, 133), where he states that the aim is to extricate "the power of truth from the forms of hegemony . . . within which it operates at the present time."

22. In *Security, Territory, Population: Lectures at the Collège de France 1977–78*, Foucault (2007a, 353) states: "the insertion of freedom within governmentality, [emerged] not only as the right of individuals legitimately opposed to the power, usurpations, and abuses of the sovereign or the government, but as an element that has become indispensable to governmentality itself. Henceforth, a condition of governing well is that freedom, or certain forms of freedom, are really respected. Failing to respect freedom is not only an abuse of rights with regard to the law, it is above all ignorance of how to govern properly."

23. In "Sexuality and Solitude" (2000b, 177), Foucault defines the technologies of self as "techniques that permit individuals to effect, by their own means, a certain number of operations on their own bodies, their own souls, their own thoughts, their own conduct, and this in a manner so as to transform themselves, modify themselves."

24. Foucault defines *poesis* as an 'art of existence': "those intentional and voluntary actions by which men not only set themselves rules of conduct, but also seek to transform themselves, to change themselves in their singular being, and to make their life into an *oeuvre* that carries certain aesthetic values and meets certain stylistic criteria" (1992, 10–11).

25. I employ this term in the Butlerian sense to mean those efforts that seek to overcome the self—acts that attempt to redirect, or enunciate a-new, the subjectivating norms through which one comes into being (see Butler, 1993, 131). This use is in line with the Foucauldian notion of practices that attempt to resist normalization. In regards to the idea of 'self-overcoming,' what must always be kept in mind is that subjectivity cannot be opposed (overcome) in a 'pure' sense. As I have discussed, this process is one that always involves reference to the terms in and through which subjects can be said to come into being. On 'self-overcoming,' see McWhorter (1999, 176–192).

26. Rabinow interprets Foucault as suggesting that problematization involves the effort to "disassemble the self, oneself." This phrasing of Foucault's project, Rabinow states, "highlights the material and relational aspects of this exercise, and introduces a notion of the self as a form-giving practice that operates with and upon heterogeneous parts and forms available at a given point in history" (2000, xxxviii).

27. For instance, Yancy (2008, 117) has argued that the "lived existential project" of black racial identity "involves and should continue to involve a continual hermeneutic reassessment of who and what Black identity means and what the social, political, cultural, and existential implications are." It is possible to claim identity and forge a politics in relation to shared histories, experiences, and enunciations, but to simultaneously insist that identity is not *reducible* to those histories or connections.

28 See McWhorter (2004, 156) for further consideration of this idea.

29. Butler does not disavow a form of intentionality, but fails to adequately explicate her position on how she imagines its operation. See *Bodies That Matter* (1993) for a general discussion of intentionality (specifically, "Critically Queer"). Also see her comment in Benhabib et al. (1995, 134–135). For further discussion of Butler's views on this topic, see Veronica Vasterling (1999).

BIBLIOGRAPHY

Abdur-Rahman, Aliyyah I. 2006. " 'The Strangest Freaks of Despotism': Queer Sexuality in Antebellum African American Slave Narratives." *African American Review* 40, no. 2: 223–237.

Agamben, Giorgio. 1998. *Homo Sacer: Sovereign Power and Bare Life.* Trans. Daniel Heller-Roazen. Stanford: Stanford University Press.

Ahmed, Sara. 1999. "She'll Wake Up One of These Days and Find She's Turned into a Nigger." *Theory, Culture, and Society* 16, no. 2: 87–106.

Ahmed, Sara, and Jackie Stacey. 2001. "Introduction: Dermographies." In *Thinking Through the Skin,* ed. Sara Ahmed and Jackie Stacey. London: Routledge. 1–15.

Allen, Amy. 1998. "Power Trouble: Performativity as Critical Theory." *Constellations* 5: 456–471.

Anzaldúa, Gloria. 1987. *Borderlands / La Frontera.* San Francisco: Aunt Lute Books.

Austin, John L. 1980. *How To Do Things With Words.* Oxford: Oxford University Press.

Banton, Michael. 1998. *Racial Theories.* Cambridge: Cambridge University Press.

Bartky, Sandra Lee. 1995. "Agency: What's the Problem." In *Provoking Agents: Gender and Agency in Theory and Practice,* ed. Judith Kegan Gardener. Urbana: University of Illinois Press. 178–193.

Beard, George Miller. 1884. *Sexual Neurasthenia.* New York: E. B. Treat.

Bederman, Gail. 1995. *Manliness and Civilization: A Cultural History of Gender and Race in the United States: 1880–1917.* Chicago: University of Chicago Press.

Bell, Derrick. 1998. "White Superiority in America: Its Legal Legacy, Its Economic Costs." In *Black On White: Black Writers on What It Means to Be White,* ed. David R. Roediger. New York: Schocken. 138–150.

Bell, Vikki. 1999a. "Mimesis as Cultural Survival: Judith Butler and Anti-Semitism." *Theory, Culture, and Society* 16, no. 2: 133–161.

——. 1999b. "On Speech, Race and Melancholia: An Interview with Judith Butler." *Theory, Culture, and Society* 16, no. 2: 163–174.

Bell-Scott, Patricia. 1982. "Debunking Sapphire: Toward a Non-Racist and Non-Sexist Social Science." In *All the Women Are White, All the Blacks Are Men, But Some of Us Are Brave,* ed. Gloria Hull, Barbara Smith, and Patricia Bell-Scott. New York: Feminist Press. 85–92.

Benhabib, Seyla, Judith Butler, Drucilla Cornell, and Nancy Fraser. 1995. *Feminist Contentions: A Philosophical Exchange.* New York: Routledge.

Benthien, Claudia. 2002. *Skin: On The Cultural Border Between Self and the World.* Trans. T. Dunlap. New York: Columbia University Press.

Bercovitch, Sacvan. 1976. *The Puritan Origins of the American Self.* New Haven: Yale University Press.

Bernauer, James, and Michael Mahon. 1994. "The Ethics of Michel Foucault." In *The Cambridge Companion to Foucault*, ed. Gary Gutting. Cambridge: Cambridge University Press. 141–158.

Berzon, Judith R. 1978. *Neither White Nor Black: The Mulatto Character in American Fiction.* New York: New York University Press.

Black, Henry Campbell, Joseph R. Nolan, and Jacqueline M. Nolan-Haley. 1990. *Black's Law Dictionary*, 6th ed. St. Paul, Minn.: West Publishing Company.

Bostwick, Homer. 1848. *Treatise on the Nature and Treatment of Seminal Diseases, Impotency, and Other Kindred Affections.* New York: Burgess and Stringer.

Bradshaw, Carla K. 1992. "Beauty and the Beast: On Racial Ambiguity." In *Racially Mixed People in America*, ed. Maria P. P. Root. Newbury Park: Sage Publications. 77–91.

Brown, Vincent. 2009. "Social Death and Political Life in the Study of Slavery." *American Historical Review* 114: 1231–1249.

Brown, William. W. 2003. *The Narrative of William W. Brown: A Fugitive Slave.* New York: Dover.

Burnham, Michelle. 1992. "Loopholes of Resistance." *Arizona Quarterly* 49: 53–73.

Butler, Judith. 1993. *Bodies That Matter: On the Discursive Limits of Sex.* New York: Routledge.

——. 1997a. *Excitable Speech: The Politics of the Performative.* New York: Routledge.

——. 1997b. *The Psychic Life of Power: Theories in Subjection.* Stanford: Stanford University Press.

——. 1999. *Gender Trouble: Feminism and the Subversion of Identity.* New York: Routledge.

——. 2004a. "Endangered / Endangering: Schematic Racism and White Paranoia." In *The Judith Butler Reader*, ed. Sara Salih. Oxford: Blackwell. 204–211.

——. 2004b. *Undoing Gender.* New York: Routledge.

Cahill, James C., ed. 1923. *Cahill's Consolidated Laws of New York.* Chicago: Callaghan and Company.

Carby, Hazel V. 1987. *Reconstructing Womanhood: The Emergence of the Afro-American Woman Novelist.* Oxford: Oxford University Press.

Carter, Julian B. 2007. *The Heart of Whiteness: Normal Sexuality and Race in America, 1880–1940.* Durham: Duke University Press.

Castronovo, Russ. 2001. *Necro Citizenship: Death, Eroticism, and the Public Sphere in the Nineteenth Century United States.* Durham: Duke University Press.

Chapman, Rowena, and Jonathon Rutherford, eds. 1988. *Male Order: Unwrapping Masculinity.* London: Lawrence and Wishart.

Christian, Barbara. 1980. *Black Women Novelists: The Development of a Tradition 1892–1976.* Westport, Conn.: Greenwood Press.

Conley, Dalton. 2000. *Honky.* New York: Vintage.

Crenshaw, Kimberlé. 1993. "Beyond Racism and Misogyny: Black Feminism and 2 Live Crew." In *Words That Wound: Critical Race Theory, Assaultive Speech and the First Amendment*, ed. Mari J. Matsuda, Charles. R. Lawrence III, Richard Delgado, and Kimberlé Crenshaw. Boulder, Col.: Westview Press. 111–132.

——. 1995. "Mapping the Margins: Intersectionality, Identity Politics and Violence

Against Women of Color." In *Critical Race Theory: The Key Writings that Formed the Movement,* ed. Kimberlé Crenshaw, Neil Gotanda, Gary Pellar, and Kendall Thomas. New York: The New Press. 357–383.

Cutter, Martha J. 1996. "Sliding Significations: Passing as a Narrative and Textual Strategy in Nella Larsen's Fiction." In *Passing and the Fictions of Identity,* ed. Elaine K. Ginsberg. Durham: Duke University Press. 75–100.

Daniel, G. Reginald. 1992. "Passers and Pluralists: Subverting the Racial Divide." In *Racially Mixed People in America,* ed. Maria P. P. Root. Newbury Park: Sage Publications. 91–108.

Davenport, Charles. 1913. *State Laws Limiting Marriage Selection: Examined in the Light of Eugenics.* Bulletin 9, Eugenics Record Office. Cold Spring Harbor, Long Island, New York.

David-Ménard, Monique. 1989. *Hysteria from Freud to Lacan: Body and Language in Psychoanalysis.* Trans. Catherine Porter. Ithaca: Cornell University Press.

Davis, F. James. 1998. *Who Is Black: One Nation's Definition.* University Park: Pennsylvania State University Press.

de Certeau, Michel. 1988. *The Practice of Everyday Life.* Trans. Stephen Rendall. Berkeley: University of California Press.

Deleuze, Gilles. 1988. *Foucault.* Trans. Seán Hand. Minneapolis: University of Minnesota Press.

Derrida, Jacques. 1981. *Dissemination.* Trans. Barbara Johnson. London: Athlone Press.

——. 1982. *Margins of Philosophy.* Trans. Alan Bass. Sussex: The Harvester Press.

——. 2000. *Limited, Inc.* Ed. Gerald Graff. Trans. Jeffrey Mehlman and Samuel Weber. Evanston: Northwestern University Press.

Deutscher, Penelope. 1997. *Yielding Gender: Feminism, Deconstruction and Philosophy.* London: Routledge.

Dews, Peter. 1987. *Logics of Disintegration.* London: Verso.

Diamond, Elin. 1996. "Introduction." In *Performance and Cultural Politics,* ed. Elin Diamond. New York: Routledge. 1–12.

Douglass, Frederick. 1973. *The Narrative of the Life of Frederick Douglass, An American Slave, Written By Himself.* Cambridge, Mass.: Harvard University Press.

DuBois, W. E. B. 2000. "The Conservation of the Races." In *Theories of Race and Racism: A Reader,* ed. Les Back and John Solomos. London: Routledge. 79–88.

Duggan, Lisa. 2000. *Sapphic Slashers: Sex, Violence, and American Modernity.* Durham: Duke University Press.

Dyer, Richard. 1997. *White: Essays on Race and Culture.* New York: Routledge.

Easthope, Anthony, and Kate McGowan. 1992. "Subjectivity: Introduction." In *A Critical and Cultural Theory Reader,* ed. Anthony Easthope and Kate McGowan. Toronto: University of Toronto Press. 67–70.

Ellis, Havelock. 1920. *Studies in the Psychology of Sex, Vol. 2.* Philadelphia: F. A. Davis Co.

Ellison, Ralph. 1995. *Invisible Man.* New York: Vintage.

Fanon, Frantz. 1967. *Black Skin, White Masks.* Trans. Charles Lam Markmann. New York: Grove Press.

Favor, J. Martin. 1999. *Authentic Blackness: The Folk in the New Negro Renaissance.* Durham: Duke University Press.

Fauset, Jessie Redmon. 1990. *Plum Bun.* Boston: Beacon Press.

Fessenden, Tracy, Nicholas F. Radel, and Magdalena J. Zaborowska, eds. 2000. *The*

Puritan Origins of American Sex: Religion, Sexuality, and National Identity in American Literature. New York: Routledge.

Foucault, Michel. 1965. *Madness and Civilization: A History of Insanity in the Age of Reason.* Trans. Richard Howard. New York: Pantheon.

——. 1970. *The Order of Things: An Archeology of the Human Sciences.* Trans. Alan Sheridan. New York: Random House.

——. 1973. *The Birth of the Clinic: An Archeology of Medical Perception.* Trans. Alan Sheridan. New York: Vintage.

——. 1980a. "Body/Power." In *Power/Knowledge: Selected Interviews and Other Writings 1972–1977,* ed. Colin Gordon. Trans. Colin Gordon, Leo Marshall, John Mepham, and Kate Soper. New York: Pantheon. 55–62.

——. 1980b. *Herculine Barbin: Being the Recently Discovered Memoirs of a Nineteenth Century French Hermaphrodite.* Trans. Richard McDougall. New York: Pantheon.

——. 1980c. "The History of Sexuality: An Interview." *Oxford Literary Review* 4, no. 2: 3–14.

——. 1980d. "Truth and Power." In *Power/Knowledge: Selected Interviews and Other Writings 1972–1977,* ed. Colin Gordon. Trans. Colin Gordon, Leo Marshall, John Mepham, and Kate Soper. New York: Pantheon. 109–133.

——. 1980e. "Two Lectures." In *Power/Knowledge: Selected Interviews and Other Writings 1972–1977,* ed. Colin Gordon. Trans. Colin Gordon, Leo Marshall, John Mepham, and Kate Soper. New York: Pantheon. 78–108.

——. 1981. "Questions of Method: An Interview with Michel Foucault." Trans. Colin Gordon. *Ideology and Consciousness: Power and Desire Diagrams of the Social* 8 (Spring): 3–14.

——. 1984. "What is Enlightenment?" In *The Foucault Reader,* ed. Paul Rabinow. New York: Pantheon. 32–50.

——. 1988. "The Ethic of Care for the Self as a Practice of Freedom—An Interview with Michel Foucault 1984." In *The Final Foucault,* ed. James Bernauer and David Rasmussen. Cambridge, Mass.: MIT Press. 1–20.

——. 1989. "Power Affects the Body." In *Foucault Live: Interviews, 1966–1984,* ed. Sylvere Lotringer. New York: Semiotext(e). 207–213.

——. 1991. *Discipline and Punish: The Birth of the Prison.* Trans. Alan Sheridan. London: Penguin.

——. 1992. *The History of Sexuality, Volume Two: The Use of Pleasure.* Trans. Robert Hurley. London: Penguin.

——. 1998. *The History of Sexuality, Volume One: The Will to Knowledge.* Trans. Robert Hurley. London: Penguin.

——. 2000a. "The Ethics of the Concern for Self as a Practice of Freedom." In *Ethics: The Essential Works of Foucault 1954–1984, Volume One,* ed. Paul Rabinow. London: Penguin. 281–301.

——. 2000b. "Sexuality and Solitude." In *Ethics: Essential Works of Foucault 1954–1984,* vol. 1, ed. Paul Rabinow. London: Penguin. 175–184.

——. 2000c. "The Subject and Power." In *Power: The Essential Works of Foucault 1954–1984,* vol. 3, ed. James D. Fabion. London: Penguin. 326–348.

——. 2000d. "What is Enlightenment?" In *Ethics: Essential Works of Foucault 1954–1984,* vol. 1, ed. Paul Rabinow. London: Penguin. 303–320.

——. 2002. *The Archaeology of Knowledge.* Trans. A. M. Sheridan Smith. New York: Routledge.

———. 2003a. *Abnormal: Lectures at the Collège de France, 1974–1975*. Trans. Graham Burchell. New York: Picador.

———. 2003b. *Society Must Be Defended: Lectures at the Collège de France, 1975–1976*. Trans. David Macey. London: Penguin.

———. 2006. *Psychiatric Power: Lectures at the Collège de France, 1973–1974*. Trans. Graham Burchell. New York: Palgrave MacMillan.

———. 2007a. *Security, Territory, Population: Lectures at the Collège de France 1977–78*. Trans. Graham Burchell. London: Palgrave MacMillan.

———. 2007b. "What is Enlightenment?" In *The Politics of Truth*, ed. Sylvere Lotringer. Trans. Lysa Hochroth and Catherine Porter. Cambridge: Semiotext(e). 97–120.

———. 2008. *The Birth of Biopolitics: Lectures at the Collège de France 1978–1979*. Trans. Graham Burchell. London: Palgrave MacMillan.

———. 2010. "Preface to *The History of Sexuality*, Volume II." In *Michel Foucault: The Foucault Reader*, ed. Paul Rabinow. New York: Vintage. 333–339.

Fowler, David H. 1987. *Northern Attitudes Towards Interracial Marriage—Legislation and Public Opinion in the Middle Atlantic and the States of the Old North-West, 1780–1930*. New York: Garland Publishing.

Frankenburg, Ruth. 1993. *White Women, Race Matters: The Social Construction of Whiteness*. Minneapolis: University of Minnesota Press.

Fraser, Nancy. 1989. *Unruly Practices: Power, Discourse, and Gender in Contemporary Social Theory*. Minneapolis: University of Minnesota Press.

Freud, Sigmund. 1894. "How Anxiety Originates." In *The Standard Edition of the Complete Psychological Works of Sigmund Freud, Volume One*. London: Hogarth Press.

Gates, Henry Louis, Jr. 1987. *Figures in Black: Words, Signs, and the "Racial" Self*. New York: Oxford University Press.

———. 1988. *The Signifying Monkey: A Theory of Afro-American Literary Criticism*. New York: Oxford University Press.

———. 1992. *Loose Canons: Notes on the Culture Wars*. New York: Oxford University Press.

Genovese, Eugene D. 1976. *Roll, Jordan, Roll: The World the Slaves Made*. New York: Vintage.

Getman, Karen A. 1984. "Sexual Control in the Slaveholding South: The Implementation and Maintenance of a Racial Caste System." *Harvard Women's Law Journal* 7: 115–152.

Gilman, Sander. 1985. *Difference and Pathology: Stereotypes of Sexuality, Race, and Madness*. Ithaca: Cornell University Press.

Ginsberg, Elaine K. 1996. "Introduction: The Politics of Passing." In *Passing and the Fictions of Identity*, ed. Elaine K. Ginsberg. Durham: Duke University Press. 1–18.

Godbeer, Richard. 2002. *Sexual Revolution in Early America*. Baltimore: Johns Hopkins University Press.

Goldberg, David Theo. 1992. "The Semantics of Race." *Ethnic and Racial Studies* 15: 543–569.

Golder, Ben, and Peter Fitzpatrick. 2009. *Foucault's Law*. Oxford: Routledge.

Gordon, Colin. 2000. "Introduction." In *Power: Essential Works of Foucault 1954–1984, Volume Three*, ed. James D. Fabion. London: Penguin. xi–xli.

Gossett, Thomas F. 1964. *Race: The History of an Idea in America*. Dallas: Southern Methodist University Press.

Gotanda, Neil. 1991. "A Critique of 'Our Constitution is Colorblind.'" *Stanford Law Review* 44, no. 1: 23–36.

Gould, Stephen Jay. 1996. *The Mismeasure of Man.* New York: W. W. Norton.

Grant, Madison. 1918. *The Passing of the Great Race or The Racial Basis of European History.* New York: Charles Scribner's and Sons.

Gross, Ariela J. 1998. "Litigating Whiteness: Trials of Racial Determination in the Nineteenth-Century South." *Yale Law Journal* 108, no. 1: 109–188.

——. 2001. "Beyond Black and White: Cultural Approaches to Race and Slavery." *Columbia Law Review* 101, no. 3: 640–689.

——. 2008. *What Blood Won't Tell: A History of Race on Trial in America.* Cambridge, Mass.: Harvard University Press.

Grossberg, Michael. 1982. "Guarding the Altar: Physiological Restrictions and the Rise of State Intervention in Matrimony." *American Journal of Legal History* 26, no. 3: 197–226.

Hacker, Andrew. 1992. *Two Nations: Black and White, Separate, Hostile, Unequal.* New York: Scribner.

Hall, Stuart. 1996a. "Introduction: Who Needs Identity?" In *Questions of Cultural Identity,* ed. Stuart Hall and Paul du Gay. London: Sage. 1–17.

——. 1996b. "The West and the Rest: Discourse and Power." In *Modernity: An Introduction to Modern Societies,* ed. Stuart Hall, David Held, Don Hubert, and Kenneth Thompson. Oxford: Blackwell. 184–227.

Hammonds, Evelynn M., and Rebecca M. Herzig. 2009. *The Nature of Difference: Sciences of Race in the United States from Jefferson to Genomics.* Cambridge, Mass.: MIT Press.

Han, Béatrice. 2002. *Foucault's Critical Project: Between the Transcendental and the Historical.* Trans. Edward Pile. Stanford: Stanford University Press.

Haney López, Ian F. 1996. *White By Law: The Legal Construction of Race.* New York: New York University Press.

Harper, Phillip Brian. 1996. *Are We Not Men? Masculine Anxiety and the Problem of African-American Identity.* New York: Oxford University Press.

Harris, Cheryl. 1993. "Whiteness as Property," *Harvard Law Review* 106, no 8: 1707–1791.

Hartman, Saidiya V. 1997. *Scenes of Subjection: Terror, Slavery, and Self-Making in Nineteenth-Century America.* New York: Oxford University Press.

——. 2007. *Lose Your Mother: A Journey Along the Atlantic Slave Route.* New York: Farrar, Strauss, and Giroux.

Hekman, Susan. 1995. "Subjects and Agents: The Question for Feminism." In *Provoking Agents: Gender and Agency in Theory and Practice,* ed. Judith Kegan Gardener. Urbana: University of Illinois Press. 194–207.

Hening, William Walter, ed. 1823. *Statutes at Large . . . of Virginia (1619–1782),* 13 vols. Richmond: Samuel Pleasants.

Heyes, Cressida. 2007. *Self-Transformations: Foucault, Ethics, and Normalized Bodies.* New York: Oxford University Press.

Hickman, Christine B. 1997. "The Devil and the One Drop Rule: Racial Categories, African Americans, and the U.S. Census." *Michigan Law Review* 95: 1161–1265.

Higginbotham, Leonard, and Barbara Kopytoff. 1989. "Racial Purity and Interracial Sex in the Law of Colonial and Antebellum Virginia." *Georgetown Law Journal* 77: 1967–2028.

Hill Collins, Patricia. 1990. *Black Feminist Thought: Consciousness and the Politics of Empowerment.* Boston: Unwin Hyman.

Hodes, Martha. 1993. "The Sexualization of Reconstruction Politics: White Women and Black Men in the South after the Civil War." In *American Sexual Politics: Sex, Gender and Race Since the Civil War,* ed. John C. Fout and Maura Shaw Tantillo. Chicago: University of Chicago Press. 59–74.

hooks, bell. 1981. *Ain't I a Woman?* Boston: South End Press.

———. 1992. *Black Looks: Race and Representation.* Boston: South End Press.

———. 2003. *We Real Cool: Black Men and Masculinity.* New York: Routledge.

Hyde, Alan. 1997. *Bodies of Law.* Princeton: Princeton University Press.

Jameson, Fredric. 1983. "Postmodernism and Consumer Society." In *The Anti-Aesthetic: Essays on Postmodern Culture,* ed. Hal Foster. Port Townsend, Wash.: Bay Press. 111–125.

JanMohamed, Abdul. 1992. "Sexuality On/Of the Racial Border: Foucault, Wright, and the Articulation of 'Racialized Sexuality.'" In *Discourses of Sexuality: From Aristotle to AIDS,* ed. Domna C. Staton. Ann Arbor: University of Michigan Press. 94–116.

Johnson, Barbara. 1981. "Translator's Introduction." In Jacques Derrida, *Dissemination.* Trans. Barbara Johnson. London: Athlone Press. vii–xxxiii.

Johnson, E. Patrick. 2003. *Appropriating Blackness: Performance and the Politics of Authenticity.* Durham: Duke University Press.

Johnson, Walter. 1990. *Soul by Soul: Life Inside the Antebellum Slave Market.* Cambridge, Mass.: Harvard University Press.

———. 2000. "The Slave Trade, the White Slave, and the Politics of Determination in the 1850s." *The Journal of American History* 87, no. 1: 13–38.

———. 2003. "On Agency." *Journal of Social History* 37, no.1: 113–124.

Jones, D. Marvin. 1993. "Darkness Made Visible: Law, Metaphor, and the Racial Self." *Georgetown Law Journal* 82, no. 2: 437–511.

Jordan, Winthrop D. 1962. "American Chiaroscuro: The Status and Definition of Mulattoes in the British Colonies." *William and Mary Quarterly* 3rd ser., 19, no.2: 183–200.

———. 1968. *White Over Black: American Attitudes Toward the Negro, 1550–1812.* Baltimore: Penguin.

———. 1974. *The White Man's Burden: Historical Origins of Racism in the United States.* Oxford: Oxford University Press.

Kaplan, Sidney. 2000. "The Miscegenation Issue in the Election of 1864." In *Interracialism: Black-White Intermarriage in American History, Literature, and Law,* ed. Werner Sollors. Oxford: Oxford University Press. 219–265.

Kennedy, Randall. 2000. "The Enforcement of Anti-Miscegenation Laws." In *Interracialism: Black-White Intermarriage in American History, Literature, and Law,* ed. Werner Sollors. Oxford: Oxford University Press. 140–162.

Kondo, Dorinne K. 1997. *About Face: Performing 'Race' in Fashion and Theatre.* New York: Routledge.

Larsen, Nella. 1986. *Quicksand* and *Passing.* Ed. Deborah E. McDowell. London: Serpent's Tail.

Lewis, Earl, and Heidi Ardizzone. 2001. *Love On Trial: An American Scandal in Black and White.* New York: W. W. Norton.

Lipsitz, George. 1998. *The Possessive Investment in Whiteness: How White People Profit from Identity Politics*. Philadelphia: Temple University Press.

Lloyd, Moya. 1999. "Performativity, Parody, Politics." *Theory, Culture, and Society* 16, no. 2: 195–213.

Lombardo, Paul. 1988. "Miscegenation, Eugenics, and Racism: Historical Footnotes to *Loving v. Virginia.*" *U.C. Davis Law Review* 21, no. 2: 421–452.

Lowe, Lisa. 1996. *Immigrant Acts: On Asian American Cultural Politics*. Durham: Duke University Press.

Lubiano, Wahneema. 1995. "The Postmodernist Rag: Political Identity and the Vernacular in *Song of Solomon.*" In *New Essays on Song of Solomon,* ed. Valerie Smith. Cambridge: Cambridge University Press. 93–116.

Macey, David. 2009. "Rethinking Biopolitics, Race, and Power in the Wake of Foucault." *Theory, Culture, and Society* 26, no. 6: 186–205.

Marriot, David. 2007. *Haunted Life: Visual Culture and Black Modernity*. New Brunswick: Rutgers University Press.

Mbembe, Achille. 2003. "Necropolitics." Trans. Libby Meintjes. *Public Culture* 15, no.1: 11–40.

McBride, Dwight. 1998. "Can the Queen Speak?: Sexuality, Racial Essentialism and the Problem of Authority." *Callaloo* 21, no.2: 363–379.

McDowell, Deborah E. 1986. "Postscript." In Nella Larsen, *Quicksand* and *Passing,* ed. Deborah E. McDowell. London: Serpent's Tail. 249–277.

McLaren, Angus. 1997. *The Trials of Masculinity: Policing Sexual Boundaries, 1870–1930*. Chicago: University of Chicago Press.

McNay, Lois. 1994. *Foucault: A Critical Introduction*. Cambridge: Polity Press.

——. 1999. "Subject, Psyche and Agency: The Work of Judith Butler." *Theory, Culture, and Society* 16, no. 2: 175–193.

McWhorter, Ladelle. 1999. *Bodies and Pleasures: Foucault and the Politics of Sexual Normalization*. Bloomington: Indiana University Press.

——. 2004. "Practicing Practicing." In *Feminism and the Final Foucault,* ed. Dianna Taylor and Karen Vintges. Urbana: University of Illinois Press. 143–162.

——. 2009. *Racism and Sexual Oppression in Anglo-America: A Genealogy*. Bloomington: Indiana University Press.

Melville, Herman. 1967. *Moby-Dick; or, the Whale*. New York: W. W. Norton.

Mercer, Kobena. 1990. "Black Hair/Style Politics." In *Out There: Marginalization and Contemporary Culture,* eds. Russell Ferguson, Martha Gever, Trinh T. Minh-ha, and Cornel West. New York and Cambridge, Mass.: New Museum of Contemporary Art / MIT Press. 247–264.

——. 1993. "Looking For Trouble." In *The Lesbian and Gay Studies Reader,* ed. Henry Abelove, Michelle A. Barale, and David M. Halperin. New York: Routledge. 350–359.

Messer-Davidow, Ellen. 1995. "Acting Otherwise." In *Provoking Agents: Gender and Agency in Theory and Practice,* ed. Judith Kegan Gardener. Urbana: University of Illinois Press. 23–51.

Mirón, Louis F., and Jonathon Xavier Inda. 2000. "Race as a Kind of Speech Act." *Cultural Studies: A Research Volume* 5: 85–107.

Morton, Patricia. 1991. *Disfigured Images: The Historical Assault on Afro-American Women*. New York: Praeger.

Mullen, Harryette. 1994. "Optic White: Blackness and the Production of Whiteness."
    diacritics 24, no. 2/3: 71–89.
Mumford, Kevin. 1999. "After Hugh: Statutory Race Segregation in Colonial America,
    1630–1725." *The American Journal of Legal History* 43, no. 3: 280–305.
Murray, Stuart. 2006. "Thanatopolitics: On the Use of Death for Mobilizing Political
    Life." *Polygraph* 18: 191–215.
———. 2008. "Thanatopolitics: Reading in Agamben a Rejoinder to Biopolitical Life."
    Communication and Critical/Cultural Studies 5, no. 2: 203–207.
O'Farrell, Clare. 2005. *Michel Foucault.* London: Sage Publications.
O'Leary, Timothy. 2002. *Foucault and the Art of Ethics.* London: Continuum.
Omi, Michael, and Howard Winant. 1986. *Racial Formation in the United States: From
    the 1960s to the 1980s.* New York: Routledge.
Pascoe, Peggy. 1996. "Miscegenation Law, Court Cases, and Ideologies of 'Race' in
    Twentieth Century America." *Journal of American History* 83: 44–69.
———. 2009. *What Comes Naturally: Miscegenation Law and the Making of Race in
    America.* New York: Oxford University Press.
Pateman, Carole. 1988. *The Sexual Contract.* Stanford: Stanford University Press.
Patterson, Orlando. 1982. *Slavery and Social Death: A Comparative Study.* Cambridge,
    Mass.: Harvard University Press.
Prado, C. G. 1995. *Starting With Foucault: An Introduction to Genealogy.* Boulder, Col.:
    Westview Press.
Pugliese, Joseph. 2010. *Biometrics: Bodies, Technologies, Biopolitics.* New York: Routledge.
Rabinow, Paul, ed. 2000. "Introduction." In Michel Foucault, *Ethics: The Essential Works
    of Michel Foucault 1954–1984,* vol. 1, ed. Paul Rabinow. London: Penguin. xi–xlii.
Raboteau, Albert J. 1978. *Slave Religion: The "Invisible Institution" in the Antebellum
    South.* Oxford: Oxford University Press.
Reuter, Edward Byron. 1931. *Race Mixture: Studies in Intermarriage and Miscegenation.*
    New York: Whittlesey Press.
Robinson, Amy. 1994. "It Takes One to Know One: Passing and the Communities of
    Common Interest." *Critical Inquiry* 20: 715–733.
———. 1996. "Forms of Appearance of Value: Homer Plessy and the Politics of Privacy." In
    Performance and Cultural Politics, ed. Elin Diamond. New York: Routledge. 237–261.
Robinson, Sally. 2000. *Marked Men: White Masculinity in Crisis.* New York: Columbia
    University Press.
Roediger, David R., ed. 1998. *Black on White: Black Writers on What it Means to Be
    White.* New York: Schocken.
Rosenberg, Charles. 1976. *No Other Gods: On Science and American Social Thought.*
    Baltimore: John Hopkins University Press.
Rottenberg, Catherine. 2008. *Performing Americanness: Race, Class, and Gender in
    African-American and Jewish-American Literature.* Lebanon, N.H.: Dartmouth
    College Press.
Saks, Eva. 2000. "Representing Miscegenation Law." In *Interracialism: Black-White
    Intermarriage in American History, Literature, and Law,* ed. Werner Sollors. Oxford:
    Oxford University Press. 61–81.
Salih, Sara. 2002. *The Judith Butler Reader.* London: Routledge.
Sawicki, Jana. 1991. *Disciplining Foucault.* New York: Routledge.

Scales-Trent, Judy. 2001. "Racial Purity Laws in the United States and Nazi Germany: The Targeting Process." *Human Rights Quarterly* 23: 260–307.

Segal, Lynne. 1990. *Slow Motion: Changing Masculinities, Changing Men.* London: Virago Press.

Senna, Danzy. 1998. *Caucasia.* New York: Riverhead.

Sexton, Jared. 2010. " 'The Curtain of the Sky': An Introduction." *Critical Sociology* 36, no. 1: 11–24.

Smith, Theophus H. 1994. *Conjuring Culture: Biblical Formations of Black America.* Oxford: Oxford University Press.

Smith-Pryor, Elizabeth. 2009. *Property Rights: The Rhinelander Trial, Passing, and the Protection of Whiteness.* Chapel Hill: University of North Carolina Press.

Sollors, Werner. 1997. *Neither Black Nor White Yet Both: Thematic Explorations of Interracial Literature.* Oxford: Oxford University Press.

———. 2000. "Introduction." In *Interracialism: Black-White Intermarriage in American History, Literature, and Law,* ed. Werner Sollors. Oxford: Oxford University Press. 3–16.

Somerville, Siobhan. 2000. *Queering the Color Line: Race and the Invention of Homosexuality in American Culture.* Durham: Duke University Press.

Spillers, Hortense. 1987. "Mama's Baby, Papa's Maybe: An American Grammar Book." *diacritics* 17: 65–81.

Stokes, Mason. 2001. *The Color of Sex: Whiteness, Heterosexuality, and the Fictions of White Supremacy.* Durham: Duke University Press.

Stoler, Ann Laura. 1995. *Race and the Education of Desire: Foucault's History of Sexuality and the Colonial Order of Things.* Durham: Duke University Press.

Taylor, Charles. 1986. "Foucault on Freedom and Truth." In *Foucault: A Critical Reader,* ed. David Couzens Hoy. New York: Basil Blackwell. 69–102.

Taylor, Dianna. 2009. "Normativity and Normalization." *Foucault Studies* 7: 45–63.

Taylor, Dianna, and Karen Vintges, ed. 2004. *Feminism and the Final Foucault.* Urbana: University of Illinois Press.

Thompson, Robert Farris. 1984. *Flash of the Spirit: African and Afro-American Art and Philosophy.* New York: Vintage.

Tyler, Carole-Anne. 1994. "Passing: Narcissism, Identity, and Difference." *Differences* 6: 212–248.

———. 2003. *Female Impersonation.* New York: Routledge.

Vasterling, Veronica. 1999. "Butler's Sophisticated Constructivism: A Critical Assessment." *Hypatia* 14, no. 3: 17–38.

Wacks, Jamie. 2000. "Reading Race, Rhetoric, and the Female Body in the *Rhinelander* Case." In *Interracialism: Black-White Intermarriage in American History, Literature, and Law,* ed. Werner Sollors. Oxford: Oxford University Press. 162–178.

Wacquant, Loïc. 2002. "From Slavery to Mass Incarceration: Rethinking the 'Race Question' in the US." *New Left Review* 13: 41–60.

Walcott, Rinaldo. 2003. *Black Like Who? Writing Black Canada.* 2nd ed. Toronto: Insomniac Press.

———, ed. 2000. *Rude: Contemporary Black Canadian Cultural Criticism.* Toronto: Insomniac Press.

Wald, Gayle. 2000. *Crossing the Line: Racial Passing in Twentieth-century Literature and Culture.* Durham: Duke University Press.

Walzer, Michael. 1986. "The Politics of Michel Foucault." In *Foucault: A Critical Reader,* ed. David Couzens Hoy. New York: Basil Blackwell. 51–68.

Warner, Michael. 1992. "The Mass Public and the Mass Subject." In *Habermas and the Public Sphere,* ed. Craig Calhoun. Cambridge, Mass.: MIT Press. 377–401.

Westley, Robert. 2000. "First-Time Encounters: 'Passing' Revisited and Demystification as a Critical Practice." *Yale Law and Policy Review* 18: 297–349.

Whitebook, Joel. 1999. "Freud, Foucault, and 'The Dialogue with Unreason.' " *Philosophy and Social Criticism* 25, no. 6: 29–66.

Wiegman, Robyn. 1995. *American Anatomies: Theorizing Race and Gender.* Durham: Duke University Press.

Wilderson, Frank B., III. 2009. *Red, White, and Black: Cinema and the Structure of U.S. Antagonisms.* Durham: Duke University Press.

Williams, Gregory Howard. 1995. *Life on the Color Line: The True Story of a White Boy Who Discovered He Was Black.* New York: Dutton.

Williams, Patricia J. 1993. *The Alchemy of Race and Rights: Diary of a Law Professor.* London: Virago Press.

Williamson, Joel. 1995. *New People: Miscegenation and Mulattoes in the United States.* Baton Rouge: Louisiana State University Press.

Yancy, George. 2004a. "A Foucauldian (Genealogical) Reading of Whiteness: The Production of the Black Body/Self and the Racial Deformation of Pecola Breedlove in Toni Morrison's *The Bluest Eye.*" In *What White Looks Like: African American Philosophers on the Whiteness Question,* ed. George Yancy. New York: Routledge. 107–142.

——. 2004b. "Introduction: Fragments of a Social Ontology of Whiteness." In *What White Looks Like: African American Philosophers on the Whiteness Question,* ed. George Yancy. New York: Routledge. 1–25.

——. 2008. *Black Bodies, White Gazes: The Continuing Significance of Race.* Lanham, Md.: Rowman and Littlefield.

Zuberi, Tukufu. 2001. *Thicker Than Blood: How Racial Statistics Lie.* Minneapolis: University of Minnesota Press.

INDEX

NADINE EHLERS is Assistant Professor in Women's and Gender Studies at Georgetown University (Washington, D.C.). Her main areas of expertise are critical theory, Foucault, and studies of the body, which are directed toward analyzing racial construction and racializing technologies as they operate in terms of gender, sexuality, and class.